Praise for *How to Teach*

'Filled with sparkling insights, a joy from start to finish. In turns witty, brilliant and irreverent, McGowan explains nothing less than the meaning of life – to his dog. If only we were all as lucky as Monty to go for long walks with the author...'

Peter Frankopan, author of *The Earth Transformed*

'Anthony McGowan's wonderful survey of philosophy... Hugely entertaining and accessible, there can't have been more delightful exponents of Socratic dialogue than McGowan and Monty, his scruffy and evidently delightful Maltese terrier.'

Tom Holland, Best Books of the Year, *New Statesman*

'For essential reading on both the meaning of dogs and the meaning of life, I can recommend Anthony McGowan's wonderful book *How to Teach Philosophy to Your Dog*, a series of conversations he had with his dog, Monty, while out walking together. The final chapter is a touching meditation on death and the existence – or not – of God, that takes in everything from Aristotle to Schopenhauer and leaves you suspecting dogs might already have had many of the answers all along. *There are more things in heaven and earth, Horatio / Than are dreamed of in your philosophy.*'

Guardian

'Genuinely profound as well as very funny.'

Alex Preston

'An accessible, amusing guide to key philosophical questions... Perfect for novice philosophers.'

Idler

How to Teach Economics to Your Dog

A Quirky Introduction

Rebecca Campbell
and Anthony McGowan

ONEWORLD

A Oneworld Book

First published by Oneworld Publications in 2022
This paperback edition published 2023

ISBN 978-0-86154-618-3
eISBN 978-0-86154-380-9

Typeset by Geethik Technologies
Printed and bound in Great Britain by Clays Ltd, Elcograf S.p.A.

Oneworld Publications
10 Bloomsbury Street
London WC1B 3SR
England

To Gabriel, Rosie and, of course, Monty

Contents

Preamble

Reader, meet Monty, who is to play a role in this book: not perhaps the star, but definitely up for best supporting actor. Monty is a Maltese. I sometimes erroneously describe him as a Maltese terrier, which is straightforwardly incorrect. Although in some ways terrier-like in his tenacity and occasionally unfocused aggression, the Maltese is from a quite different family of dogs, and belongs on the lap, not down tunnels hunting for rats. It's always struck me as odd that Maltese are always referred to as 'Maltese dogs'. This seems rather unnecessary: no one is going to mistake Monty for a Maltese rabbit, or Maltese guinea pig, although I suppose you might mistake him for a Maltese muff. He's fluffy and white and when washed and blow-dried resembles a dandelion clock. At other times he can appear a bit scraggy and bedraggled, like a heavy sneeze come to life. And the tendency of Maltese to develop dark tear stains below their eyes, for all the world like run mascara, makes him look like an albino goth in the midst of an emotional crisis. Although Maltese are not renowned for their intellect, Monty has a quizzical, enquiring sort of look, and often cocks his little head to one side, which makes him at least appear to be a good listener.

So much for Monty's appearance, but here we're more interested in his character. I expect that you, if you're a dog owner, chat to your dog. Perhaps it's mainly a matter of endearments and encouragement, interspersed with demands that they come or sit or stop chasing that postman. I also suspect that for some of you at least, your dog talks back. Perhaps he does it by the traditional canine mediums of barking, yowling, growling and tail-wagging. Perhaps it takes a more eloquent form, the words appearing in your mind, in a way that you can then articulate. 'What's that? You want a biscuit? And you want it now?'

Monty is an unusual dog in quite how well he manages to convey his thoughts. This was a skill he developed in a series of walks recorded in *How to Teach Philosophy to Your Dog*, which gave Monty a thorough grounding in the dialectical method, in other words, how to learn through conversation.

Now, one understands that there might be, in the mind of the reader, a small degree of scepticism (a subject, incidentally, dealt with at length in the aforementioned book) about the extent to which a mere pooch could engage in relatively sophisticated intellectual debate. In that case I will offer you an alternative. In *The Third Policeman*, the great Irish novelist and humorist Flann O'Brien describes the process by which a man and a bicycle can, by means of the simple scientific truth of Brownian motion – the jiggling about of molecules in any substance – combined with the close contact of the fundament and the saddle, become so intertwined and enmeshed that no clear distinction between the one and the other can be drawn. This leads to the many instances of human-like behaviour in bicycles – that tendency, for example, for bikes to nestle next to radiators in hallways during inclement weather. Something similar undoubtedly occurs with a dog and its owner. Those hours of stroking and lap-sitting (which is where Monty is right now, by the way, having his post-supper nap) have inevitably taken us to the point at which Monty is, to some unspecified degree, me, and me, Monty. So, in the walks that follow, you are at liberty to imagine either a McGowan-infused Monty, or a Monty-infused McGowan, as the junior partner in these discussions.

Following our philosophical perambulations, it was quite clear that Monty wanted more. Philosophy is many things: a way to polish the blunted tool of your rationality; an engaging series of stories about what may make up the nature of reality; a guide to living a more ethical life. However, it could be argued that philosophy leaves much of the reality of existence out of the picture, everything on the small scale about our daily struggle to earn a living, to, on the larger, the way in which societies should be organised to bring the maximum benefit to the greatest number of people. This is quite a big hole in the understanding of any person (canine or human). It is the job of economics to fill this gap, hence the title of Robert Heilbroner's classic book on the history of economics, *The Worldly Philosophers*.[1] It is economics that gives we philosophers a sharp kick in the pants, redirecting our attention from the clouds to ground level.

In our lives, we are enmeshed in complex economic forces, generated by the way things are made, traded, sold. These forces determine the kind of lives we are able to lead. Of course there is an underlying humanity connecting us all, but the infinitely complex texture of modern life, how we spend our working days, where we live, what we wear, what we eat, how finally we spend our retirement, is determined by these vast inhuman forces. Economics is the greatest tool we have (and, as a philosopher, this stings, it truly does) for understanding these forces.

What follows is a series of walks in which Dr Rebecca Campbell, who flitted in and out of *How to Teach Philosophy to Your Dog*, tries to explain economics to Monty and, through him, to me. And you. Although intended as a friendly and welcoming primer to the subject, *How to Teach Economics to Your Dog* actually follows quite closely the structure of a typical introductory course that an undergraduate might take in the first year of an Economics degree. And like such a course, it falls roughly into two halves, dealing first with microeconomics and then macroeconomics. Don't worry, these terms will be explained shortly, but for now, the micro just means the little stuff – the causes and consequences of the economic decisions individuals make – and the macro the big stuff, such as the policies of governments and national banks, concerning things like interest rates and government spending.

Economics and politics are, obviously, closely entwined. Decisions about economics have political consequences, and decisions about politics economic ones. So I should point out that, as with every successful marriage, ours is one based on violent disagreement. Dr Campbell is a big fan of markets and the capitalist system, which she believes, not without some empirical justification, to have transformed the lives of literally billions of people for the better. I am some sort of irresponsible anarcho-syndicalist, with Marxist tendencies. Last Christmas I asked for a Che Guevara beret and a 'This machine kills fascists' sticker to put on my guitar. (I got a SodaStream and a pack of M&S underpants, since you ask.) Monty, being infused with those McGowan molecules, will, to some extent, challenge some of Dr Campbell's pro-market assumptions, but the fact remains that economics is, at its heart, the study of how markets work, and that will be the central focus of this book.

Perhaps another few words about the domestic economy of the McGowan/Campbell family. Economists like to employ down-to-earth examples to help explain difficult concepts. One of the most famous of these (in the sense that even non-econo-mists like me have heard of it), used by Adam Smith at the start of his masterpiece, *The Wealth of Nations* (1776), involves pins. Making a pin, you might think, if you've thought about it at all, is a relatively straightforward process. But you would be wrong. 'One man draws out the wire, another straights it, a third cuts it, a fourth points it…' The list goes on, until we have eighteen dis-tinct operations, each performed by some poor drudge who does that, and *only* that.

This specialisation, although it may well take away much of the natural delight of pin-making, means that productivity is massively increased. Ten men working together, Smith reckons, could produce over 48,000 pins in a day. One person working alone might make only twenty. What fool would stand in the way of such progress?

Margaret Thatcher (about whom, as you can probably imagine, Dr Campbell and I have rather differing views…) was fond of comparing managing a national economy to managing a household budget, balancing up income and expenditure, saving here to spend there. Quick spoiler alert: this is nonsense. Running a national economy is nothing like running a house-hold. However, in both, there's a role for specialisation.

And so in our household, we all have our particular roles. Our daughter, Rosie, supplies the joy, the exuberance and enthusiasm. Our son, Gabe, is there to add a certain dry, laconic coolness to proceedings. Rebecca (aka Dr Campbell) handles organisation, getting things done, paying bills, ensuring that the household doesn't descend into chaos. Monty bathes everything in love, in the way that only a dog can. Traditionally, my jobs have been to wander around turning off lights left on by the others, and to restack the dishwasher, on rigorously scientific principles/cranky theories of my own devising. Oh, and to take Monty on the long walks that nobody else fancied, and which formed the basis of *How to Teach Philosophy to Your Dog*. But now Rebecca is taking over those duties, and I shall step back, although you should feel free to imagine me in some mysterious sense lurking in Monty's head. And, as Marx (the Groucho version) may or may not have said, outside of a dog, a book is a man's best friend, and inside of a dog it's too dark to read.

The Toaster

What we talk about on this walk: What one man's attempt to build a toaster can tell us about markets and, more broadly, economics.

It was one of those frantic family breakfasts, with everyone in a fractious mood. The Philosopher has a way of carrying chaos around with him the way a snail schlepps its shell. He seems to think that this is a creative chaos, as if you could make a cake by pulling the pin on a hand grenade and tossing it into the kitchen. Rosie and Gabe were fighting over who had to sit on the broken kitchen stool, a battle won by Rosie, as all battles of the will are won by Rosie. Gabe grumpily stumped off to the toaster, ramming some too-thick slices into the slot. In a few seconds the toaster started to smoke, then there was a bang and the lights went out.

'Don't panic!' yelled the Philosopher in a panicky way. He has few DIY-type gifts, but one is an ability to switch a blown fuse back on (or whatever the right terminology is – it involved rummaging in the coat cupboard, swearing and muttering). But today the problem wasn't solved by throwing a switch.

'It's the toaster. The dilithium crystals have become contaminated with carbonised fragments of ionised disaccharides,' he said, or something like it. I wasn't really listening. He then uttered the words our family has come to dread. 'I'll get my toolbox.' Gabe groaned, Rosie wailed, I put my face in my hands. Monty ran to the bedroom and hid under a pillow.

Half an hour later, the toaster was in bits and the kitchen looked like a junkyard in a *Mad Max* movie.

'Come on, Monty,' I said. 'Let's get out of here.'

It wasn't destined to be one of our longer park walks, but just a pleasant stroll through the quiet side streets of West Hampstead in the autumn sunshine. The Philosopher has devised a game he calls 'Hedgerow Russian Roulette', to be played at this time of year. The game involves randomly plucking and eating fruits and berries he sees growing in urban hedges and accessible gardens, even if he does not know what the fruit or berry is. His rationale is that no one berry or bite is likely to kill you, and you pretty soon know if something tastes poisonous and can spit it out. His worst experience was with what turned out to be the pulpy outside of a walnut, which he'd convinced himself was an unripe peach. He went into spasms, and regurgitated it, saying it was like licking piss off a nettle, though he didn't die. I, of course, don't play, and I suspect there's something instructive here about the obvious superiority of economics over philosophy, as a discipline.

'OK, Monty,' I began. 'Let's talk toasters.'

Monty raised his eyebrows. He definitely has eyebrows, and, for that matter, a sort of moustache, and both moustache and eyebrows are surprisingly eloquent.

I'm assuming this is some sort of illustration, a wotsit, parable, rather than your analysis of who's to blame for blowing our toaster up?

'You got me. Let's think of this as a gentle introduction to economics.'

Sneaky.

'First a quick definition, before we get toasting. Economics can be defined broadly as the science of how people make choices, and how those choices affect society. This involves thinking about trade-offs and how people respond to incentives. Much of economics is concerned with how markets work. And when they don't…'

I assume you're not just talking about Camden Market, where Rosie goes to buy her Doc Marten boots and the Philosopher goes to get his rare vinyl from that record stall?

'I don't *only* mean that. A market is any place, online or in the real world, where people interact to buy and sell: to exchange goods or services for money. But Camden Market is actually a good example. Importantly, market exchange is only possible because of the wider framework, the institutions and infrastructure, that enables trade. This wider framework oils the wheels of commerce in Camden, but also facilitates that grander vision of the market, and we'll devote much of our time to it, on our later walks.'

A little advance hint about what sort of things you mean…?

'Money, and a legal system that helps regulate commercial transactions, and which takes a dim view of purloining things without paying for them.'

I thought you'd finished with the cheesecake!

'Yes, well, let's pass over that. I gave what was left to the Philosopher… As I say, we'll talk about markets at much greater length later on, but for now, let's think about economics as the study of markets, how they succeed, and how they fail.'

Seems a little narrow.

'That's because your own view of what a market is, and how important markets are, is too limited. But this is precisely why I want to talk about that toaster.'

Good save. OK, hit me.

'A few years ago a British designer called Thomas Thwaites decided to try to build a toaster from scratch.[1] It's not, he reasoned, as if he were trying to build a lifelike android or a supercomputer. Just a toaster. How hard can it be?'

Let me guess, this didn't go well?

'Thwaites's attempt to build his toaster was a comical disaster. He started by buying the cheapest toaster he could find (£3.99 from Argos) and then tried to reverse-engineer it. Once it was disassembled, Thwaites found that this basic appliance contained four hundred separate parts, made out of more than a hundred different materials. Unable to source all these raw materials, he did the best he could with just five: steel, mica, plastic, copper and nickel. Bearing in mind that this was a gifted designer, with more technical skill and ability than most of us, you'd think he might be able to at least get close.'

Er, no. I predict a fiasco.

'Fiasco it was. Thwaites's toaster looked like some kind of mutant sea creature. He turned it on, once, and it did start toasting for about five seconds until the element melted. It cost £1,187.54 to make. The moral: working alone, no one individual, however much of a genius, could produce a toaster or, by implication, any other of the many domestic appliances we take for granted. Yet the market, that complex, subtle machine for getting things done, could produce one for what amounts to loose change. And it's not just toasters. The whole of modern life is a kaleidoscope of these miracles. We know that we can walk into any of the cafés here in West Hampstead and order a cup of coffee. No one knew in advance that you were going to want that cup of coffee; it was just there for you. The beans were grown in Colombia; the milk comes from cows in Devon; the water reaches us purified, through hundreds of kilometres of underground tunnels; the sugar comes from beets grown in East Anglia; the chocolate for the cappuccino is made from beans shipped in from West Africa.'

Wait just a moment. Now, you know what the Philosopher would say if he were here. He'd point out that these very pleasant things, toasters and coffee and chocolate and all that, all come with a hidden cost. Maybe they're so cheap for us because people aren't being paid much to pick those beans. Some people get stupidly rich on the sweat and poverty of others. And what about the huge environmental cost?

'And, as usual, he'd have a point. We're not going to be ignoring the downsides of the market system and international trade. Markets enable cooperation on a vast scale, and that has led to huge advances in human well-being. This system is clearly not perfect, but the way to deal with that is first of all to understand this wonderfully complex machine. Only then can we hope to fix it. Taking that toaster apart might not have meant that Thwaites could make a toaster, but he might well have been able to fix ours, without blowing the fuses.

Some have argued that markets are so important to our prosperity that government should be as small as possible and get out of the way.[2] My preferred interpretation is that we are all part of a collective system (the market system), and so we should try to ameliorate some of the inequalities that inevitably result from such a system.

I suppose the market system is a bit like having a dog...'

Oh, here we go.

'There are undoubted benefits. Everyone finds that their life is better, happier, fuller, richer. But there are also downsides...'

Very minor!

'Walks when it's raining, dog poo to pick up, the occasional accident indoors, every now and then an unfussy flea or two.'

Nobody's perfect.

'So the key thing is to make sure that the good things are spread as widely as possible, and the bad things don't all fall on the shoulders of a few unlucky drudges, i.e. me.'

Feels a bit shoehorned, but fair enough. You're teaching economics to a dog, so this kind of thing is going to happen.

'My point is just that neither the deification of the market nor its demonisation is our goal, but its *understanding*. And sometimes you have to go back to go forwards, so we'll begin with a couple of walks delving into the history of economics, looking at some of those towering figures, the founding fathers. And sadly "fathers" is the right term – they're all male, I'm afraid, no notable women economists until the twentieth century. Although familiar, these figures are often much misunderstood, their teachings simplified or distorted to fit in with later ideological positions they could not have held. After our history lesson, we'll discuss microeconomics, which is that branch of the subject that looks at how individuals – and for our purposes that can be actual individual humans, or households or firms – make decisions and interact in the market. Then we'll talk about macroeconomics, which takes a broader look at economic policy, examining issues like unemployment, growth and international trade, and the ways in which governments can help, or hinder, the economy.

But now, how about we pop into this café and sample the products of those international networks of trade?'

Walk 2

Part I: A Short History of Nearly Everything

What we talk about on this walk: On the first part of this walk we work our way towards a definition of economics, and discuss the historical development of the market economy. In the second part we look at some of the 'big dogs' whose ideas shaped the subject.

Our first walk was to be the familiar path through the woods around Golders Hill Park, a pretty, semi-detached offshoot of Hampstead Heath. It's our standard walk, taking in some rather grand streets until we reach the trees and the paths that wind between. If the Philosopher (i.e. my husband, Anthony McGowan) was with us he'd be showing off, identifying birdsong ('that's a male chiff-chaff... two years old, just returned from winter in... yes, going by the accent, Chad') or unusual fungi ('this one's the death's stink cap, tastes of burnt almonds, causes immediate suffocation and death, unless taken as a suppository, in which case there's little more than a mild tingling')

14

or animal droppings ('weasel, easy to tell from stoat by the smaller size and the taste of burnt almonds'). But he's not, so it's just Monty and me and economics.

There was a little rain in the air, but not enough to give us an excuse to stay indoors. I wrapped us both up well, putting Monty in the waterproof coat that he seems to regard as a blow to his masculinity (*It's pink!* 'No, it's cerise.') and off we went.

'Well, Monty,' I said, when we were in the safe seclusion of the woods, 'you've had your fun with philosophy, but how about learning something useful?'

Monty gave me one of his eloquent looks. He's famous, in our house, for these. It's amazing how much he can squeeze into a raised canine eyebrow, or a curl of his doggy lip.

Kinda depends on what you mean by 'useful'.

'Philosophy really has spoiled you, hasn't it?'

There's useful to me, and there's useful to you.

'Fair point. This is going to be useful for me. But it's not a zero-sum game.'

A what now?

'A zero-sum game means whatever I win, you lose. When a lion meets a zebra, that's a zero-sum game. But here there's something in it for both of us.'

You're saying you'll make it worth my while?

'I'll make it worth your while.'

Cheesecake?

'In your dreams. Dog biscuit.'

The Philosopher's a lot more generous.

'You mean soft? Well now we're playing *my* rules.'

Three?

'What?'

Dog biscuits.

'Good negotiating tactic. Go in with a high demand, expecting to have to give a little. You can have two.'

Deal. But, er, remind me what we're doing again…

'Economics.'

Okaaaaay… And economics is?

'Well, that is a harder question to answer than you might think, and economists don't always agree among themselves.'

Somehow I knew you were going to say that!

'Give me a chance, we've barely started yet, and I've got to get some steam up. Right, a professor at the LSE, Lionel Robbins (1898–1984), famously defined economics as, "the science which studies human behaviour as a relationship between ends and scarce means which have alternative uses".'

Sorry?

'Yes, I don't love that definition either. It is probably enough to make most normal people – and dogs – run a mile. But let's unpick what he's trying to say. We have a limited amount of cash (the *scarce means* bit) and we have to decide what we want to spend it on (the *ends*). This necessarily means we have to make choices, deciding to buy one thing rather than another – a yacht, say, rather than a Ferrari.'

Sure.

'Joking. Let's say a pair of shoes rather than a handbag.'

Definitely much more you.

'And it also means that we will respond to incentives. If you make something cheaper, let's say cheesecake, as you've planted the image in my head – we will probably buy more of it.'

I'm not arguing.

'Embedded in that definition is the idea that economics is a science, by which he means a reliable way of getting at the truth, using evidence and testable hypotheses.'

And is it?

'I have my doubts on that. It's very difficult to do controlled experiments in economics, dividing populations up and subjecting one half to one economic policy, and the other half to a different one. But history has provided us with some actual experiments, such as the post-Second World War divisions of Germany and Korea, and we can also do thought experiments to tease out the logic of certain arguments. Rather than obsessing over the degree to which economics is a science, it's best to regard it as a *method*, a way of analysing how people make rational choices about scarce resources. And of course economics often involves a lot of maths, which can give the impression that it's truly scientific.'

Groan. Look here, I can count, sorta – I know when you have short-changed me on the treats front – but if this walk is going to be all about algebra and calculus, then we can just go back home now.

'Don't worry, Monty, we'll stick to the ideas. No equations...'

Phew!

'I think the easiest way to begin to understand economics is to look at the origins and history of the subject. And understanding the history of economics means getting to grips with economic history.'

By which you mean... ?

'Well, not the history of kings and queens and battles and great men doing great things, but the changing ways in which societies have organised how food and goods and services are produced and distributed and paid for. But why not have a bit of a run-around first, to use up some of that surplus energy?'

We'd reached a favourite spot, a stand of tall, austere beech trees, with a permanent crunchy layer of old beechmast on the ground. Monty scampered and sniffed, while I plodded and pondered, trying to get the story straight in my head. After a while, I saw that Monty had stopped by a bench on a patch of slightly higher ground, with a pleasant view over the treetops. I sat down and let Monty clamber up next to me.

'Ready?'

As I'll ever be. But you promise no equations?

'Promise. OK, at its most basic, economic thought has traditionally been concerned with the problem of how we manage to produce everything we need, and get it to the people who need it or want it. For most of history this was both a more important, but also a less complicated, question. More important because the struggle for existence was far more brutal. But far less complex as people were more self-sufficient. For the first couple of hundred thousand years of human history, families and small groups of humans produced pretty much all they needed for their own consumption through hunting and gathering. But as settlements developed, and societies began to diversify and stratify, with different roles for different groups within those societies, the need grew for more intricate systems of cooperation.

If you look back over history you see that there have been three basic ways that societies have attacked this problem: tradition, command and markets.

Probably the oldest way that societies solved the economic problem – who does what (and who got what) – was through tradition. You do what you do, because that's what you've always done. Sons followed in their fathers' footsteps, and this continuity ensured that important skills were passed down. For example, the Indian caste system dictated your occupation from the moment of your birth. Traditional systems worked because they were stable and helped to maintain social order. But they were very static (not to say unfair). If your dad shovelled manure, you shovel manure.

The second way of solving the economic problem is command. You tell people what to do.'

Sounds like what happens in our house – you tell everyone what to do.

'Yeah, well, the Philosopher likes to feel the smack of firm government. Think pyramids. Pyramids in Ancient Egypt did not get built because some enterprising entrepreneur saw a market in it. They were built because the Pharaoh said: "Build!"

And the Soviet system for much of the twentieth century was a command economy. Although there were limited markets, most decisions about who did what, and how much you were paid, and what you were able to buy in the shops, were made by a central planner.'

I'm guessing from your tone that this wasn't an entirely good thing?

'In periods of crisis, wars or famines, say, command may be the only way to get things done. And, as we will discuss later, there are times when markets work badly, where we might prefer a central planner to make rational decisions on our behalf. As recent events have shown, there is nothing like the threat of a global pandemic to make governments step in and take control. But there are at least two problems with the command system. The first is ethical: in a command economy you can't decide yourself what to make or sell or buy, and that means a huge part of your life is fundamentally *unfree*.

A second objection is that command economies are simply a hugely inefficient way of managing incredibly complex situations. This is an argument made by the Austrian economist and philosopher Friedrich Hayek (1899–1992). But we will return later to that, and to him.'

I can hardly wait.

'Lowest form of humour, sarcasm, you know.'

Give me a break, I'm a dog. You should be glad I don't eat my own vomit and hump the cushions.

'I'll give you that. Where were we? Yes, the third way of organising things, and the one that most of us live under now, is a market-based system. Here, decisions about resources – what we do and what we get – are not made centrally by some authority, or inherited from the previous generation. It's the market that decides.'

You know I'm going to need a bit more about what you actually mean by 'the market decides'. At the moment it's just words.

'And you'll get it. But for now we're taking in the lie of the land, like this view here.' I made a broad sweeping gesture, though Monty, being a dog, looked at my hand, and not the view. 'Just focus on the fact that markets are the key. Most of us take for granted the quite astonishing way that markets coordinate economic activity. Remember the toaster? Remember the coffee? So many things that make our lives bearable are only possible because of markets. And this is why economics focuses on markets – when they flourish and when and how and why they fail.'

OK, but if this market system is so great, why did it take so long for societies to come up with it?

'Because history isn't a matter of rational, steady progress towards some ideal state. In ancient societies, most people lived a rural existence that was almost cashless. The route to wealth was religious or military power. If people thought about money and commerce they were often focused on the moral aspects, struggling with the idea of what is the "just price".'

The just price…?

'It's a concept you find in the work of the medieval philosopher Thomas Aquinas, but it goes back to Ancient Greek thought. It's the idea that things have a natural value, and that's what the tradesperson should charge. An example Aquinas gives is building materials. There's a "right" price for stone and mortar, and it's wrong to charge more for these things after say an earthquake, when everyone wants to rebuild, and the greedy stonemason could put up his prices. Nothing could be further from the market way, in which the price of a good emerges from the myriad interactions of sellers and buyers.

Economic activity and trade was considered somehow dishonourable. Cicero summed up the prevailing attitude: "Sordid too is the calling of those who buy wholesale in order to sell retail, since they would gain no profits without a great deal of lying."

If we skip forward to economic society in the Middle Ages, in many ways it takes a step back. There was the loss of political stability caused by the fall of Rome. Old trade routes decayed, as Europe split into warring states. The feudal system also limited the development of markets.'

Hold on! The feudal system is…?

'Very quick and grotesquely oversimplified historical sketch alert. Thinking just about Europe, northern Africa and the Middle East, first we have Rome, reasonable stability, established trade routes, rule of law, cities, all that jazz. That all goes to pot, and we get the Dark Ages. Chaos, war, madness. Gradually things settle down again, and we find ourselves in the Middle Ages. Reasonably stable kingdoms, but we're not back to the complex international trade of the Roman Empire. And there's a lot more political fragmentation. Consequently, people fell back onto self-reliance. The Big House – the manor – became the basic unit of economic organisation.

In ancient society, slavery was universal, but by the Middle Ages this had evolved into the concept of serfdom. A serf was also (more or less) the property of his master, but there were reciprocal bonds and obligations. The master gave protection, the serfs gave labour. Serfs were permitted to farm a small plot of land for their own family's subsistence, and in return they had to provide labour or a proportion of their produce. There were some guilds of workers who were paid for work that was too specialised to be supported by even the grandest manor. But in general goods and services were produced and distributed in response to law and custom, not market price. The ruling ethos was perpetuation, not progress.'

So, what changed?

'The next period of economic history, roughly from the middle of the fifteenth century to the middle of the eighteenth, is sometimes referred to as "merchant capitalism" or "mercantilism". Itinerant merchants were bringing ever more exotic products from ever more remote places; commerce was growing, markets were proliferating. You see the rise of merchant towns such as Venice, Florence and Bruges. Merchants were becoming influential and (a little) more respectable. You also see the rise of the nation state. Europe's fragmented political entities were slowly forming into larger wholes. England, noticeably, enjoyed a single unified internal market, and this was one factor behind its emergence as one of the first great industrial powers. At the same time, you see the breakdown of the manorial system. As towns grew, they increasingly paid for their food with money. Gradually the old feudal obligations became monetised. Payments previously made in kind – days of labour or chickens or eggs – were transformed into hard cash. A growing pool of people who are paid for their labour in turn provides an expanding market in which vendors can sell their products.

Finally, there was also a change in the religious climate.'

What's religion got to do with it? Isn't it the opposite of economics?

'Today we tend to think of them as quite separate fields. But this is very recent. Christian thought before the Reformation rejected worldly concerns – though of course the obscene wealth of the Church rather undermined that. Earthly existence was transient, and it was our next, eternal life that was of value. Consequently, the pursuit of money and possessions was vanity. According to Max Weber, this changed with Protestantism.[1] Diligence and hard work became a measure of your spiritual worth. Just as significantly, wealth was not to be wasted on sinful luxuries, but to be saved and invested.'

So that was all that was needed to change?

'Not entirely – I think there is one more intellectual shift that we need to discuss. The attitude to competition. To the extent that merchants themselves were powerful, they supported state intervention to limit competition. They called for monopolies and restrictions on trade wherever they could. They were also strongly against imports. If they had heard the term laissez-faire they would have resisted it.'

Er, hello – English dog alert. I ain't no poodle or no French bulldog.

'Sorry. Laissez-faire literally means to "let do", i.e. let people do as they please. It has come to be one of the most influential and contested ideas in economics – that governments should refrain from intervening in private exchanges, for example through regulation, subsidies or any but the most minimal taxation. The term was first used in the eighteenth century by the Physiocrats, a group of radical French thinkers. They believed that the only source of wealth was agriculture, but their most lasting contribution to economic thought was this idea of free exchange. Their guiding principles were the protection of private property and freedom of trade. Their rallying cry was *laissez-faire* – let the market alone. The government should butt out of the economic sphere, and restrict itself to law and order and national defence. This brought them into conflict with the mercantilists.

By the late eighteenth century we are moving into a world that looks much more recognisably capitalist. However, there are still some curious anomalies, even in a country as advanced as France. In the late eighteenth century, only those with a royal charter were permitted to sell cooked food, thereby limiting it to a privileged clique who could charge high prices. But cunning French caterers found a way round this. They started to sell meat broths (and the odd side dish) as "medicinal" or "restorative". And the French word for "restorative"? Restaurant! So, commerce finds a way, and we see tradition and command being supplanted by the "invisible hand" of the market. And the man who coined that term, our friend Adam Smith, was to provide the first great explanation of the workings of this new world.'

Er, I sense that this is what you might call a natural break. How about I have a quick sniff'n'wee, and then we go home? You can tell me all about this Smith geezer on the way.

So I let Monty go on one of his urinary rampages, democratically spraying both towering ash and diminutive shrub.

Part II: The Big Dogs

'You ready?'

All peed out.

'OK, we're going to have to discuss some of the Big Dogs in the field.'

Monty growled, menacingly. His only fault… OK, not his only fault, but one of his few… oh, OK, he has lots of faults, and this is just one of them, is that he has a somewhat inflated opinion of himself as a brawler, and what he most likes to do is to have a quick snarl and snap at any hulking great dogs we come across. He never makes any contact, and he hasn't, in his old age, got enough teeth left to do any damage anyway. But it's all very embarrassing, and doesn't reflect at all well on his owners. So at the mention of big dogs, Monty bristled and got ready to yap. After he'd checked all compass points for worthy adversaries, he relaxed.

Metaphor?

'Yep.'

These are people, aren't they?

'Yep.'

Famous economists?

'Can I go on?'

Proceed.

'I'm going to give you a quick run-down on the three classical thinkers who between them built the foundations of modern economics: Adam Smith, Thomas Malthus and David Ricardo.

Adam Smith is regarded as the inventor of economics. He wrote two great books: *The Theory of Moral Sentiments* (1759) and *The Wealth of Nations* (1776). The first is about ethics, the second, on which his fame depends, is about political economy.'

What does political economy mean?

'Good question. People toss these terms about without really understanding what they mean. As it developed, economics became increasingly mathematical. And this meant that it became much more abstract, perhaps losing touch with lived reality. In contrast, political economy focuses on how economic issues play out in the real world. It is not just considering how markets work in the abstract but how they interact with government, law and culture.

In *The Wealth of Nations* Smith explores what it is that makes nations richer. And in Smith's world, where small children worked fourteen-hour days, pregnant women were treated as beasts of burden dragging carts of coal underground, and bands of starving poor roamed the countryside in search of work, there could hardly be a more pressing question. It is a huge and digressive book, but there are at least four key ideas.

The first is that the hidden mechanism that would increase productivity, and so a nation's wealth, was the *division of labour*. Remember our pin factory?'

No…

'Oh, sorry, yes, that was before you got involved. To cut a long story short, it's much more efficient if you break down the manufacturing process, say of pins or cars or—'

Toasters?

'…into many small sub-routines or jobs, each performed by a different person.'

Is this like when you finally crack, and stomp around telling everyone that they have to clean a different bit of the house?

'Er, well, yes, a bit, I suppose. It's better if I do the kitchen and the Philosopher does the bathroom, and Rosie her bedroom, and Gabe hoovers the hall. But it's probably easier to think of making things. Whenever a big job can be broken down into smaller specialist tasks, productivity goes up.

The second key idea in *The Wealth of Nations* is that this way of organising ourselves is driven by our natural propensity to "truck and barter, and exchange one thing for another". Division of labour and specialisation are only possible (and so increases in wealth are only possible) if you have some way to exchange products, and this means markets. The bigger the market, the more specialisation is possible. He brings you in here, Monty.'

Me? Really – I always knew I was special.

'Well, not literally you, Monty. Dogs in general. He points out that humans are unique: "Nobody ever saw a dog make a fair and deliberate exchange of one bone for another with another dog".'

Don't be ridiculous. Why would I give my bone to another dog? But hang about – when I give you the full soppy-eye thing, you give me bits of bacon. Does that count?

'Well, Smith has an answer for this objection. He says that when an animal wants to obtain things from his master, it will fawn upon him. And he notes that people often do the same, if they have to. Everyone knows a toady or two. But Smith points out that this is a limited and unreliable way to get people to cooperate with you, and a complex society, based on the division of labour, requires a system that can coordinate millions of transactions.

The third, somewhat counterintuitive idea is that a system based on *self-interest* is much more likely to get us what we want. That when we work hard in pursuit of our own self-interest, without intending it, without knowing it, we advance the interest of wider society. Here we have another of Smith's most famous quotes: "It is not from the benevolence of the butcher, the brewer, or the baker, that we expect our dinner, but from their regard to their own interest. We address ourselves, not to their humanity, but to their self-love, and never talk to them of our own necessity but of their advantages."

His fourth great idea is the *invisible hand* of the market. He describes how the market naturally regulates itself, without anyone explicitly directing it. If sellers bring less to the market than buyers want, free competition means that buyers will bid up the price. If sellers bring more to the market than buyers want, the price will be bid down. Price is the outcome of the forces of supply and demand. Competition also provides a check to our self-interest. If you try to charge too much for your goods, you will find yourself without any customers. If you pay too little to your workers, you will find yourself without any labour.

He also outlines how the market price will further regulate the supply of goods. As the price moves, sellers/producers are naturally prompted to shift their attention to making goods with a high price and away from those with a low price. As high price follows on from scarcity, this mechanism will help to fix that, without the need for a central planner. No bureaucrat has to order people to produce more of this or less of that: the market decides. Smith, following those Physiocrats, makes clear that the main job of the sovereign is to establish the rule of law and get out of the way.

Here we have our free market economic system in a nutshell, fuelled by self-interest, regulated by the invisible hand of the market.'

So, Adam Smith thought selfishness was good, markets are great, and that the government should stay out. Is that right?

'That's how his ideas have been caricatured by some ideologues of the right, but it is more complex.'

How did I know you were going to say that?

'Smith certainly did not think that greed is good, and he was scornful of our hunger for money and power. There is a lovely section in *The Theory of Moral Sentiments* where he describes a man who spends his entire life in the unrelenting pursuit of wealth only to realise that he has sacrificed his youth for nothing. But Smith's genius is revealed at the end of this devastating critique when he suddenly pivots: "And it is well that nature imposes upon us in this manner. It is this deception which rouses and keeps in continual motion the industry of mankind." Our own shameful selfishness is what, paradoxically, motivates us to "invent and improve all the sciences and arts, which ennoble and embellish human life". Private vice can result in public virtue.

And he certainly didn't think that markets were always fair. When he writes about wages, he is clear that there is a big imbalance in bargaining power between the landowner and the labourer. Labourers are by definition poor, and landowners rich. In a dispute, the one can bide his time, the other must feed his family.

This is a crucial point. Modern proponents of laissez-faire economics frequently base its moral legitimacy on the idea that *free and fair* exchange is by definition good. If a deal entered into freely did not improve both sides' position, then it simply wouldn't happen. The logic seems solid. Unless both sides to the exchange expect to benefit, why would they go ahead? Of course the side with more bargaining power is very likely to get the better end of the deal, but if even the weaker gets something out of it, then what's the problem? But Smith was not blind to the power imbalance, or the inequality of outcome that must result.

Nor did Smith think governments should never intervene in markets. He explicitly thought the state should provide for public goods like the education of the common people, which is something that embarrasses his modern, market-fundamentalist advocates.

Adam Smith believed in the power of markets to make our lives better, but he was no blind adherent of laissez-faire. He did not oppose all state intervention and nor did he think selfishness a virtue. But you can discover what you want in his voluminous writings, finding support for both laissez-faire and government intervention.

I've gone on so long about Smith partly because he's often misrepresented. But he is not the only important thinker of this period. I want to quickly introduce Thomas Malthus (1766–1834) and David Ricardo (1772–1823). We'll have done with them by the time we get home.'

Fine. But make it snappy.

'Adam Smith had a sunny disposition. He looked at the world and saw the possibility for improvement. His successors Malthus and, to a lesser extent, Ricardo were rather gloomier in outlook.

Malthus, a clergyman, noticed that he was baptising many more young than he was burying old. And he saw how much poverty there was in his parish. He linked these two observations, and meditated on them in *An Essay on the Principle of Population as it Affects the Future Improvement of Society* (1798). His conclusions were profoundly depressing. Firstly, population is limited by the means of subsistence. As he bluntly put it: "it is the quantity of food which regulates the number of the human species." Secondly, the population will increase when the means of subsistence does. All well and fine, except that the two have very different rates of increase. Population goes up geometrically, subsistence arithmetically (or linearly, as we'd say now).'

This is sounding a bit mathematical...

'I'll try to make it easy for you. Imagine a happily married man and a woman, living in a farm with a field they cultivate. Our couple are blessed with four healthy children. Those four children, if they have, in turn, four children each, will produce sixteen children. If those sixteen children have four each, we reach sixty-four children. Our population has gone from two to sixty-four in four generations. That's a geometric increase. Malthus thought food production could never keep up, increasing at best in a linear fashion. If you begin with one field to feed those original two people, each new generation might bring one more field into cultivation. In four generations, we go from one field to four, and whereas at the start, each person could live off half a field, now each person has to scratch a living from a mere 6.25% of a field for their spuds and carrots. But even this might be optimistic. Malthus saw diminishing returns in each new field brought under cultivation. The best land would always be farmed first, and any new fields would, almost by definition, be less productive than those already in use.

This led to Malthus's third melancholy conclusion, that if sickness, disease or war did not keep populations in check, famine was waiting in the wings.'

Well, you were right. Nothing as depressing as an empty bowl…

'And that is not the worst bit. Malthus also argues that it is pointless to try to help. He thought that if you try to improve the lot of the masses, then they will only have more children and inevitably return to their former desperate condition. Charity was merely cruelty in disguise.'

And was he right?

'Short answer, no. Much of the modern world has escaped the Malthusian trap. Although overall living standards will not improve if a country's population is growing faster than its output, and there have certainly been terrible famines in the two centuries since Malthus wrote his *Essay,* the world is not a hungrier place than it was in his time, despite the massive growth in population. Birth control (a taboo subject in his day) played its part, as did advances in agricultural practices, and improved fertilisers, which boosted food production in ways Malthus couldn't have foreseen. But economic and political changes were just as important. In an agricultural economy, children are assets, every pair of hands is useful. This no longer holds in an increasingly industrial economy, where to do well you have to be educated. Which is expensive, and so the logic leads to smaller families.'

Oh, so not so gloomy after all…

'So, Monty, we are nearly home, but I think there is time for us to talk about one more of the Big Dogs before the end of our walk. Malthus's ideas may be gloomy, but they are joyfully simple to explain. It is a harder job with Ricardo, but let's give it a go. Ricardo and Malthus were good friends, but lived very different lives. Malthus's means were always limited, and he had to keep a close eye on his purse. In contrast, Ricardo made a fortune in business, retiring at forty-two with enough to be comfortable for the rest of his life.

Ricardo's focus was on land, the source of all wealth and a necessarily limited resource. Adam Smith had been concerned with how wealth was generated. For Ricardo, the key question was how this wealth was to be distributed between the three classes: workers, landowners and capitalists.'

Workers and landowners I understand, but capitalists?

'Let's keep it simple for now, and call them factory owners. Ricardo concluded that different classes would tend to get a very different slice of the pie. This uneven distribution of wealth followed logically (he believed) from the theory of rent he developed.

Ricardo argued that land only has value because it is limited and varied in quality. And, following on from the world of his old pal Malthus, it is limited because of the pressures of population. As Ricardo says, if land was like air or water "unlimited in quantity and uniform in quality, no charge could be made for its use".'

OK, I get the first bit – why no one would pay for something that was unlimited. But what has a difference in quality got to do with it?

'Good question. Once again Ricardo builds on Malthus. As the growing population demands to be fed, inferior agricultural land comes under cultivation. And at this point rent will increase, because farmers will always prefer more fertile land to less fertile and will be prepared to pay something for that difference. Rent arises from the difference between the best land and the worst, in a world where there is never quite enough land to go round.

The lot of the worker, for Ricardo, must always be grim. If wages drifted up, then living standards would improve, and the population would increase. Inevitably, this would mean that more workers were pursuing the same number of jobs, and so wages would ratchet back down again. It's as if the worker has not so much a chain, as a piece of elastic tied to his neck. He can stretch it, up to a point, but sooner or later it will drag him back again.

The entrepreneurial class – our capitalists – while responsible for progress in society, would have their gains competed away: population increases would inevitably lead to food price increases, as increasingly unproductive land was forced into use. Thus wages would have to rise in order to pay for this new more expensive (but no more abundant) subsistence living for the workers. Wages that came out of the capitalists' profits.'

You'll forgive me if I hold back a little on my sympathy for the factory owners, when you've just explained how their workers are going to starve.

'Fair point. But Ricardo sees both the capitalist and the worker ultimately as losers. The winners are the landlord class, the old aristocracy, with its near monopoly over land ownership. Holders of a scarce and essential resource, they could just sit back and collect their ever-increasing rents, like a fat spider in the middle of a web, sucking the juice from any fly that blunders into the trap. It is a tribute to Ricardo that, despite being a considerable landowner himself, he was prepared to look at the issue dispassionately.'

Are all economists this miserable? Can we have some cheery stories please?

'Well, Ricardo was famed for his ability to understand the underlying logic of a complex, messy system. But it turned out that his predictions were as wrong as Malthus's. Industrialisation not only put a brake on the rate of increase in the population, it also enormously increased our ability to raise food from our existing land. So, the story has a happy ending. Or rather, it didn't lead to the sort of gross unfairness Ricardo predicted, with the landowning class creaming off all the good stuff.'

You've been quite critical of Malthus and Ricardo. It feels a bit like I've asked you a question, and you've usefully told me two of the wrong answers.

'Hah, well, yes, I suppose I have. Adam Smith is still a "living force" in a way that Malthus and Ricardo aren't – which isn't to say that they're not studied, and don't have some influence, but there aren't many Malthusians or Ricardians in university Economics departments. Perhaps they're most interesting in that they looked rationally at the economy, and the society of which it formed a crucial part, and tried to find scientific laws both to explain the hugely complex processes at play, and to make predictions about the future. In this they were influenced by Newton's scientific revolution, and both wanted to be the Newton of economics. Interestingly, this failed attempt to find scientific laws to explain the battle for survival in human societies did have one incredibly important impact on science. Charles Darwin came back from his round-the-world trip on the *Beagle* in 1836, and quite soon began to work on his theory about how one species might transform into another. What he lacked was any notion of the forces that would drive this process. Then, in 1838, he read Malthus's *Essay* and found in the depiction of too many mouths striving for too little food just such a force. The relentless struggle for existence, combined with random variation in a population, would mean that any small advantage would enable an individual to survive, and pass on that advantage to the next generation. So Malthus's ideas may not be at the heart of economics, but they have found a place in evolutionary biology.

Look, Monty, we're almost home. Let's see if you have been listening. What is economics then?'

Oh, I didn't know there was going to be a test… Markets. Something to do with them? And money? And making stuff and distributing it. And, and…

'Not bad. But here's a nice snappy definition to end on, from another of the great economists, Robert Heilbroner (1919–2005): "Economics is the study of how market-driven society works".'

Easy peasy lemon squeezy. What's next?

'A bit more history. Adam Smith, Malthus and Ricardo are very different thinkers, but, as Heilbroner points out, all three regarded the working class as essentially passive victims. There was no hint in their writing that the suffering classes might take it into their heads to fight for change. On our next walk we can see what happened with the Industrial Revolution, and what Karl Marx and others had to say about it.

And here we are, back in our own street. Thank heavens. This walking and talking is quite hard work.'

You're telling me.

'You've earned a biscuit. And I've earned a cup of tea.'

Walk 3

Part I: The Industrial Revolution

What we talk about on this walk: The Industrial Revolution and how this led to an unprecedented increase in productivity. Why are we 500,000 times better at producing light than our ancestors? We also look at the dark side of the Industrial Revolution: the human costs of working seven-year-old children for fifteen-hour days. In Part II, we visit Karl Marx's grave and learn why he thought revolution was not just desirable but inevitable. Finally, we discuss how economics shifted from moral philosophy to science.

Another day, another walk. But at least the sun was shining.

And what intellectual delights do you have for me today? asked Monty as I battled to hook his lead onto his collar.

'Two main bases to cover: the Industrial Revolution and Karl Marx. And as it isn't far, it might be nice to pay the old boy a visit.'

Huh?

'Marx: buried in Highgate Cemetery. It means getting the bus...'

I love the bus!

And he does. Despite his age, he's still thrilled by the sights and smells, and enjoys the fussing of little old ladies who find him irresistible. But of course we had to wait till we got off the bus before our conversation could begin. The rule is that you're allowed to talk publicly to your dog about what a good boy he is, or what a naughty boy, or to say fetch (not that Monty has ever fetched anything), but going into detail about the means of production is considered... eccentric. But finally we were alone on the outskirts of the cemetery, with just the occasional jogger to interrupt our dialogue.

'Let's kick things off with the Industrial Revolution, which began to get creakily under way around the middle of the eighteenth century, and saw the transformation of an economy based on agriculture and commerce to one in which industrial manufacture became the dominant part of economic activity. From horse power to horsepower.'

Eh?

'Sorry, that works better on the page. The Industrial Revolution led to an unprecedented increase in productivity and, ultimately, a rise in living standards the like of which the world had never seen before, but also saw much human degradation and misery, as the urban poor toiled and laboured in often terrible conditions.

The Industrial Revolution, and the demographic changes that flowed from it, is why Malthus's grim predictions did not come to pass. Imagine a graph that plotted living standards from the year 1000 to today. What you would see would be a long flat line with a sudden uptick at the end – imagine a hockey stick on its side. Actually, I've never liked that analogy – it sounds too American for me, as I suppose they have in mind an ice hockey stick, which has a much longer end bit thingy, whatever it's called. I like to think of it as a dead clown.'

A WHAT?

'You know, a clown… big shoes… lying on their back… feet sticking up. Might not be dead. Could be having a nap. But the point is, more or less flat, with a sharp rise at the end. Got it?'

Sure. But don't kill any more clowns.

'Whatever. Starting from the year 1000, real living standards flatlined for 700 years. Then, beginning in the UK around 1750, things began to change. Productivity surged, connectivity (the speed and ease with which information flows around the world) skyrocketed. Today in the UK living standards are about twenty-five times higher than they were 300 years ago.'

And this happened because… ?

'It was down to a wave of new ideas, new discoveries and new methods that simply meant that we could produce more stuff, for less sweat. Some of the important early breakthroughs were in the textile industry, with John Kay's flying shuttle (1733) and James Hargreaves' spinning jenny (1764) both massively boosting cloth production. From the late 1770s, James Watt developed steam engines that could drive the water pumps that kept coal mines from flooding and powered textile looms. Each of these innovations was important, but taken together they were utterly transformative. Another *illuminating* example was what happened with lighting.'

Groan – OK, I got what you did there.

'For most of human history the night was lit only by the moon, stars, and the flickering of a campfire. The first breakthrough came with oil lamps. Then came candles, made from animal fat, or, if you were rich enough, beeswax, which burned more cleanly and didn't stink the place out. Then there was a big advance when gas lighting was developed in the nineteenth century. But the most dramatic leap forward was electric lighting, introduced in the last quarter of the nineteenth century.

Each stage made lighting a little more efficient, but it remained out of reach for many ordinary workers. To pay for an hour's worth of candlelight in 1800, a typical worker would have to labour for fifty hours. And so, of course, they stayed largely in the dark. By 1880, that figure had come down to three hours' work, for one hour of light. Still beyond the reach of many. Now, how long do you think a typical person (in the developed world) has to work for an hour of electric light?'

I hate these kinds of questions. Just tell me.

'One second.'

OK, that's undoubtedly a thing. But if it's so cheap, how come the Philosopher is always complaining about lights being left on?

'He likes to complain. And he's saving the planet. But mainly it's the complaining.

The same thing has happened in many other fields. Think about how long it takes to send information. In 1860, when Abraham Lincoln was elected President of the US, it took almost eight days for the news to get from Washington DC to California. Or consider how easy it is to physically move stuff – which, after all, is what trade is all about. The invention of container shipping has made it almost incomprehensibly cheap to shift goods from A to B – even where A is China and B is Peru.'

OK, I sort of get what happened, but I was wondering what, er, you know, caused it? The Industrial Revolution, I mean. If the world had just been pootling on for thousands of years what caused the change?

'Ultimately what's going on here is specialisation and innovation. And both of those rely on markets. When people and factories specialise, they need some way to exchange all the different goods they make. Back to Adam Smith's pin factory: specialisation increases productivity. This huge increase in productivity is pointless unless you can trade the excess (who needs 4,800 pins a day?). And this is only possible if you have markets. A teacher or nurse can only specialise in their profession if there are systems in place to supply them with all their material needs, their food and clothing, their transport to work. Their glass of wine to decompress when they get home.'

Ah, that's what you call it.

'You *could* try to do this through direct command. The government could order me to be a teacher, and tell other people to be miners or builders. They could control what farmers grow. They could decree exactly what clothes are made. But the lesson of history is that this has not been very effective. Or you could try to have a system where things were bartered through families and communities (through gifts and sharing). Again, we do see this to a certain extent; a lot of childcare is done exactly in this way. But it was only when markets and firms developed that specialisation really flourished, facilitating unplanned cooperation on a global scale. The people who made my phone did not know or care about me. No bureaucrat decided that I needed it. The people who made it did so because they are better at making phones than me. I ended up with it because I paid for it, which meant *they* could buy the goods that they need or want.'

I get why you need exchange if everyone specialises, but how does innovation depend on exchange?

'No one will put the expense and effort into developing innovative new products just for their own personal use. Inventors need markets, both to reward them for their endeavours and to supply them with the necessities for life.

But innovation and exchange are not the only drivers for this huge increase in productivity and the prosperity that followed on from it. The final part of the puzzle was what is called the demographic transition. Remember Malthus?'

The increase in population equals an increase in misery and starvation guy?

'Yeah, him. Increased productivity is great, but overall living standards will not improve if a country's population is growing faster than its output. And in the early stages of the Industrial Revolution populations exploded. In 1810, the average English woman of childbearing age could expect to have between five and six children. But by the late nineteenth century birth rates had tumbled, and by 1930 on average each woman would have two children. Since then there have been a couple of upward ticks in birth rate, but now we are well below two.'

Why? You might think that kids are expensive, so the richer you are, the more you can have.

'There are lots of explanations. Kids are handy on a farm: chickens have to be fed, crows scared off the fields. In an increasingly urban environment children aren't quite so useful. As economic living conditions begin to improve, parents are less worried that their children might die, so they have fewer. Education becomes more important, so having children is more expensive. As women's status changes and they become more active in the workforce, they have less time to raise children.'

And this is all good, right?

'Generally, yes. But it does throw up some interesting problems. Fewer children means fewer future workers. People are living longer, and those old folks need to be looked after. At the moment almost all developed economies have birth rates that have slipped well below replacement levels. These problems certainly aren't unsolvable, but it may well take some ingenuity, and it's likely to involve major movements of populations from developing to developed countries. But I'm confident that the market is a key part of the solution; it's a brilliant mechanism for bringing together workers and the work that needs to be done. But this is something we'll investigate further when we talk about globalisation on a later walk.'

Right, so can we conclude, without your usual qualifications, that the Industrial Revolution was a Good Thing?

'We can. But the increased productivity took time to feed through into increased incomes for ordinary people. For two to three generations things got no better, and for some may have got a lot worse. For many it was brutal to live through. The economic historian Arnold Toynbee (1852–83) estimated that in 1840 the wages of a labourer would come to eight shillings a week, which was six shillings less than needed to cover the bare necessities of life. The difference was made up by sending his wife and children to work. By 1870 working conditions had begun to improve. Wages crept up enough to enable workers to cover and even exceed the cost of basic food and lodging. And work hours, though still very long, had begun to fall. But this effect was by no means even. Those steam-powered looms we talked of drove hand weavers to destitution. Ultimately, though, the corner had been turned.'

All the time we had been winding through the cemetery, stopping every now and then to admire a mournful monument or gloomily Gothic mausoleum. Monty was beginning to look a little tired.

Have we by any chance turned a corner, too… ?

'We have. We'll head back now, but we'll go via one of the most famous graves in the world.'

Part II: Marx and the Revolution That Didn't Happen

'When I described the Industrial Revolution at the start of our walk as being the shift from agriculture and commerce to industrial manufacturing, what that meant for the people actually involved was a move from the field to the factory. Factory working conditions were grim and required a huge adjustment for the people who worked there. Many violently resisted this change, attacking the machinery and burning the hated mills and sweatshops.

And if the factory was bad, the slums where people lived were worse. Life expectancy in Manchester at the start of the nineteenth century was seventeen years. The squalor and poverty were almost unimaginable. A report on conditions in Glasgow in 1839 described narrow streets clustered around stinking dunghills, bare rooms in which fifteen to twenty people huddled together, some clothed, some naked. Some historians argue that this urban poverty was no harsher than what had gone on before in the countryside, it was just now more visible. And this visibility began to attract public sympathy. This sympathy, along with grassroots organisation through unions and other mass movements, pushed politicians into introducing laws limiting working hours and restricting child labour. Both factors reduced the supply of labour, which in turn nudged up wages. The franchise was gradually expanded, although it wasn't until 1918 that all men over twenty-one were given the vote (all women followed in 1928).

But for some, gradual reform was not enough: they wanted revolution. In the words of *The Communist Manifesto* (1848): "Let the ruling classes tremble at a Communist revolution. The proletarians have nothing to lose but their chains. They have a world to win."'

With perfect timing, we had arrived at Marx's grave: the mighty bust of his head, set high on a marble plinth.

'So here he is, Monty. Well his monument at least. Not really an economist, more a philosopher, but someone whose ideas had a bigger impact on the twentieth century than any economist. Some of the greatest crimes and horrors of the age were committed in his name, but the tragic irony of it was that Marx's economic philosophy was based on believing the best *of* people and wishing the best *for* them. While a market system, which takes for granted their greed and selfishness, has led to far happier outcomes. You see what is written on the plinth?'

No, I am a dog. I can't read.

'Yes of course. You are such a clever chap I keep forgetting. It quotes from Marx: "The philosophers have only interpreted the world in various ways; the point, however, is to change it." And in this he was very successful. For much of the twentieth century at least four out of ten people on earth lived under governments that considered themselves Marxist. On our last walk we talked about Adam Smith, Malthus and Ricardo; in different ways they were all concerned with the plight of the working man. But despite the French Revolution they did not really think about the possibility that the suffering classes might fight back. Well, Marx was about to change that.'[1]

OK, give me some background – when was he around?

'Marx (1818–83) was born in Germany but spent much of his life in exile in England. His two most famous works were *The Communist Manifesto* (1848), which he wrote with his lifelong friend and collaborator Friedrich Engels, and *Capital* (1867–94). Marx questioned the "science" of economics, which he argued simply assumes things such as private property and a system of competitive markets, rather than questioning them. He saw the capitalist system as one with an unavoidable conflict at its heart, a conflict that would inevitably lead to revolution. For Marx, modern society was divided along class lines, each class defined by its relationship to the means of production. The capitalist class owned the factories, the mills, the mines and the forges. The worker has only his or her labour. This labour is bought by the capitalist. The capitalist's wealth comes from the difference between the wages paid to the workers, and the value of what they produce. Let's imagine that I'm the owner of a factory producing metal choke chains of the kind used to discipline unruly dogs.'

Did you actually twirl an imaginary moustache there?

'Might have…'

You're really getting into this Evil Capitalist act, aren't you?

'I'm trying to channel the Philosopher, here: this is more his area than mine. So going a bit method. Anyway, naturally, I want to make a healthy profit on the sale of my choke chains. I have certain costs, for the materials involved. There's not much I can do about that, other than encourage the politicians who represent my class to go out and expand the Empire, to make sure we have access to the rubber and the iron and whatever else I need. Besides the materials, the other cost is the wages of those who toil in my sweatshops. The less I pay them, the greater my profits. And there's something else, an idea that Marx took and adapted from Adam Smith and Ricardo. The cost of the materials in a choke chain is £1. My worker makes ten choke chains an hour in the sweatshop, so I've had to cough up £10 in materials. Let's say I pay my worker £10 an hour, being a generous soul who also likes to keep the maths easy. I sell my choke chains for £10 each. So, in an hour, I have paid out £20, and earned £100. That's a profit of £80.'

Nice work.

'For Marx, that profit, that *surplus value*, can only have come from the labour of the worker. His labour, in other words, is worth £90, but I've paid him only £10. And right there we see the roots of the conflict between the worker and the capitalist. The capitalist steals that surplus value from the worker. The worker wants to be better compensated for his labour. The capitalist wants wages kept as low as possible. Ergo, class conflict.'

Would it be fair to say that you've simplified all this a little?

'It would. Marx is a complex thinker, whose work encompasses history, philosophy and psychology as well as economics, so this is a bit of a caricature. One could easily have a whole series of walks on *How to Teach Marxism to Your Dog*. But we've got a lot more ground to cover. Even those of us who aren't Marxists by any stretch of the imagination can feel the power in much of his critical writing about the reality of capitalism in the nineteenth century. His work contained detailed descriptions of the horrific nature of factory life, much of which was taken from government publications. The most gripping parts of *Capital* are the descriptions of "The Working Day", which show the human cost of brutal working conditions imposed not just on adults, but on small children.

Capitalism, he claimed, enslaves its workers. For Marx the only real difference between capitalism and a slave society was in the way that surplus was extracted from the worker. Workers might appear to be free, but in reality they must take the terms offered by the capitalist or starve. This is inevitable. It is not because the capitalists are cruel or greedy (although some may be) but because the laws of competition coerce capitalists as much as individual workers.'

Hmmm… that all sounds pretty persuasive. I think I might be a Marxist… Wait, hang on, I feel a pun coming – a Barksist!

'Terrible!'

Sorry. But did he have an alternative to all this misery and exploitation?

'He rejected gradual reform, the idea that the workers' lot could be enhanced by higher wages or incremental improvements in conditions, which he thought would be "nothing but a better slave-salary". His solution was a radical transformation, beginning with the common possession of land and the means of production. He argued that, ironically, capitalism would make this transition easy. It had already concentrated wealth into the hands of a few, so all that is needed is for the working class to expropriate these expropriators. But Marx gives almost no detail about what communism in practice might look like. He makes clear, though, that all humans are degraded by private property and regards the aim of human history as being human freedom. He thought that when private property was replaced by communal ownership and socially organised means of production, greed and envy would disappear. And as one's individual interests would now be the same as the interests of society, people would voluntarily cooperate with each other and there would be no need for the state as we know it.'

Too optimistic?

'Perhaps. Marx's failure to even sketch out the new form society would take created great problems for his followers. If we no longer use markets, how do we ensure that the difficult jobs get done? Who cleans the drains? Who digs the coal? Who collects the rubbish? Can the hugely complex webs of trade that bring us our food and clothes and other necessities be replaced by some spontaneous organisation of local people, with no coercion, no monetary incentives, no hierarchies?

Nevertheless, Marx had a brilliant insight into the worst aspects of a ruthless capitalist system. He showed us that "free labour" was much less free than it sounded. That a system of private property and free markets was not an immutable natural order, but created by humans, and that we should question who benefits, who loses out.'

This revolution Marx predicted, how come it never happened?

'Well, of course it did – just not where or when he thought it would. Marx thought revolution was most likely in a developed capitalist society, where capitalism would be at the decadent point where change must come, but also where the workers would have achieved a degree of enlightenment and consciousness of their own strength. In fact it happened first in the least developed part of Europe. There are many suggestions as to why this was the case. Western colonialism played a part: Western economies have exported their exploitation to developing countries, so can afford to treat their domestic workers a bit better. Competition in many industries, especially those where markets are dominated by a few large firms, is less cut-throat than Marx expected. These large firms are able to use some of their market power to pay their workers better. Perhaps most significantly, the state, which Marx dismissed as the executive committee of the ruling class, has increasingly enacted many reforms that have given workers more rights. And so capitalist democracies have been able to broker a stable trade-off between profits and welfare.[2] Hence no revolution, and no Che Guevara beret for the Philosopher.'

Are we done with Marx and revolution?

'Yes, but one last thing before we get home. Marx strongly believed that his system was scientific, that he was discovering laws of human history that would enable him to predict the future state of the world. In fact the part of Marx that has most survived is his early humanistic writing, in which, rather than looking for scientific laws, he was observing and condemning the unfairness and cruelty of the capitalist state, and its despotic governments. But other economists, arguably with more success, have tried to put the subject on a scientific basis. And the key person here is Alfred Marshall (1842–1924), one of the founders of the school of neoclassical economics. His aim was to put the hard numbers into economics, to use the clean, bright light of maths to cut through the confusing murk of human economic activity.'

Hmmm… you've been saying that economics is all about people making decisions. From what I've seen of you lot, there's not much science in that. How many times have you sent the Philosopher out for bread and milk, and he's come back with beer and crisps? Not much sign of the clean, bright light of maths there.

'Marshall acknowledged that there are no economic laws that are as exact as those in physics and chemistry. Economics is the study of human behaviour, and we can never predict exactly what people will do. Nevertheless, he argued that we should at least try to approach economic questions with as much rigour as possible. To this end, he argued that economics should attempt to set out "as best we can well-thought-out estimates, or provisional laws, of the tendencies of human action".[3]

So you can't one hundred percent predict how people behave, but you can at least try to make estimates of what people are more or less likely to do?

'Exactly. He gave the example of the tides. We know that the tide rises and falls twice a day. That there will be strong tides at new and full moon. We can calculate beforehand when a tide will be at its highest, and roughly where that will be. But no one knows enough to say to the inch how high the water will come up on Brighton beach, at a particular hour on a particular day. And this was what he hoped for with economics, so that we might be able to set out economic laws or statements of what we might expect people to do in different situations.

Marshall radically changed the study of economics. His *Principles of Economics* (1890) was for many years the standard introductory textbook for students. It's a book filled with diagrams and equations, generating a strong impression of scientific rigour. He was the first to come up with the standard supply and demand graph. He also introduced key ideas of marginalism and elasticity, which we'll touch on later.

But Marshall did not want the numbers to swamp the ideas, and he took great care to make his work relevant and comprehensible to the layperson, or dog. He wittily summed up his approach in six points.

1. Use mathematics as shorthand language, rather than as an engine of enquiry.

2. Keep to them till you have done.
3. Translate into English.
4. Then illustrate by examples that are important in real life.
5. Burn the mathematics.
6. If you can't succeed in 4, burn 3. This I do often.'[4]

So did he make his case? Is economics a science?

'Economics is the study of human behaviour and, as Marshall said, humans are fickle and unpredictable. People do not follow simple laws the way falling apples do. And this means that there's scope both for arguing that economics needs to be scientific, and for asserting that it can never be. There are certainly times when economists rain blizzards of equations, which seem to obscure more than they illuminate. The term "physics envy" has been coined for this ceremonial donning of the white lab coat.[5] But I am behind Marshall's conviction that there's value in the numbers, and that the difficulty in finding objective laws is worth the effort. Half a loaf, as Orwell put it, is better than no bread, and just because we don't understand everything, that does not mean we understand nothing.'

I looked down at Monty. His little legs were very wobbly. I stooped, and scooped him up – he is a very carriable dog.

'Let's get that bus home, boy. We've done quite enough history. From now on our walks will focus more on how economics is practised today, how it affects our lives, how those numbers beloved of Marshall can shed light on the forces that shape our society.'

Markets: Who Is in Charge of the Bread Supply for London?

What we talk about on this walk: Why markets are so useful. How economists model a simplified (well behaved) market. When markets are not so well behaved (bubbles, bitcoin and bog roll). How markets balance supply and demand. When market outcomes are good. And what can go wrong.

It wasn't destined to be one of our energising park walks but just a stroll through the highways and byways of West Hampstead. When we first moved here, nearly thirty years ago, the high street was a collection of useful, rather old-fashioned shops: a butcher, a fishmonger, a hardware shop, even a little record shop. Now it's pretty much all cafés and charity shops, with the occasional nail bar and a hairdresser or three for variety. It has a bookshop, though, so we should be grateful for small mercies. And it's still quite pretty, in the sunshine. Mildly interesting fact: until the coming of the underground, this area was called West End, and the high street is still called West End Lane. But when the station for the new Metropolitan line was built, they realised that the name West End could confuse passengers who might think they'd reached Theatreland, and so the name West Hampstead was invented.

'OK, Monty,' I began, as he took a slightly disturbing amount of interest in some black bin liners left out on the street, 'I think we are now finally ready to talk some crunchy, contemporary economics. But before we start, let's quickly recap. We've discussed the three main ways that societies have used to solve the economic problem: tradition, command and markets. And then we talked about how the development of a market *system*, where people were able to specialise and exchange goods, resulted in huge increases in productivity and innovation. And on our last walk we talked about the Industrial Revolution, which brought about the most extraordinary leap in living standards that the world has ever seen (remember the dead clown). But, as Marx described, those advances came at a cost, and it was paid, as costs so often are, exclusively by the poor. The horrors of the Industrial Revolution engendered communism, which ultimately proved to be a failed economic experiment. But part of the reaction was also the "invention" of economics as the study of markets. We've seen economics move from moral philosophy (Adam Smith) to a more formalised science of how markets work (Marshall).'

And today? (Monty had dragged himself away from the olfactory delights of the rubbish.)

'Today I want as an hors d'oeuvre to talk about how economists model market behaviour, and then, for the main course, how the combined forces of supply and demand determine price and quantity.'

I've heard you mention models a couple of times now. I assume you're not talking about the Warhammer models that Gabriel used to make...

'When economists talk about a model what they mean is some simplification of reality, a stripping away of the distracting irrelevances, to leave a meaningful core. Sometimes things are so simplified that they seem to lose touch with reality. But this lack of realism is not necessarily a bad thing. What goes on in an economy is overwhelmingly messy and complex, the result of millions of actions and interactions. To even begin to understand the big picture you need some way to simplify it all. Think of economic models as like the London tube map. The reality of hundreds of miles of twisting track is simplified to give you all the key information you need: the number of stops between stations and interchanges, a rough idea of direction.'

Got it. I think.

'OK, Monty, so let's imagine that an economist is trying to understand the way the market works for some particular good or product. Let's say it's—'

Cute dogs like me?

'Sure. So in trying to understand the market for cute dogs, economists construct a hypothetical model of what they term a *perfectly competitive market*. This tells them what would happen if there were nothing to get in the way of free competition. They assume that each of the goods that is being bought and sold is identical. So, in our example all the dogs would be exactly as cute and lovely as you.'

Impossible!

'Remember, we're being hypothetical. And they assume that there are many buyers and many sellers, and that none of them are so powerful that they can have an impact on supply and demand by themselves. They also take it for granted that people act rationally, and are able to make the choices that most benefit them. They assume that there are no externalities.'

No what, now?

'By externalities I mean there is no positive or negative impact on people who are not party to the exchange. But don't worry, we'll join the dots on that a little later, as it's really important.

Finally, they assume that the buyers and sellers understand exactly what they're getting, and how much it costs.'

A lot of assumptions. I've heard you tell Gabe and Rosie more than once that to assume *makes an* ass *out of* U *and* me.

'It's true that these assumptions seem to be pulling us away from reality. But it's a distance that brings perspective and clarity. Remember that tube map? It really is easier to understand than if the map contained the reality of twisting and jumbled lines.'

OK, I'll give you that. So what does this simplified model of the perfectly competitive market for cute dogs tell us?

'First let's think about it from the buyer's point of view, or, in economist talk, the *demand* side. A central idea in economics is that people respond to financial incentives. If the price of something falls, then buyers will want more of it. As cute puppies get cheaper people will tend to buy more of them.

From the seller's perspective, or the *supply* side, it is also plausible to think that as the price goes up, sellers will want to sell more. If I'm getting £100 for a puppy, I might not be inclined to work my socks off to get them to the market. But at £1,000, I'm busting a gut.'

Nothing too shocking in all that.

'Nope, but this is just the build-up. We're about to hit a really important point, so I hope you're paying attention.'

All ears.

'OK, drumroll: economics predicts that the price of a good – that's our cute little puppy in this case – will tend to settle at the point where the demand equals supply. This is called the *equilibrium*.'

Not sure that's quite drumroll material. Spell it out a bit more?

'Some people are hard to impress. What this is really saying is that there is a dynamic relationship between the quantity demanded, the quantity supplied and price. If demand for puppies goes up, more people will be chasing the same number of puppies and, all other things being equal, the price will rise. This is exactly what we saw happen during the pandemic. Many of us were stuck at home and decided that we needed the love of a canine companion, demand soared and the price of desirable puppies more than doubled.'

Not a hundred percent happy with this commerce in my canine brothers. Can we make it a bit less personal?

'OK, let's shift sideways into dog food. Imagine that for some reason the price for dog food was temporarily above the equilibrium point where demand equalled supply. At this high price you would have more sellers than buyers. There would then be an excess of dog food on the market. Warehouses would fill up. Eventually sellers would start undercutting each other's prices to get rid of all those tins. The price would fall until – you guessed it – it reached the equilibrium where quantity demanded equals quantity supplied.

Now imagine the reverse. The price is below the point where quantity demanded equals quantity supplied. The tins are cheap, so dog owners rush to stock up. Now you have a situation where too many people are chasing too little dog food. There will be shortages, so suppliers might start ... ?'

Increasing the price.

'Until?'

You reach equilibrium.

'Excellent. You're now an economist. The beautiful thing here is that the system automatically self-regulates. If prices rise, causing higher profits, then, over time, sellers will shift their attention to producing this good. If prices fall, then sellers will be prompted to provide other products. And here we have Adam Smith's model of the naturally self-regulating system of supply and demand that would be familiar to any first-year economics undergraduate.

Another important point is that economists will describe markets like this as *efficient*. If markets are efficient then buyers will not have to wait in a queue to buy what they want, and sellers won't have surpluses sitting on a shelf. But this is not the same thing as the outcome being fair, and economists certainly do not think that nothing can or should be done to intervene.

This principle is often called the *law of supply and demand*, although that really should be two separate laws: the law of demand, which says that at higher prices, buyers will demand less of an economic good; and the law of supply, which says that at higher prices, sellers will supply more of an economic good.

Adam Smith famously grappled with the slightly unintuitive idea that price comes not from the intrinsic value of a thing, but from this interaction of supply and demand. He used the example of diamonds. Why would we value diamonds so much and water so little? Common sense might suggest the reverse. One is necessary for life, the other a mere frippery. The answer, put crudely, is that there are many people who are prepared to pay a lot for diamonds and the supply is very limited. In contrast, water is something that is vital, but because the supply is (for now) so plentiful compared to demand, water is extremely cheap. For an economist the price of a good is a function of our demand for it (how much we are prepared to pay for it) and the supply of it (how plentiful or cheap it is to provide). It's worth stressing here that economics has no view on the moral aspect of all this. For economists intrinsic value has no meaning. Value is exchange value, nothing more.'

Any chance of a diamond-studded collar…?

'Bit bling for a scruffy old dog like you.'

Not necessarily for me. There's a certain Pekinese who's moved in down the road…

'Penelope?'

Possibly, I didn't quite catch her name…

'Not sure we can run to diamond necklaces, I mean collars. Perhaps I should change the example again. Let's look at how two different taxi markets work. London is famous for its black cabs. They are safe, comfortable, and the drivers know the whole of London like you know the lampposts on our street. But the cost of taking a black cab is quite inflexible. There's a set tariff, and that's what you pay. This is an example of a market that does not look much like our model of perfect competition. Black cabs do charge a bit more at weekends, bank holidays and in the evening, but apart from that the price is fixed. This means that there are often shortages, and there will be times when it might be almost impossible to get a black cab. Before Covid, catching a black cab when you came out of the pub at closing time was a lottery. And at other times there would be more cabs than passengers, with the drivers waiting around in bored ranks.

Uber works completely differently. They developed a very sophisticated algorithm that allows them to increase fares depending on the scarcity of drivers. The goal for their pricing is to find an "equilibrium" price that matches passenger demand with the supply of drivers. And it works. One of the consequences is that you get very large surges in prices. When the demand for Uber goes up, so do the prices. They are a (rare) example of a real market that looks pretty like that hypothetical model of perfect competition.'

But I seem to remember the Philosopher going on about how evil Uber were – something about how they exploited workers…

'Good point, Monty. The Philosopher is, for once, not entirely wrong. There are some valid criticisms of Uber. Consumers might have benefited from a cheaper ride back from the pub, but for the drivers the picture is less rosy. For a long time Uber argued its drivers were self-employed. This meant that the company could minimise their tax, and their drivers did not get holiday pay, sick pay or pensions.[1] It is worth repeating that when economists set out the model of perfect competition, they are not all saying that this is what all markets should look like. We may well want to intervene. They are just posing the question: does this model help us to understand anything about the underlying forces of supply and demand in our economy?'

Hmmm… I think I'm with you. But you humans being fickle creatures, don't you demand change all the time? Remember when the Philosopher went on some weird diet and only ate cornflakes for a month? And when you both do dry January, I imagine that's a pretty big blow to the West Hampstead wine trade.

'Cheeky. If demand (or supply) changes then you will see – in a market where prices are flexible – a change in price and quantity. What happened with Covid-19 in the spring of 2020 gives us lots of examples. Suddenly, for some strange reason, people decided to stockpile toilet paper.'

So, come the apocalypse, is a dirty bum really going to be the worst of your problems?

'Yes, the loo paper thing was a bit strange. But, for whatever reason, Covid-19 caused a sudden increase in demand for various goods. Face masks, hand gel, medicines, storable food, and even dogs. In some cases, there were big price surges. However, this was deeply unpopular with the public, and authorities sometimes stepped in to prevent "price gouging". In New York, they fined shops that hiked prices on hand sanitiser and cleaning products. In other cases, prices did not change but you simply could not buy the product, and many shops introduced rationing. Both of these reactions (price rises or rationing to deal with shortages) are precisely what the simple model of a market would predict.

One last bit of jargon I want to get across is the idea of *elasticity*. I started out by saying that if the price of a good is high, we would expect people to buy less of it; if the price is lower we would expect people to buy more. So the question is, just how sensitive are people to changes in price? Marshall came up with the term *elasticity* to describe this sensitivity to price. We call demand *elastic* when it is very responsive to changes in price, and *inelastic* when demand does not react much to price changes. We're going to talk much more about this on our next walk, which will be about how people respond to incentives, but for now just remember that *elasticity* is the norm: if the price goes up, demand will go down.'

OK, got it – I think. Markets are clever. Price tends to settle where demand equals supply. If demand or supply shifts then prices or availability will change, and elasticity tells you how much prices will adjust. Do markets always work this way?

'Everything described above is how you might describe a well-behaved market. But, no, as with dogs and children (and

Philosophers), not all markets are well behaved. In particular, markets for assets can be … strange.'

Assets?

'Things we buy not to consume, like an ice cream, but to keep, to sell on, or as an investment.'

Got it. Like a bone I bury, rather than scoff.

'Sorta. If you are buying something to consume, then rising prices will generally reduce demand. However, if you are buying something as an *asset*, this can change. If you think a high price today is a signal to expect even higher prices tomorrow then that can become a self-fulfilling prophecy and you end up in a bubble. At least for a time. But eventually the bubble pops.'

Bubble … ? Who doesn't like bubbles?

'A bubble is when the market goes crazy for something not because of its intrinsic value, but because buyers spot a careering bandwagon and desperately jump aboard.'

Bubbles? Bandwagons? I think you may be mixing your metaphors a bit …

'Sorry, yes. An example or two may help. The first famous bubble was the tulip craze in Holland in the early 1600s when a mad passion for tulips took hold of a whole society. Some rare tulips sold for more than the price of an Amsterdam mansion.[2] More recently we have had the dot.com bubble of the late 1990s, when stock in tech companies massively increased in value, and then, in 2000, almost as suddenly collapsed. Because that's the thing about a bubble: in the end, it bursts. The US housing market bubble of 2007 is another example. Exponential rise, followed by sudden collapse. Many think that the next potential bubble waiting to pop is bitcoin (of which much more, anon). Robert J. Shiller, a Nobel Prize-winning economist who was famous for predicting earlier bubbles, certainly thinks that bitcoin is just the latest example of collective irrationality. Shiller has likened bubbles to mass delusions, and argues that like a mental illness they can be best defined according to a checklist of symptoms. His checklist for a bubble includes:

1. a time of rapidly increasing prices;
2. people telling each other stories to justify the reason why the price increase makes sense this time;
3. people telling each other stories about how much money they are making;
4. people feeling envy and regret that they did not get involved.'

I am sort of confused; you said earlier that markets are why we are all so rich, and you talked about perfect markets. But then you started talking about bubbles. And I know I'm a dog and that money does not play a big part in my life, but that tulip example is insane. So what is it, are markets all-knowing, or are markets idiots?

'Sometimes markets work well, sometimes they work badly. The trick is to grasp how they work, so that you can understand and improve the economic system. But with asset markets you do clearly get some periods of mass delusion.'

So sometimes the market goes mad. Does that not suggest that maybe we ought to use some other system? Something sane and rational?

'The main alternative that has been tried is central planning.'

Oh, the command thing from our second walk?

'That's the one.'

Was pondering that. Surely it makes sense to have someone clever in charge to plan something as important as the economy?

'In some ways this does sound appealing. On the surface, markets seem a very anarchic way to organise things. And it is not obvious that a system that is based on everyone just trying to get the best deal for themselves would be so much better than central planning. There is a nice story about a Soviet official who visited London in the 1960s. He asked, "Who is in charge of bread supply for London?" The answer is, of course, no one.

Should this worry us? Well generally, no. London does fine for bread. During Covid-19, there was a period where the system did break down, and the government became involved. But fairly quickly, shops did sort out supply. I think it might be easier if I give you a couple of examples.

It is hard to think of a country that makes less use of markets than North Korea. And as North Korea effectively split from South Korea in 1945 one also has a standard to judge it against. Before the Second World War, the two regions were similar in economic development. But by 2017 GDP per capita, measured in US dollars, was about $32,000 in South Korea and less than $2,000 in North Korea. (Oh, and don't worry about exactly what GDP means – we'll go into detail on that on another walk… For now just take it as a rough measure of a country's prosperity.) And while money is not everything, there is little doubt that, at least up to a certain minimum level, GDP is correlated with quality of life.

Or take East and West Germany. After the Second World War, Germany was divided into two different economic systems: capitalism in West Germany, central planning in East Germany. Before this division they had very similar living standards and shared the same language, culture and capitalist economy. Once again we have a natural experiment of central planning versus an economy that made much greater use of markets. In 1989, when the Berlin Wall fell, East Germany's GDP per capita was less than half that of West Germany's.'

OK, let's assume that you're right and that free markets lead to faster economic growth than planned economies. What's the explanation?

'One of the most famous champions of the free markets was the Austrian economist Friedrich Hayek. I mentioned him earlier. Generally, people argue that centrally planned economies don't work because of incentive problems. Why flog your guts out if everyone gets given the basic needs of life? Hayek pointed out a more subtle problem with command economies. He argued that price is a signal; it tells you how relatively scarce a good is. And that it is this information that is lost in a centrally planned system. He gives the example of a small businessman deciding whether he should use tin in his factory. Suppose, for whatever reason, there is a shortage of tin. The businessman does not need to know why there is a shortage of tin, all he needs to know is that tin has got slightly more expensive and that he'll save money if he uses something else. And this small decision will rapidly spread through the whole economic system, influencing not only how people use tin, but also how people use its substitute, or the substitute of the substitute.

Leaving aside the greater efficiency of markets, there's also a moral aspect. Markets are all about freedom. For economists like Hayek and Milton Friedman, markets provide a way for people to voluntarily cooperate rather than being told what they can or cannot do by a government bureaucrat.[3] Free markets reduce the area of our life that is subject to political power.'

Hmmm. Well that all sounds very nice. But what happens if you don't have enough money to buy anything in a market? That does not sound very free to me.

'That is a really good point. Adam Smith was keenly aware that the difference in bargaining power between landlords and workers meant that it was clear which side was going to get most of the benefit of any exchange. But this is such a huge (and important) subject, I think we should give it its very own walk. Let's just keep to markets for now.'

I'll look forward to it. From what you've been saying, markets are all butterflies and flowers. Can they really do no wrong?

'Getting rid of markets completely would be a really bad idea (not even North Korea has been able to do that), but that does not mean they are perfect. There are many areas of life where, for good reasons, we do not use markets. Most interactions between family and friends don't involve markets. Gabriel and Rosie don't have to buy parental services from the Philosopher and me. In some cases, we actively forbid markets, for example with illegal drugs and human organs. Finally, even the most ardent supporters of free markets acknowledge that the government plays a very important role, not least in providing a framework of rules without which markets could not exist.

There are probably two main reasons why not everything should be organised through markets: questions of fairness and questions about whether the assumptions we made when first talking about our model of a market are satisfied. We'll focus on fairness and inequality in another walk. But if the assumptions we made earlier are not reasonably satisfied then markets will work less well. So, Monty, can you remember what the assumptions for a perfectly competitive market were?'

Me, oh yes, absolutely. I was definitely listening. So the first assumption was… er no sorry, I've got nothing.

'Don't worry. Look, we are nearly home, let's have five minutes sitting on this bench and I will go through them. I said that we should assume that people are the best judges of what is good for them. But is this always the case? If people are not making the "right" choice about what they buy, then markets might not be a very effective way of increasing human welfare. But the big question is, if we don't trust people to make important decisions about their own lives, then who do we trust? I would argue that even if people do not always make the right choices for themselves, the alternative – that government officials will choose for you – may well be worse. And even if the government is acting rationally, on things like healthy eating, say, should a person be compelled to do what they don't want to do, even for their own good?

Another assumption we made was that individual buyers and sellers are small in relation to the size of the market. And this matters because it means no buyer or seller is big enough to impact the market price. But reality is often different. An extreme example of this would be a monopoly, where one company totally dominates the market, and can set whatever prices it wants. We talked about Uber earlier. They have been accused of using very aggressive tactics to drive their competitors out of the market. Another company with a reputation for playing tough is Amazon. In the early days of the internet, two school friends, Marc Lore and Vinit Bharara, set up Diapers.com, selling, well, diapers – nappies – and other baby products to time-pressured new parents. Amazon liked the look of their business and offered to buy them out. The founders wanted to remain independent and turned the offer down. Subsequently Amazon dropped prices on nappies by thirty percent. Every time Diapers.com changed their prices, Amazon would change its prices accordingly. Amazon were ready and able to lose a huge amount of money for a long time. There was no contest. In a bruising series of negotiations Diapers.com eventually sold out to Amazon.'[4]

Sneaky.

'I also said that the perfect market assumes that there are no externalities...'

Remind me, what's an externality?

'An externality is where some commercial or industrial activity has an impact on third parties, without that being reflected in the market price. The classic example is pollution. But this is a big subject and I think we should have a whole separate walk about it. (See walk 8)

The last standard assumption was that of perfect information: that buyers and sellers know the price and the quality of the good that they are buying. The market will not generally be efficient if there is imperfect information. Again, more on this later. (See walk 9)

As you see, Monty, all of these assumptions can be questioned. There is probably no market in the real world that looks like the textbook model of perfect competition. But realism is not the point of the model. The point of the model is to help us to think about the underlying forces of supply and demand, to focus our minds on where markets might work well, where there might be problems and what we might want to do about it.

There are also more profound critiques of the market. Some have contended that markets themselves corrupt us. Michael Sandel argues that markets are bad as they encourage people to see themselves only as individuals cut off from the rest of society, careless about the consequences of their actions. Laissez-faire economics sees each of us as an economic unit, rationally maximising our own interest, a sort of selfish robot.

And you do have to question if material wealth is the only measure of a good life. Love, friendship, family, all these things are important, and all hard to place in that intricate web of commercial transactions that makes up the market.

But for now I think the key idea is that while material wealth is not everything, it does correlate pretty highly with lots of other things we value. It's hard to be happy when your only source of heat and light at night is a choking fire made from dried animal dung, as it still is for millions of people around the world. And if markets can fix that, then we have a moral duty to understand them and the benefits they potentially bring.'

Hang on, animal dung? That's not why you collect mine in bags, is it?

'No, but best not to mention it to the Philosopher or he'll try to use it as a way of reducing our fuel bill.'

Household Behaviour: You Can't Always Get What You Want, But if You Try Real Hard...

What we talk about on this walk: How people respond to incentives. In a world of limited resources this involves making trade-offs. We discuss the exceptions to the rule: Giffen goods and Veblen goods. We examine how demand for different types of goods is impacted by increases in income (and Monty realises that he is a luxury good). Finally, and perhaps most importantly, how do we make choices when it comes to our most valuable resource of all, our time? Was Keynes right or wrong?

It was a drizzly sort of day, good for the garden but bad for walking, so I snuggled down with Monty on the sofa. In his old age he probably prefers this to a dank walk, although he'd never admit it.

Admit what?

'Oh, nothing. Was I talking to myself again?'

Kinda. So what's today's topic?

'Remember how yesterday we were talking about how markets work?'

Mm hm.

'I said we can generally assume that if the price of something went down, people would buy more of it. This is sometimes referred to as the *law of demand*.'

Yes, I remember. And its best mate, the law of supply.

'Good, but today we're focusing on the demand side. Distressing though it is for economists, these laws don't work like the laws of physics, but as generalisations go, the law of demand is pretty solid. What I want to dig into a bit more today are two key ideas. First, the fact that we respond to incentives. Second, that this involves making trade-offs. In Mick Jagger's immortal words: "You can't always get what you want" (incidentally, he studied at the LSE). In the jargon, this is referred to as "opportunity cost", in other words the unavoidable trade-offs that you have to make in the presence of scarcity.

Steven Landsburg has said that most of economics can be summarised in four words: "people respond to incentives"; the rest is just commentary. This ties back to Hayek's famous insight that free markets work because price contains information as well as a reason to respond to it.'

I'm a dog. I respond to treats, walks, belly rubs. You are going to have to give me some examples about prices.

'In 2015 the UK government introduced a 5p charge for plastic bags. The result has been an estimated eighty percent drop in their use. In 2003 London introduced a congestion charge. The result, after ten years, was a traffic reduction of ten percent. In Mexico in 2014 they put a tax on sugary drinks and sales fell by nearly ten percent by the second year. These are all examples of what are sometimes called "sin" taxes, taxes on things that society wants to discourage. These taxes are seen as a double win, as they are a way to both improve public health and raise money. The point I want to make is not really whether these taxes are a good idea or a bad one (some argue that sin taxes punish the poorest hardest), rather that they are effective, demonstrating that we respond to price signals. If the price of something goes up, we buy less of it.'

I can see that if a soft drink gets more expensive you might cut down. No one needs Coke. But what about other stuff, stuff you do actually need?

'Good point, Monty. The idea that people respond to incentives may be true, but we also want to know how much they respond. Sometimes people are very sensitive to changes in price, other times not so much. Remember we talked about *elasticity*?'

Oh, yeah. If the price goes up, and demand goes down, that's elastic. Like the Philosopher putting on the trousers with the elastic waist when you go out with the girls and he orders a 16" pizza.

'Lovely image, thanks. As you point out, with a soft drink you might expect demand to be very responsive to price. There are loads of very similar soft drinks to choose from, and you can easily do without a drink. So if one brand increases their price, people will react by switching to other brands. But let's say you have a job where you need to drive to work, then you might be less responsive to price changes in petrol (demand might be relatively *inelastic*).'

And now I'm wondering if the market for elastic is elastic or inelastic? Inelastic, I suppose. I mean, without it, the Philosopher's trousers would fall down, wouldn't they?

'Moving on… in answer to your question, Monty, although it's harder to use less petrol than to switch brand of cola, people do adapt. They might carpool, or switch to a more fuel-efficient car, or buy a bike. As a consequence of all this, firms are very aware of how elastic the demand for their product is. Netflix has been spending enormous amounts on developing new content and has been gradually increasing its prices in the US. It is gambling that demand for its product is relatively inelastic – that those higher prices will not result in it losing too many of its subscribers.

Governments also have to be aware of elasticity. If a tax hike is supposed to raise money (as opposed to changing behaviour), there's no point targeting something that's very price sensitive. You might just find that you end up reducing demand so much that the revenue goes down. The window tax that England introduced in 1696 is a good example.'

Hang on, a tax on actual windows? Like, the more you have, the more you pay?

'Exactly that. Intuitively, a window tax might sound like a good idea. It is a difficult tax to avoid as it is pretty hard to hide how many windows you have. And it sounds fair: the richest people are generally those who live in big houses with the most windows. Yet the results were, to an economist, predictable. People started bricking up their windows. This led to especially wretched conditions for the poor living in tenement buildings, where in some cases landlords removed windows from entire floors. The tax made windows more expensive, so people "demanded" fewer windows. Charles Dickens spoke out against it, arguing that a tax intended for the rich was depriving the poorest of both air and light. The window tax was eventually repealed in 1851.'

So that was curtains for the window tax.

'Very good. We also respond to *how* we are paid. When we are paid on commission we often work harder. One particularly brutal example of this was the transportation of convicts to Australia. Initially private ships were paid a flat rate by the UK government to transport the convicts, and between 1790 and 1792 twelve percent died on the journey. As the ships' captains could sell any unused provisions once they reached Australia, there was actually an incentive to let the convicts die, and die early. On one ship thirty-seven percent perished. How to solve this problem? The English government decided to appeal to financial self-interest and gave captains a bonus for each convict who reached Australia alive. The result was that death rates fell to almost zero.'[1]

OK, you have me convinced about this incentive thing, and the law of demand. But you said there were some exceptions?

'The law of demand is pretty much the most ironclad rule that there is in economics. But, yep, there are a couple of interesting exceptions. One special case is a *Giffen good* (named after a nineteenth-century British civil servant, Sir Robert Giffen). A Giffen good is where increasing the price of something paradoxically increases demand.

So why would this happen? Imagine that you are really poor and can afford only two types of food: some staple like rice, which provides most of your calories, plus a small amount of meat. Now imagine that the price of rice goes up. You are only just getting enough calories as it is, and if you still bought the meat, you'd have to cut back on rice. But that will leave you with insufficient calories to survive. Your only option is to stop buying the meat and buy more rice – even though it is now more expensive.

Another situation in which demand increases as the price goes up is with a so-called *Veblen good*. But here it happens for a very different reason. Some people might argue that you are a Veblen good, Monty.'

I don't know what it means but I like the sound of it. But a Veblen good is actually good, isn't it? Because, to be honest, the Giffen good was pretty bad, all things considered.

'I will let you decide. Veblen goods are named after the economist Thorstein Veblen (1857–1929), who coined the term "conspicuous consumption". An example might be an Hermès bag, or indeed you, Monty, as you are a very superior dog indeed.'

Too true, but conspicuous consumption means… ?

'Buying things to show off, basically. With a Giffen good the reason demand increased as price did was because of a poverty trap. Here it is exactly the opposite. It is the desire to signal status. People want these goods not *despite* the fact they are expensive, but *because* they are expensive and, crucially, other people know it. Hermès bags can come with a price tag of over £10,000, and are kept deliberately in very short supply. You can't just walk into an Hermès shop and buy a Birkin bag. You must order it, and there is a long waiting list. But if they were available for a tenth, or even a hundredth, of the price on every department store shelf, arguably demand would fall.'

And that's me? A status symbol?

'Well, certainly *some* dogs are. Anyway, I hope all these examples have convinced you that, bar the odd exception, we respond to price incentives in some predictable ways.

Another key concept here is that consumers have to make trade-offs. Most of us have limited resources, of both time and money. We have to make choices about how we use those resources. And to do one thing means closing off the possibility of doing something else. Economists refer to these "missed opportunities" as *opportunity costs*. Opportunity costs are easy to overlook. When people consider the cost of, say, going to university, they'll tot up their tuition fees and living expenses. But they might well ignore how much they could earn if they worked rather than studied. That is the opportunity cost. If I decide to take you for a walk this afternoon, then the opportunity cost is the money I could be earning while we were out.'

OK, got it.

'We all have a budget, and within that we will try to find a combination of different goods and services that best suits our preferences. So one question is, what happens to demand when our budget increases, when we get richer? Economists approach this question by looking at how the demand for different types of goods responds to increases in income. They classify goods into *inferior goods* and *normal goods*.'

Sounds a bit judgy…

'I suppose it does, and it is! Inferior goods are goods where, as income rises, demand will fall. Think of cheap food, or unbranded supermarket products or, historically, at least, a bike. Another example would be taking out a payday loan, when you can't borrow from a more reputable source. These are all things that people buy because they can't afford what they really want.

In contrast, with normal goods, demand rises with income. "Normal" because this is what we would expect: if you get a bit richer you tend to buy more of things. Normal goods are further divided into *necessity* and *luxury* goods.

Luxury goods are the kind of things on which people spend a higher proportion of their income as they get richer.

An example would be sports cars, watches, holidays, or fancy dogs like you, Monty. If you're poor, you just don't waste your money on these things. If you're rich, you can, and usually do.

When it comes to necessity goods, demand will also rise as income rises, but not as much as your income rises. Food or utilities would be an example.'

Can you explain that bit about demand rising but not as much as your income?

'Sure. Take food. Generally, as people get richer, they do spend more on food. They buy more of it (they throw away more of it too) and they tend to buy more expensive types of food. But they do not increase their spending on food by as much as their income increases: there's only so much you can eat.

Talking of eating, how about we go to the café and share a bacon sandwich?'

Monty loves bacon more than an economist loves, well, I don't know, a spreadsheet showing bacon production figures in the third quartile of the last tax year. He galloped off and grabbed his lead from the hall chair. I've said before he looks down on most doggy tricks, but fetching his lead is one he's mastered. I got him harnessed up and we ventured down to the high street. The complex interactions of rent, rates, demand and supply have, as I've observed before, turned what was once a varied selection of useful shops into, if not a monoculture, then a triculture, with cafés, charity shops and hairdressers dominating the ecosystem, much as rats, cockroaches and pigeons will take over once the apocalypse comes. We went to one of the more established non-chain cafés, and found a comfy corner.

'OK, Monty, so far today we have been talking about what economists call "decision making under scarcity". And what is the ultimate scarce resource?'

Dog biscuits?

'Our time.'

Oh, sure. You know, from a dog's perspective, you humans are weird. All this time sitting hunched in front of your computer to earn money when you could just be taking me for a walk. Never mind these people who actually pay someone else to do it. It's like paying someone to eat your dinner for you.

'You are a wise chap, my friend. But this whole work/life balance that we responsible adults have to negotiate is a bummer. Imagine that you had a job for forty hours a week paying you £10 an hour. So you have £400 a week to spend on stuff.'

Er, income tax?

'What?'

I don't know really what it is, except that the Philosopher thinks everyone should pay more, and you think everyone should pay less.

'Fine. Let's just pretend there's no such thing as tax. Right, now imagine that by some stroke of luck your hourly wage was increased by six times, to £60 an hour. Would you carry on working forty hours and enjoy the extra spending power – you've now got £2,400 a week in your sweaty paws. Or would you decide that you don't want any more stuff and would rather have the time? In which case you could now cut your working week to fewer than seven hours a week. What would you do?'

Well, I'm a dog, so I'm definitely going to take the time. And second, how realistic is that? An increase of six times sounds extreme.

'I chose an increase of six times deliberately as this is roughly the increase in average hourly real earnings for Americans over the twentieth century. In 1930, John Maynard Keynes wrote an essay: "Economic possibilities for our grandchildren".[2] He was writing this during the Great Depression, a time of profound economic pessimism. But Keynes was an upbeat guy – he said that his only regret in life was not drinking more champagne. In this essay he made two bold predictions about what life for his grandchildren would be like in a hundred years' time. Which is basically now. First, Keynes predicted that, because of techno-logical advances, we would be between four and eight times better off. Second, that as a result, we would only need to work for fifteen hours a week.'

I'm not keeping count, but you humans all seem to work more than fifteen hours a week…

'Keynes was pretty much spot on with his first prediction. Incomes in the US, as I said, increased more than six-fold during the twentieth century. But Keynes clearly got the second bit wrong. A journalist tried to track down his grandchildren to ask them how many hours they worked.'[3]

And…?

'Turned out he didn't have any. But they found his sister's grandson, which was close enough. Keynes's great-nephew is Nicholas Humphrey, now retired, but he was a professor of evo-lutionary psychology. He estimated that he worked fifteen hours a *day*.'

So how come Keynes got it so wrong?

'Richard Freeman, Harvard University economist, argued that Keynes's mistake was to think about leisure as if it was a luxury good. Remember we said that what makes a luxury good a luxury good was that the more money you had, the more you would spend on it? So if leisure is a luxury good…'

The richer we become the more of it we 'buy'.

'Exactly. Keynes anticipated that as we all got wealthier we would take more time off. This is what economists call *the income effect* – as we get richer we buy more of something. But very often we do not see this happen. Look at famous film or sports stars. Arnold Schwarzenegger got paid $29 million for the third Terminator movie. LeBron James, a basketball player, was expected to make $94 million in 2021. Why don't they both quit and lead a life of leisure?'

Perhaps because they enjoy what they do?

'That's certainly one reason. There is no doubt that Keynes ignored this element. Some of us find purpose and meaning in our careers. Keynes probably had in mind the ordinary working person, slaving in a factory or bored to death in an office. And he didn't follow his own advice. Despite the champagne quip, and the fact that he had a pretty adventurous private life, he worked notoriously hard until the day he died.

But there is another economic effect in play here, pulling in the opposite direction. And that is the *substitution effect*. This says that as something gets relatively more expensive (leisure, in our example), people will switch away from it. Time for another hypothetical question. Imagine your daily rate is £500, and you have the choice of working (and earning that £500) or going to the park on a beautiful sunny day. What would you pick?'

Well, I do like the park, but £500 is a lot of money. Suddenly it seems kind of expensive to go to the park…

'Exactly, and this is our substitution effect. In making the trade-off between work or leisure, when you earn a lot, taking time off can feel like you're burning money. Of course, you are not literally charged for your free time, but remember when I mentioned the idea of opportunity cost? The opportunity cost of your free time increases when your wage increases. When your wage goes up, two things happen. You get more income for each hour you work. This is the income effect. With the same amount of free time, you can now have more consumption. But your free time has now got more expensive, so you have an incentive to work more and take less time off. This is the substitution effect.'

So what will happen? Does the income effect or the substitution effect win out?

'One way to answer that is to look back over time and see what actually happened. The Industrial Revolution led to a dramatic increase in wages. Did people use this to buy more free time or more stuff? The crude answer is a bit of both.

Working hours first increased steeply during the Industrial Revolution. The worker's day might easily last eighteen hours. In England, a committee of Parliament set up in 1832, to look into factory conditions, described children working nineteen-hour days with barely any breaks. Then, from about 1870 to 1950, hours of work decreased dramatically across all developed countries. Things get interesting from the 1950s. In Europe, working hours continued to decline but in the US, the rate of decline flattened out. Currently Americans, despite being richer on average, work longer hours than people in many other advanced countries. In fact, over the last part of the twentieth century working hours actually *increased* slightly in America.'

So, if I have understood right, in general people chose a bit of both, but in America they chose to buy more stuff, in Europe people chose to buy more time.

'Exactly. As a rough estimate, in the US over the course of the twentieth century hourly wages increased about six-fold and working time decreased about a third. While Keynes was wrong about us all working fifteen-hour weeks, we have taken some of the productivity increases of modern capitalism in the form of more leisure. Keynes's prediction looks better if we consider not weekly, or even annual, working hours, but the amount we work over a lifetime. Compared to earlier times we spend far longer in education. We also live longer and have a long period in retirement. Before the twentieth century, retirement did not exist other than for the very wealthy. Most people worked until they dropped.'

So, some of you work less over a lifetime, but others still work long and hard. How come?

'First, you have to question whether we have as much choice over our working hours as economists sometimes assume. Second, there's a distinction between our needs (which may be fairly easily satisfied) and our wants (which may be almost insatiable). Considering the first issue, working hours are about the balance of power between employee and employer. When the bosses have the whip hand, when it is harder to get jobs, when unions or labour regulations are weaker, then employers have more power to set hours of work. You might be able to choose your job, but you can't usually choose your hours.

The other really important factor is our very human tendency to compare ourselves to others, which can lead to an arms race of competitive consumption. As the wit H.L. Mencken once put it: a wealthy man is one who earns $100 more than his wife's sister's husband. And it's an arms race that's spiralling out of control. The economist Juliet Schor argues that the middle class has gone from trying to keep up with the Joneses to trying to keep up with the Kardashians. That can only lead to a vicious Darwinian competitiveness, and consequent debt.[4]

When Keynes made his predictions, he did note this issue (which he referred to as our desire for superiority compared to our fellows). But he clearly underestimated its strength. He thought that once our absolute needs had been met, we would turn our attention to what he called the real permanent problem: how to use our economic freedom "to live wisely and agreeably and well".'

That sounds like a good place to finish.

'OK boy. Home we go. I think we should both take the afternoon off!'

Firms: Monopolies, Oligopolies, Collusion and Competition

What we talk about on this walk: One of the key players in an economy: the firm. What is it, and what forces act upon it? How do firms set their prices? How can we ensure proper competition and avoid monopolies and oligopolies?

'On our last walk we talked about demand. Can you remember any of it, Monty?'

Er, if we have more money, we buy more things. Not ordinary things like sausages, but luxuries, like, er, Hermès bags, whatever they are. And diamond collars. And I seem to recall that elastic is involved in some way, not just to keep the Philosopher's trousers from falling down. One thing everyone thought we were going to buy more of was nothing, I mean leisure time. But we all still work too hard because of Opportunity Knocks.

'Costs, opportunity costs! Sometimes I wonder if... But, well, yes, that's more or less it. On today's walk, I want to look at one of the other main players in an economy: the firm.'

Hold your horses. Quick definition of 'firm' please?

'Good boy, there's always a danger we might skip over these things. A firm is an organisation that seeks to make a profit by manufacturing or selling products or services to consumers. It ranges from a sole trader flogging flip-flops at the local market, to a multinational company flogging iPhones to half the world's population. Back in Adam Smith's time, most firms were small and markets were local. There were some exceptions. The East India Company accounted for half the world's trade by the early 1800s. Typically, however, the markets familiar to Smith would have been made up of lots of small sellers, none of whom had enough power to control the price. This type of market resembles the market model that economists now call *perfect competition*.

Things have changed. Today, many markets are dominated by very large firms. Occasionally you see a market where there is just one supplier – a monopoly. More often you see markets where just a few big suppliers control things – an oligopoly. Sometimes firms within an oligopoly will compete viciously, as with Coca-Cola and Pepsi. Sometimes they collude, as, notoriously, with the auction companies, Christie's and Sotheby's.'[1]

Collude? Sounds a bit dodgy...

'As Adam Smith noted, "People of the same trade seldom meet together, even for merriment and diversion, but the conversation ends in a conspiracy against the public, or in some contrivance to raise prices."[2]

This is exactly what happened at Christie's and Sotheby's in the early 2000s. It is a story full of double-crossing, Picassos, private jets and class warfare, which ended with the owner of Sotheby's being sent to prison (although save your tears; he flew there in his private jet being served hot dogs and caviar by his butler). By the 1990s Christie's and Sotheby's had an effective cosy oligopoly, with ninety percent of auction sales passing through their books. But then the market went through a rocky patch and they found themselves in a bitter fight, offering sellers lower and lower commissions to get the sale. At some point, someone (and it is disputed who) thought that it might be better for both of them to fix their commission. The American authorities became suspicious and Christopher Davidge, the CEO of Christie's, shopped his opposite number at Sotheby's in exchange for immunity.'

This sounds more like politics or drama than economics…

'You're not wrong, Monty, I have rather started in the middle. Let's decide where we want to walk and I will start at the beginning.'

We've not been to Primrose Hill for a while. Lots of pretty poodles there. And excellent trees…

Another short bus ride later we were sitting on a bench atop Primrose Hill, with a view over Regent's Park and the zoo, and beyond that to the towers and ziggurats of the City.

'All set?'

All ears.

'Traditionally, economics has focused on markets, on how sellers and buyers interact in a free economy. What actually goes on *inside* firms has been neglected. But the fact is that many of society's most important economic decisions are not taken by individuals choosing to buy or sell, or, for that matter, by governments, but inside large organisations with complex, bureaucratic decision-making structures.'

One of your examples would be helpful here.

'Sure. The glasses I am wearing came from Specsavers, who employ around 33,000 people. John Lewis, where I bought your collar and lead, employs nearly 100,000 people. The coffee in my hand is from Starbucks, which employs 349,000 people.[3] In the US Walmart employs 2.2 million people, McDonalds 1.9 million. Within these, and hundreds of other mega companies, there's a huge amount of commercial activity, to which economics has turned a blind eye. Even when you look at international trade, a significant amount of it is made up of internal transfers going on *within* a firm, not market exchanges *between* firms. Car manufacturers and aeroplane makers ship wheels and wings from one plant in Europe to another in the US. And all of these crucial, multi-billion-pound transactions are decided not by the invisible hand of the market, but by the very visible hand of the manager.'

But I guess if these managers messed up, then their cars or planes or whatever would be crappy, and the market would then decide not to buy them. So doesn't the market kind of 'see' into the firm that way?

'Absolutely, Monty, but that still begs the question, how do firms work on the inside and has neoclassical economics got anything useful to say about it? Or is this an area better left to psychologists, sociologists or even political scientists?'

And Philosophers?

'Let's not go mad. In fact I think there are at least two useful things that economics has to say about firm behaviour. The first is about costs and pricing, the second is about the structure of different markets.

Let's start off with the traditional economic perspective on how firms set their price. The neoclassical story would go something like this: consumers have a clear idea of their preferences, and after considering prices and their budget they will choose a bundle of goods and services that maximise their happiness. Firms exist solely to make profits. Every firm aims to maximise profits in the same way: by producing exactly the level of output where the cost of making one more unit (the marginal cost) is equal to the increase in revenue from selling one more unit (marginal revenue).'

Back up a bit there. What do you mean by marginal cost *and* marginal revenue *and what did you mean about that bit about profit maximisation?*

'The first key thing to note is that economists divide costs into *fixed costs* and *variable costs*. Fixed costs are all the costs that have to be paid even when a firm is producing nothing. If you set up a dog grooming business you need to pay the rent on the building whether you groom one or one hundred dogs. Variable costs are the costs that change with the amount of output. For our dog groomer, that might be things like the workers you need to employ to do the grooming, or the shampoo you need to wash the dogs. This then leads to two more important concepts: *average costs* and *marginal costs*. Average costs are, well, your average costs (your total costs divided by the total number of groomed dogs). Marginal costs are how much total costs increase when you produce one more unit of groomed dog. Both of these costs will vary with the level of output.

So, that is the cost side of the equation. Looking at the revenue side, marginal revenue is the extra revenue you get from selling one more unit. And if you put the two together there is a lovely simple, logical formula: profits are maximised where marginal revenue = marginal cost.'

No, I'm lost.

'Think about it, Monty. If producing and selling one more of something brings in more money than it adds to your costs, you do it. If it does not, you don't.'

OK, I think I get it. Making stuff incurs costs. As long as those costs are less than the profits, you keep making more.

'That's pretty much it. Add in a lot of graphs and messing around with calculus and this is the neoclassical view of the firm.'

And is this realistic?

'I think you have to accept that the theory is a grotesque simplification. But again, this simplification is the point of the theory, not a drawback. Economics is really the study of an important subset of human behaviour and, as human behaviour is overwhelmingly complex, it has to be simplified if we are to have any hope of understanding what is going on. Whatever ethical or other commitments a firm has, unless it makes a profit, it goes bust. That applies to publishers of books as well as producers of widgets. Every businessperson thinks about costs and revenues. If they don't, they're out of a job.'

Dog eat dog…

'I said earlier that economists are really focused on markets, and one hugely important factor for firms is what type of market they're in. How many other firms do they have to compete with? And, crucially, how free are they to set their own prices? Economists refer to this as market structure. At the start I talked about monopolies, oligopolies, perfect competition…'

Yeah, I think you might need to run these past me one more time.

'Let's start with perfect competition. This refers to a type of market we discussed earlier: many firms all selling an identical product, each too small to influence the price. If one firm tries to charge above the market price, the consumer shops elsewhere. There is also free entry and exit to the market, so that it is impossible to prevent new firms coming in to compete. As a consequence, price will be driven down to very close to the cost of production, and profits will be low. This is more a theoretical ideal rather than a reality: competition is rarely this perfect. But you do see some markets that get close. Markets for commodities such as wheat or gold tend to work like this. Or the old-fashioned markets for produce that Smith would have been familiar with, a small-town market with farmers and others coming in on market day to sell their cabbages and cheese or whatever. If Farmer Giles sells his cabbages for a shilling, then if Farmer Bob tries to charge two shillings, he'll be left with a cartful of cabbages at closing time.'

And this sounds good for the humble consumer.

'It is. The consumer will tend to get a good deal, as prices will be competed down to the lowest possible level that enables the firm to stay in business.'

Downsides?

'While it is great for consumers, it can be tough on workers. The producers will attempt to drive down wages and conditions to increase their competitiveness.'

Ouch. So much for your perfect competition. And what about the others, monopoly and oligopoly?

'We've discussed them both a bit already, but to recap, a monopoly is where you have just one firm that controls a market, and an oligopoly is where you have a small number of firms that dominate a market or an industry. Sometimes they will really compete against each other, sometimes they will collude, like Sotheby's and Christie's before they fell out. In the world of sports clothing and kit there is a virtual duopoly: Nike and Adidas dominate, and no other firm comes close. Almost all the world's passenger planes are made by either Airbus (a European company) or Boeing (US).

If we look hard enough we can find examples of perfect competition, monopolies and oligopolies, but the type of market arrangement that's most familiar is called *monopolistic competition*. In monopolistic competition, rather than selling essentially the same stuff, firms can differentiate their products in some way. This gives them some degree of market power: they can raise prices a little and not lose all their customers. Think of the independent restaurants in a local area. They all bring something a little different to the table, and you may have your favourites. Price isn't everything in this situation. You might fancy an Indian, or a pizza or sushi, and that will be a key part of your decision. But you're also likely to check the prices on that menu in the window, and if your favourite pizza joint suddenly starts to charge way over the odds for your margherita or quattro stagioni, then you'll look elsewhere.

Monopolistic competition is the natural home of branding. When companies spend a lot of money on logos, slogans, advertising, or getting celebs to wear their clothes or perfumes, that is because they are trying to create a kind of monopoly for themselves, by persuading you that their products are unlike any others. Chanel is not just any perfume, it is the perfume that was worn by Marilyn Monroe. Adidas don't just make any football boots: they make the football boots worn by Lionel Messi, the world's greatest footballer.'

Woah, that was unexpected!

'Well, he's kinda cute…'

Focus! I see we've come back to monopolies. Is that the Holy Grail, then, for any firm? Do they all want to be the one big beast in the jungle?

'If you can pull it off, then yes. Typically monopolies will use their market power to restrict their output and sell it at a higher price than would be the case in a more competitive market.

For much of the twentieth century the De Beers Group had a near monopoly in diamonds. Before the late nineteenth century diamonds were rare and this scarcity, along with their intrinsic qualities of beauty and hardness, made them valuable. But in 1870 large diamond mines were discovered in South Africa. The investors realised that they had to band together to control production to protect the illusion of scarcity. De Beers was created and managed to control prices until the end of the twentieth century. In a famous early campaign ("A Diamond is Forever") De Beers cemented the idea that diamonds were a gift of love, and the larger the diamond the greater the expression of love. In the 1950s, when diamond mines were found in Siberia, De Beers brought them into the cartel. These diamonds were much smaller than those from South Africa, and so to create a market for all the smaller gems they invented the "eternity ring". De Beers' research showed that women were conflicted. On one level they recognised the vulgarity in such a display of conspicuous consumption. But at a deeper level, the status of a diamond as a universal signifier of wealth and success was seductive. A "surprise" gift meant that a women could pretend she did not really participate in the decision – she both retains her innocence and gets the diamond. The final piece of the puzzle was to make sure that people did not try to resell their diamonds. Customers had to be conditioned to hang on to their diamonds – otherwise the illusion of scarcity would again be shattered.'[4]

That's all quite sneaky.

'And all done to establish and maintain a monopoly. De Beers eventually lost their stranglehold, as producers in Australia and Canada broke away and concerns grew about the origins of De Beers' gems (many came from war-torn African states – the notorious "blood diamonds"), but they had an extraordinarily long run. Many now argue that the modern tech giants such as Microsoft, Google and Amazon have followed the De Beers playbook, and have become dangerously close to monopolies.'

I can see that this monopoly lark is nice work if you can get it. But, well, how exactly do you get it? And if you've got it, how do you keep it?

'In general, for a monopoly to last you need some kind of barrier to entry. This can be from gaining a patent, they can arise through collusion (for example the diamond racket created by De Beers), or the government can deliberately create monopolies. Or, perhaps most commonly, you can achieve a natural monopoly due to economies of scale.'

What's a natural monopoly?

'A natural monopoly arises when it's simply more efficient for one firm to serve an entire market. An obvious example would be a water company. The fixed costs of building the infrastructure to deliver water are huge, but once you have done so the marginal costs (the cost of delivering one extra unit of water) are low. It would be very hard (and arguably wasteful) for another company to come in and build a duplicate infrastructure. The key idea here is that there are large economies of scale.'

Sorry, you are going to have to explain that to me.

'Large firms can be more efficient simply because they can make things more cheaply. This can happen because of large fixed costs that have to be paid however small or large your production, as with the water pipes. Other examples would be things like research and development spending, or marketing costs. Think of an aircraft company. It's hugely expensive to design and build that first jumbo jet. But once you've got the assembly line up and running each subsequent plane will be much cheaper to build. The key idea is that an industry where there are increasing returns to scale will tend towards an oligopoly or a monopoly. You will not see a perfectly competitive market in this case.'

I don't quite see why not?

'Because increasing returns mean that large firms just have an enormous cost advantage over small firms. The more general point is that market structure is very dependent on the technology in a particular industry. Dog grooming is low tech, with low fixed costs, so you do not see increasing returns to scale. As a result, you are likely to have a market in which there are lots of small competing firms. In an industry in which there are huge fixed costs, you will be much more likely to see fewer very large firms.'

OK, got it.

'There may also be *demand* advantages to scale. People may be more willing to buy a product from a large firm, because of reputation or network effects. You see this with the tech giants. I am on Facebook and Twitter because lots of people I want to connect with are also on Facebook and Twitter. The more people use Google the more effective its search engine becomes, so the more people use it. In other words, with a network effect the value of the good rises with the number of people using it.

Both these cost and demand advantages can lead to a winner takes all market. It also means that companies can be willing to lose money for a very long time in order to 'buy' the prospect of a future monopoly. That's the path trod by Amazon and Uber. Amazon has very effectively exploited the returns to scale associated with its logistics and delivery to push out smaller rivals. Every Uber trip loses Uber money, but its strategy is to force rivals out of the market and leave it, eventually, with a near monopoly.'

So, are monopolies always a bad thing?

'Often yes. Just how badly can you treat your customers if they're stuck with you come what may? The basic issue is that under perfect competition price will be very close to production costs, but in all other markets prices will float up. And we would expect price to be highest under monopoly. Take the iPhone. You would probably not describe Apple as a monopoly: there are plenty of other mobile phones to buy. However, it does have a huge amount of market power. When Rosie and Gabriel were at school, they clearly regarded it as social death to have anything other than an iPhone. And this market power is reflected in Apple's ability to set very high markups. For example, the iPhone 11 Pro Max that was released in 2019 sold for around £1,000 in the UK and cost about £385 to make. In a perfectly competitive market, that retail cost would be much closer to the production cost.[5]

Government monopolies often get an even worse reputation. In the late 1970s my parents set up a small business. They needed a phone line to operate that business. In the UK at the time British Telecom had a government monopoly and so had little incentive to worry about customer service. My parents were told that the wait for a new telephone line was one year.

For this reason, some people argue that the government should not be the sole provider of any good or service unless there is a compelling reason that the private sector will fail in that role.'

I kind of get the feeling that you are now going to come up with a 'but'...

'You know me so well Monty! Monopolies get a bad reputation for price gouging, or poor service. But there are some cases where the benefits of monopolies outweigh their costs. A typical justification for monopoly rights is to encourage innovation. You can see that people would be reluctant to spend a lot of time or money on an invention if they thought that anyone could just come along and copy their hard work. Patents give investors a period of time in which they have exclusive rights to sell their invention. In fact, patents used to be called patent monopolies.

Another key issue with monopolies is contestability. Monopolies may not be ideal, but as long as there is *potential* competition to keep these firms on their toes, they may still deliver value to consumers. Someone might just design that iPhone killer...

Finally, with natural monopolies, where one large producer can supply something at a much lower cost than several smaller ones, it can be more efficient to allow only one provider. It would make little sense to have more than one set of pipes delivering gas to your home. It would be inordinately wasteful (and annoying) to encourage different companies to collect rubbish on the same route. In this case governments will typically allow just one firm to operate.'

Right, so, monopolies, generally bad. So what do we do about it?

'Ultimately governments have to decide when to support and when to suppress a monopoly. Where there is a good reason to think that it makes sense for one firm to be the sole producer (as with a natural monopoly) then there are essentially two options: first is public ownership. The theory being that if there's a natural monopoly, it should be run by the people, for the people, so you won't get the exploitation of customers – for example by charging very high prices.'

Sounds sensible.

'It does. For some time the political consensus was that publicly run companies tended to be inefficient and wasteful. So the trend was to allow the private sector to run natural monopolies, but regulate them, by, for example, imposing limits on the prices they are allowed to charge. The UK does this with many utilities such as water, electricity and gas.

However, the political pendulum is swinging back, and some are now arguing that privatised monopolies should be brought back into public ownership. For example, there are some sensible arguments for taking the UK railway, privatised in 1993, back into public ownership. Currently our railway is split into two parts. The infrastructure (the track, signalling, bridges and stations) is a publicly owned not-for-profit company. The rail services, however, are run by private train-operating companies, generally on a franchise. In contrast, most European railways are under public ownership. Unsurprisingly, rail fares in the UK are among the highest in Europe, and because of all the different franchises it can be very hard to understand ticket pricing or timetables. The argument goes that, under public ownership, the state could think more strategically about where to invest in the rail network. A rail network is a natural monopoly and there are wider economic and social benefits to a well-functioning (and affordable) transport system. The state is likely to take a longer-run view than shareholders. Renationalisation in this case need not be ruinously expensive either; it could take place gradually, as each existing rail franchise comes up for renewal.

Where it does not make any sense for there to be a monopoly structure, then governments can step in to make industries more competitive. The nuclear option is to break a monopoly up. Standard Oil was set up by John D. Rockefeller in 1870, and by 1890 it controlled nearly ninety percent of the US oil market. The US government argued that it was artificially lowering prices to put competitors out of business and, once it had killed the competition, raising its prices to exploit its customers. In 1911 it was ruled an illegal monopoly and broken up into thirty-four companies. The big tech companies are clearly worried that the same thing might happen to them.

There are less extreme ways of encouraging competition. Governments normally monitor industries to make sure firms don't exploit market power. They will watch for collusion, where firms agree with each other to set higher prices, or predatory pricing, where firms will set low prices to force rival firms out of business. Another example of bad behaviour is collusive tendering, where firms agree with each other to take turns in submitting the winning bid for a contract. In one South Asian country, after a strong nudge from the government, four pharmaceutical companies agreed to take turns in providing medical supplies for projects financed by international donors. They met four times a year to agree on whose turn it was. A US pharmaceutical company noticed the high prices and submitted a bid at much lower prices. So the four original members invited it to join the club, which it did.'[6]

So there's a constant fight between the authorities and the big firms. Who's winning?

'There is some concern that markets have become much more concentrated and need to be better regulated. Elizabeth Warren has argued that the US economy is rigged. Lazy firms are earning monopoly profits at the expense of the consumer. There are rival explanations. In one camp the argument goes that this is because ultra-competitive firms are pushing aside unfit competitors, and so this is nothing to be worried about. Others argue that this is not due to survival of the fittest, but rather because the largest firms have been allowed to get away with anticompetitive behaviour by weak regulators.'

So which is it?

'That is a hard question to answer. But it is certainly the case that you cannot expect markets to run themselves. Regulators need to very carefully watch what is going on. You know, Monty, I teach in a business department. In one lecture hall economics students will be taught about the efficiency of perfectly competitive markets. In another lecture hall they will be taught strategy and marketing and how *not* to compete. As Peter Thiel (a venture capitalist) said: "Competition is for losers".[7]

And on that note…

'Yes, boy, I feel you shivering. Home we go.'

Walk 7

Winners and Losers: Capitalism, Markets and Inequality

What we talk about on this walk: How markets can lead to gross inequality in wealth and power. Can anything be done about this, or is market efficiency the only goal worth striving for? Does capitalism need inequality?

Bright autumn sunshine falling prettily through the windows meant that this was a day for a long walk. And a long walk meant a big subject.

'How about we go the long way round the Heath today, Monty?'

Suits me.

Once again, it was impossible not to be struck by the wealth on display in the elegant streets leading up to the Heath. Elsewhere in London, many of the big old houses are subdivided into flats, but here most of them retained their original unity. Black-windowed SUVs stood at the kerbsides, occasionally with a heavily built security person in shades leaning against the bodywork, smoking. These streets are out of the reach even of doctors and lawyers. This was the land of the oligarch and the hedge fund manager. If the Philosopher were here, he'd often stoop and pick up a stone and go through a little mime of hurling it through a window. 'These people don't pay any tax. At least if I smashed a window they'd have to get a local firm in to replace the glass. They might even be stuck with the VAT.' But the stone would make its way to his pocket, and later he'd drop it among the trees, his shoulders slumped in defeat. He's a little old for smashing windows and other acts of revolution.

'OK, Monty, even those of us who believe in the free market system have to concede that capitalism generates inequalities. In other words, there are winners and losers.'

Meaning rich and poor?

'Yes, but we should probably clarify a bit of terminology. First, inequality is not the same as poverty. Inequality is about the gap between rich and poor. Poverty is about whether people fall below a certain level of income and can be measured either in absolute or relative terms. Absolute poverty is when you try to come up with some defined income that you would need in order to buy the essentials of life. If you fall below that, you're objectively poor. Relative poverty is when you define poverty in relation to how much everyone else has in society. In the UK, for example, relative poverty is defined as a household income that is below sixty percent of the median income. As society's view of what is an acceptable minimum income changes over time, generally relative poverty measures are preferred. And it's also true that how content we are with our lives depends to an extent on where we feel we are in relation to everyone else. The evidence is that more equal societies tend to be happier.

The second definition that I want to get clear is the difference between income and wealth.

Wealth (or capital as some call it) is the stock of all assets that are held by private individuals. So, any property you own counts as wealth: your house, shares or any other assets. Income is the flow of money coming in: wages, state benefits, any investment income. Wealth and income are obviously connected: sometimes directly, as in the income you get from renting out your property. Think of it like a bath. The water coming out of the tap is income, the height of the bathwater is the wealth. And the plughole is your spending.[1] Generally, wealth tends to be much more unevenly distributed than income.'

Why is that?

'Wealth takes time to accumulate. It often sticks in families, as each generation builds on the wealth of the previous.

Now we have got that out of the way we can talk about how economists measure inequality. One method, which is a little easier to grasp than some of the others, is to divide the population into groups according to their income, and then to ask what share of total income goes to each of these groups.'

I think I'm with you. Ish.

'Imagine you've lined up everyone in society in order of income, from poorest to richest, and then you put them into ten equal groups, or *deciles*. The first decile would have the poorest ten percent, the last decile would have the richest ten percent.'

OK.

'Then you see how much income goes to each decile. Obviously, in a totally fair and equal world, each decile would get the same amount of income. The reality is rather different…'

You don't say.

'The French economist Thomas Piketty used this approach to look at how patterns of wealth (and inequality) have changed over the past century. His research has really focused attention on the gains that have been made by those at the very top. In the 1970s the richest one percent of people in the UK and US received about eight percent of total income; but by 2010 the share going to the richest one percent had roughly doubled.

Piketty's data really helps to illuminate and therefore politicise the issue of inequality. What he shows is quite clear. From the last decades of the nineteenth century up until 1914, inequality was high: the gap between the richest and the poorest was very wide. Various economic shocks then occurred: the First World War, the Great Depression and the Second World War, which all hit the richest, at a time when many Western governments also brought in policies to help the poor. So, by the 1970s, inequality was at a historic low. Then in the UK and America, but also in many other Western countries, that equalising process was deliberately reversed. Economic policies were brought in that encouraged the massive accumulation of wealth by those at the top, whereas wages and benefits were squeezed for those at the bottom and the middle. As a result, from the 1980s we have returned to something like the levels of inequality that existed at the start of the twentieth century.'

OK, that's quite stark. So why is there so much inequality?

'Because of imbalances in power. Milton Friedman – one of the most committed ideologues on behalf of unfettered capitalism – argued that the most important single fact about a free market is that no exchange takes place unless both parties benefit.'

Yep, remember him. The point being that no one has to enter into a contract, so they'd only do it if they got something out of it. You tickle my tummy, which is nice for me, and I roll around looking cute, which is nice for you.

'Just for that, I'll give you a free tickle now! Friedman's insight really helps to clarify what goes on in a market transaction, but what it obscures is that in practice it is the side with the most bargaining power that will capture most of the gains.

Let me give you an illustration from the Industrial Revolution. In a labour market the power is generally with the person who owns the business and is offering the job. The worker can only accept or reject the offer. And for workers in the nineteenth century, the only alternative was the poorhouse. So, while the productivity of labour began to increase in Britain around the middle of the seventeenth century, it took until the middle of the nineteenth for workers to acquire the bargaining power to raise wages, through a combination of a shift in the supply and demand for workers, unionisation and new legal rights. And this power imbalance happens in many market transactions.'

Can this be fixed? Is it possible to make markets fair? Or are we stuck with the inequalities?

'One way to come at this is to break it down into two questions—'

Two? I thought these things always came in threes? You know, bang one, bang two, bang, three. Job done.

'That's How to Teach Rhetoric to Your Dog. Now, where was I?'

Two questions.

'Thank you. 1. is an outcome *efficient*? 2. is an outcome *fair*? Let's start by thinking about whether an outcome is efficient. One useful way to think about this was suggested by Vilfredo Pareto (1848–1923). Pareto argued that a distribution is efficient if there is no way to rearrange things to make at least one person better off without making anyone worse off.'

Can't quite get my little head around that… Example time.

'What is your most, and least, favourite thing to eat?'

Easy. I really don't like vegetables. Don't think I don't notice when you try to hide broccoli in my food. And as for the best, that's easy. Bacon. I love bacon.

'Perfect. Right, imagine you have got ten heads of broccoli and I've got ten rashers of bacon. I—'

Hold on, I'm imagining… mmmmmm bacon.

'Done drooling? OK, suppose I am a vegetarian so don't really want the bacon. And as we have already established, you don't like broccoli. This existing distribution is clearly *inefficient*. We could easily improve our situation by trading, and getting to an outcome that both of us prefer. Once we've exchanged, our world is now Pareto efficient. This, according to Pareto, is the market functioning optimally. If we are all free to trade, then inefficiencies like this – me stuck with bacon, you with broccoli – should be traded away.'

Sounds good. What's the catch?

'The catch, Monty, is that Pareto efficiency says nothing about fairness. The Pareto criterion is useful in that I think almost everyone would agree that society should avoid situations that are not Pareto efficient. When something can be done to make at least one person better off without making anyone else worse off, then we should do it. The problem is that it is a rather low bar for judging different outcomes.

An imaginary game might help to get across how power differences lead to inequalities.'

Does it involve chasing an imaginary stick?

'No.'

Good. Even real sticks bore me.

'In this game, called the ultimatum game, one of us is randomly chosen to be the "proposer" and the other is chosen to be the "responder". The proposer – me – is given, say £100, and can propose to you how we split it. The catch is that you have to agree. If you don't agree to my suggested split, we both get nothing. It is a take it or leave it offer. For example, if I offered you £50 would you accept it?'

Sure. But, er, can we use biscuits instead? It'll keep me focused.

'Fine. Now imagine that I offered you twenty biscuits not a hundred. Would you still accept?'

Well, that's not fair, but I guess twenty is better than no biscuits. If I don't agree we both go biscuitless, right?

'Yes.'

Then twenty biscuits it is, even if I grumble about it.

'Good, eighty for me. But suppose I offered you five biscuits?'

And you get ninety-five? Outrageous!

'Maybe. But would you take the deal?'

Without the actual biscuits here, it's hard to say. But at some point I'd tell you to get stuffed, just to punish you for being mean.

'But if you were completely economically rational, and I offered you one biscuit, with ninety-nine for me, you should accept it, as your only other option is to get nothing. More seriously, if you were starving, and the biscuits were your only chance of a dinner, how could you reject the offer? In the ultimatum game any split that we can agree on – even one biscuit to you and ninety-nine to me – is Pareto efficient, in that at least one of us gains and no one is made worse off. But who gains the most from the split is a very different question. And Pareto is silent on that. We might also want to ask, is it fair?'

If you get ninety-nine and I get one, then, no.

'And that seems intuitively right. Any normal person would think it was unfair. But now let me complicate this a bit. What if I said that the person who offered you one biscuit had four hungry children and was living in poverty, whereas you, in this example, are living the life of a pampered lapdog and really don't need the biscuits?'

Hmmm… I see what you did there.

'And what if someone offered you exactly half, would that always be fair?'

I am assuming that this is a trick question…

'Maybe. If the person had offered you half only because someone else had a knife to their throat, then you might think that was not very fair. The point I am trying to get across here is that fairness is *complicated*. It's not a simple unitary thing, but a cluster of ideas, and whenever you use the term, you need to be clear about exactly what you mean by it. Are you talking about whether the process is fair, or are you talking about whether the outcome is fair? And how are you measuring the outcome? In money (or biscuits)? In happiness? Or even in freedom?'

OK, I get that it's tricky. In fact this is beginning to sound like one of the walks I used to take with the Philosopher. But I'm guessing you can answer some of these questions…

'I'll have a go. Let's start with two famously opposing positions on *distributive justice*, i.e. ideas about how we should divide the cake, or biscuits, taken by John Rawls (1921–2002) and Robert Nozick (1938–2002).

Nozick's position, set out in his libertarian classic *Anarchy, State and Utopia* (1974), is beautifully clear. My stuff is my stuff, and the state has no right, except in extremely limited circumstances, to get its sticky hands on it, either directly or through taxation. It doesn't matter if the state is doing it for its own nefarious purposes or, in some benign way, for my good: when it comes to my property, the state just has to back off. My right to hold on to my legally acquired personal property trumps any notion you might have about fairness. For Nozick, if people enter into voluntary exchanges, no one else has the right to forcibly intervene, even if some people become inordinately wealthy as a consequence, and others are made destitute.'

Hardcore.

'It is, but it's also a really useful challenge to those of us with a more collectivist mindset.'

You're talking about the Philosopher?

'Yes, but also centrists like me. Nozick – who happens to be a beautifully elegant and engaging writer – forces you to think about something that we tend to take for granted: the right of the state to confiscate our money and use it for things that we might not agree with. He poses a clear challenge: why is it OK for the state to do this?

Rawls rises to that challenge. Where Nozick worships liberty, Rawls gives priority to equality. His most important argument concerns the "difference principle", which states that "all social values… are to be distributed equally unless an unequal distribution of any… is to everyone's advantage".'

Huh?

'Rawls conceded that we might want some economic inequality. If everyone got the same amount of money no matter how hard or how little they worked, then society as a whole might be worse off, and everyone would lose out. But he argued that inequality should be tolerated only if it made the worst off in society as well off as they could be. Forget about the rich, he tells us, they'll always be OK. Concentrate on helping the poor. Rawls justified this argument using a thought experiment involving what he called the *veil of ignorance.*'

Sounds intriguing…

'It's a good one. Say you've bumped your head, and woken up in hospital with no idea who you are. So, you've been deprived of all knowledge about yourself, whether you're rich or poor, born ill or healthy, clever or stupid, lazy or hardworking. This is the veil of ignorance. In that situation, Rawls says, any rational person would choose rules for a society that maximise the position of the least well-off person.'

Why?

'Well, because you'd want to ensure that your life wasn't unbearably horrid. If it turns out you're rich and talented, great. But if you're not, then you'd want society to lend you a helping hand. And as you don't know which you are, you'd have to choose that safety option.'

I guess. Though this veil of ignorance thing seems a bit… unnatural. I haven't just woken up not knowing who I am. Almost nobody has.

'I suppose the point is to try to find some objective way of assessing fairness. Anyone who can imagine themselves in that position would come to the same conclusion, based on nothing more than rational self-interest.'

Right, so Nozick says that if I get my biscuits legally, I can keep them all, even if you have no biscuits. And if you try to take my biscuits, that's basically stealing from me. And Rawls argues that the state should take some of my biscuits and give them to you, justifying it by saying that if neither of us knew how many biscuits we were going to get in advance, then we'd both probably opt for a system that took biscuits from the person (or dog) with the most and gave them to the other dog (or person). Have I got that right?

'Er, well, yes, actually.'

But unless I missed something, what we haven't decided is how many biscuits you take from one to give to the other. Just enough to stop them from starving? Or more than that, to even things up?

'Excellent point. One view, sometimes called (a little inelegantly) sufficientarianism, argues that we should forget inequality and focus on making sure that everyone has enough. Why does it matter if you have a collar from T.K. Maxx and that pampered pooch Penelope has one from Tiffany? The important thing is that all members of society have enough to lead a dignified life. So, society should redistribute to ensure that everyone's basic needs are met, and then stop worrying about it.'

This is all a lot to take in. On the one hand we have efficiency, which free markets achieve by matching up buyers and sellers, and then we have fairness, which, if you accept the Rawls argument, or even the ideas of the sufficientarianism guys, pulls in a different direction… Is it possible to arrange things so that they are both efficient and fair?

'That would be ideal, Monty, but nothing is that simple in life. It is often very hard to make one person better off without making someone else worse off. And there is a trade-off between efficiency and fairness.'

You mean making something fairer makes it less efficient? Why should that follow?

'In capitalist countries, the main way of making economic outcomes fairer is to use redistributive taxation, and some argue that this impacts economic incentives to work hard and innovate. And the bureaucracy involved in redistribution is expensive – all those civil servants and legislators working out how to shift money from one group to another. And when governments directly provide services, they are normally monopolies and, as we've seen, monopolies can be inefficient, and deliver a bad deal to their customers. So, finding that balance between fairness and efficiency is a real challenge.'

But you economists are a clever bunch, aren't you? There must be a way, or what's the point of you?

'An omniscient economist could tell you how to do it: promote equality up to the point where the added benefits of more equality are just matched by the added costs of more inefficiency. In reality, of course, there is no way to calculate this. The real consequences are uncertain and debatable and probably very influenced by your political perspective. To test your attitude towards the trade-off, the economist Arthur Okun (1928–80) proposed a thought experiment he calls the "Leaky-Bucket Experiment."[2]

Imagine that the bottom twenty percent of families in the income distribution have an income of less than £14,000 (averaging £10,000). And that the top five percent of families in the income distribution have an income of more than £56,000 (averaging about £90,000). A proposal is made to levy a tax on the richest five percent; that would average about £8,000. As there are four times as many families in the poorest group than there are in the richest group, if you redistributed this money, then the average poor family should get about £2,000.'[3]

Sounds fair. Take some biscuits from those with plenty, and hand them out to those with few.

'However, this programme has a problem. The money must be transferred from the rich to the poor in what Okun calls a "leaky bucket". So not all the money gets to where you want it to be. So how much leakage would you accept and still support the redistribution? Say if ten percent of the money leaked out, would you still support the programme? This would mean that the average poor family only got £1,800.'

Yes, I think I would. A loss of ten percent does not seem so terrible and the poor families still get a big benefit.

'But what if fifty percent was lost? Or seventy-five or even ninety percent? Where would you draw the line? Your answer cannot be right or wrong any more than (as Okun put it) your favourite flavour of ice cream can be right or wrong. The leak here represents economic inefficiency.

The point is to illustrate that Rawls's position would imply that you must keep transferring that money into that bucket until ninety-nine percent of it is leaking out. For him, equality is all. Friedman, in contrast, would prioritise efficiency, and I guess he would stop the transfer when the leak was very small. And someone like Nozick, who believes any redistribution is illegitimate, would stop the transfer on principle – no matter whether the leak was small or big.'

And what about you, what do you think?

'It's not an easy question. Anyone who thinks it is hasn't pondered enough about it. But I think this comes down to a political choice, as our friend Okun put it. Economists can just try to clarify the issues, and set out the consequences of whatever choices you make.'

Oh, get off the fence!

'But I like it on the fence. It has the best view.'

Cop-out.

'So far we have been rather philosophical about this issue. We saw that Pareto-efficient outcomes can be highly unequal. And that differences in power can really impact who gets to capture the economic surplus. But there's another side to this, returning to that earlier question about whether inequality is in itself a bad thing. If we look at China, focusing on the period after 1990, we see a massive increase in inequality between the richest and the poorest, but also a pulling up from terrible poverty into relative comfort of the majority of the population. Could that have been achieved without the increase in inequality, caused by moving to a capitalist system?'

From the way you ask that, I'm guessing you think no.

'As we've brought up China, it's also interesting to think about inequality not just within developed states, but between nations across the globe. An economist called Branko Milanović has tried to work out how much, on average, those in different parts of the global income distribution have fared. And what emerges is not a simple message that the rich have got richer or the poor are getting poorer. The wealthiest ten percent, and within that most strikingly the top one percent, have, predictably, become even richer. Another group has done well over recent decades: those in the bottom half, but a notch up from the poorest. These are people mainly from China, Malaysia and India who have been lifted up by the rising tide of their economies.'

OK, those are the winners, who have been the losers?

'Again, two groups stand out. As predictably as the success of the very richest, the very poorest have done badly. These are often people who live in failed states like Afghanistan, Haiti or Somalia. The other group that has not done particularly well in terms of income growth are the middle classes of developed countries.

This is the group that sits roughly at the seventieth to eightieth percentile globally. While these groups are by no means poor compared to the rest of the world, their income has remained static, or, in some cases, fallen. The rise of right-wing populist movements, from Trumpism to Brexit, might well stem from this sense that the middle classes have of losing status. Those things which they had taken for granted, university education for the kids, a house, a new car, have become increasingly hard to afford.

But turning back to the winners, even though those people we mentioned in China and India have done well in terms of the percentage increase, in absolute terms the increases have been less impressive.'

Er, I am not sure I quite understand that… can you give me an example?

'Imagine you had an income of £100 a year, and your income grew by a hundred percent. That sounds great: your income has doubled, hurrah! But in absolute terms you got an increase of £100. Now imagine that you had an income of £100,000 a year and your income grew by half as much, increasing by only fifty percent. But in absolute terms you would have had an increase of £50,000. To make that clear, Milanović has calculated that between 1988 and 2008 more than half of the total gains in wealth went to the top five percent of the income distribution. What this means is that for every extra £1 that the world produced, 27p went to the richest one percent, 25p to the next richest four percent.[4]

Many people look at this and think that an economic system that produces that kind of inequality must be broken.'

Oh, I can see why some people might be unhappy about that. This may be an obvious question, but do economists know why there's this increase in inequality?

'When you study the data, you can see that inequality began to increase in many countries around the late 1970s. There are a number of theories. Some argue that due to changes in technology and increasing globalisation, markets are now "winner takes all" contests. Those individuals and companies who are the very best at what they do can capture most of the gains.

Let me give you an example. Before football had a televised global audience, many more people went to watch their local teams play. Even if people preferred to watch more famous and better players, there was a limit to how many people could get into the stadium and so to how much footballers got paid. Once you have satellite TV everyone can (and will pay) to watch the very best. And so the most successful teams will capture most of the money.

Others point to the fact that taxation on the richest has fallen in many countries. In the 1970s, in the US and UK, the rich were taxed at over eighty percent on their income. Since then taxes have more or less halved. And, of course, the rich have become very good at sheltering their income, so much of it isn't taxed at all. Inheritance taxes have also fallen in many countries.

At the same time, the legislation and institutions that protect the poorest – unions, minimum wages and employment regulations, for example – have been weakened in many countries.

Financial deregulation is another factor driving the rise of the super-rich. Many of those in the richest one percent either work in finance, or in industries connected to finance.[5]

Finally, Piketty has argued that the accumulation of wealth (capital) has become more important. In times of high inflation, the value of wealth can be eroded – that was one of the reasons, Piketty argues, for the surge in equality in the post-1945 period. But since the 1980s, policies aimed at curbing inflation have had the effect of increasing the value of assets such as property. Income is by its nature fluid, but property tends to stick. Stick in families, stick in classes.'

That all sounds a bit depressing. Are the rich destined to carry on getting richer?

'Walter Scheidel, a historian, is not terribly optimistic.[6] He argues that if the past 1,000 years of history are any judge, then only four things have ever managed to significantly reduce inequality: war, revolution, state failure and pandemic.'

Well, they don't sound like much fun. Is there anything else that you can do to reduce inequality that doesn't involve lots of people dying?

'The obvious thing to do is to tax the rich. But it might be hard to increase income taxes much more. The very richest already pay a lot of income tax; increase it any more and they might just move. For example, the top one percent already pay twenty-nine percent of all income tax in the UK.[7] Some countries have thought about taxing wealth, rather than income. Piketty, for example, advocates much higher inheritance tax and a global wealth tax. Others argue you should strengthen labour market institutions, and many countries are implementing or increasing their minimum wages. It probably goes without saying that you should do all you can to fight gender and race discrimination that might lead to inequality.

One radical idea that has been getting increasing attention is for a Universal Basic Income, which would involve governments giving every person a certain amount of money each month, whether or not they're in employment. The Covid-19 pandemic saw many rich countries experiment with far more generous income support. So perhaps Scheidel is right, and it needs the shock of something like a pandemic to change thinking.

Oh, look, we're pretty much home. You've done well to follow all that. Assuming you have been following…'

Normally I leave the following to bloodhounds. But, yes, I think I've taken most of that in.

'Care to summarise?'

O ye of little faith. OK, I'll give it a go. You argued that market outcomes might be efficient, but they would not always be fair. Markets can increase the size of the economic pie (the efficient bit), but how that pie gets divided will depend on your bargaining power (the fair bit). In that example you gave with the ultimatum game, the side that had the power to dictate the offer only had to offer something a tiny bit better than the other side's second-best option (in the game this was getting nothing) to capture most of the surplus. And without fairness, you end up with more inequality, unless some disaster comes along to mix things up.

'That's pretty good, Monty. I suppose the point is that free markets always generate inequalities, and if we want to do something about that, then it will involve hard political choices. But for now your choice is simple: tummy rub or ear-stroke?'

Is both an option?

'Not usually, in economics. But I'm not dogmatic.'

Walk 8

When Markets Fail: Externalities, Public Goods and Common Pool Resources

What we talk about on this walk: Externalities: the positive and negative spillovers from private exchange. Why both are a problem and what to do about it. We discuss public goods (like defence) and common pool resources (like fishing). In both cases, markets will be problematic. The moral? We have to find ways to come together to either provide these goods, or limit their overuse, or we will all be worse off.

Autumn, like a good Chancellor of the Exchequer, likes to balance its books, and so every sunny day has to be paid for with a foul one. The wind was blowing, and dark clouds scudded across a sky the colour of a beached whale. It was a day fit only for the shortest of our walks: down to the miserable little green at the bottom of our street, called, for obvious reasons, the Poo Park.

Of course Monty was just as happy with the grotty old Poo Park as with a country ramble, despite the fact it was full of plastic bottles, takeaway cartons and cigarette butts. Someone had even left a bag of dog poo hanging from a holly bush, like a satanic Christmas decoration. Monty excitedly sprayed anything within range, and then made a dart for what looked like the remains of a kebab.

'No, Monty. Don't you dare!'

We'd lived the colonic consequences of Monty's strange unpickiness about street food before – ironic, given his extreme fussiness about which tins of dog food he'd be prepared to nibble at.

Spoilsport.

'You'll thank me for it later. Anyway, this might be a good time to talk about what economists call *externalities*. I think I have probably already said that markets are... remarkable.'

I think you might have already mentioned that.

'Well, they are. Markets are an extraordinarily effective way to coordinate hugely complex human interactions. But sometimes markets don't work. They "fail", as economists would say.'

Hold on a sec. What do you mean by markets 'failing'? Do you mean failing as in resulting in inequalities, as we talked about on that last walk?

'No, this is different. When economists use the term *market failure*, what they mean is that for some reason or other markets are not working as they should in their ideal form. And one important reason they fail is because of the problem of externalities.'

Tell me again, what's an externality?

'An externality is when an exchange between a buyer and a seller has an impact on a third party who is not part of the exchange. Why it matters is because one of the main arguments in support of a free market is that if a buyer and seller voluntarily conduct a transaction, both sides must benefit, otherwise that transaction would not take place. This obviously does not hold if a third party, who has had no say in the transaction, who is *external* to the deal, is affected. This is what economists mean when they talk about externalities.'

I think some examples might help…

'The obvious one is pollution. The garage sells me petrol, I'm happy, the garage owner is happy, but my car spews out toxic gases, poisoning the atmosphere for everyone – a bit like what would have happened if I'd let you eat that kebab. Or a nightclub playing thumping music all night destroying the quiet of the neighbourhood. A fast-food lover who leaves his takeaway cartons in the park. A dog owner who "forgets" to pick up his dog's poo. In all of these cases negative outcomes have been imposed on third parties.'

OK, I get it. Sometimes when we buy and sell in the market, there are bad consequences for people not party to the deal. But does this really mean that the market has failed?

'Markets work, they are efficient, when the price of a good reflects *all* the costs and benefits of a good – not just the private costs and benefits. When you are deciding to drive somewhere, you will take into account your own personal costs. But these aren't the only costs. There are costs that fall on others – the pollution, the noise, the congestion – and unless these costs are in some way included in that market valuation, then the market is not working efficiently, in the technical sense used by economists.'

Just so I can get this straight, this isn't about fairness, but efficiency – the thing that markets are supposed to be good at?

'*Exactly.* When we talked about inequality, we were looking at outcomes and asking if they were fair, which boils down to ethics and then politics. Here we are talking about how well the market works on its own terms. When there are externalities, never mind fairness, markets may not even be efficient.'

You said costs and benefits? I thought we were just talking about bad things?

'Good spot, Monty. Externalities can be both positive and negative. In the case of a negative externality, you get too much of a bad thing. In the case of a positive externality, you don't get enough of a good thing. The key idea is that if externalities lead to market failure, then, on the grounds of efficiency, we might want to intervene to fix it. We can talk about positive externalities later but first let's consider a very real example of a negative externality. Why don't you pop up here next to me on this bench, to keep you away from that nasty old kebab.'

Hey, if you had to eat tinned dog food you'd leap at the chance for some nice cold kebab.

'Touché. As I said, Monty, pollution is the classic example of a negative externality. In the 1980s the French authorities authorised the use of a particularly nasty pesticide called chlordecone in the French Caribbean islands of Martinique and Guadeloupe.[1] Chlordecone was death to the dreaded banana weevil, and plantation owners used it as it was a very effective way of increasing their harvest. They got higher profits, banana buyers got lower prices. A win for both buyer and seller. But as the pesticide washed off the land, it contaminated the water of nearby fishing communities.'

And did the plantation owners know about this?

'They certainly did, as did the French government who were in charge. Production of chlordecone was stopped in the US in 1975 when it was linked to neurological disorders. But it was only in 1990 that the French authorities finally banned it, and even then they still allowed the farmers to use up their stocks of the wretched stuff until 1993, and possibly beyond.[2] Chlordecone is one of the family of "persistent organic pollutants", also known as "forever chemicals", and it can take centuries to break down. As a result, much of the land on Martinique will remain useless for food production for generations. High levels of cancer on the islands have been attributed to the pesticide.'

Point made. Externalities can be very bad indeed. So what's to be done?

'In principle, when it comes to dealing with negative externalities there are three basic solutions.

The first involves making property rights clear. This is an approach much in favour among free-market enthusiasts. Let's think about air pollution. The property rights people say that air pollution is an issue because nobody actually *owns* the air. If they did, then you wouldn't be allowed to pollute it – for example with the kind of noxious gaseous expulsion that would have followed if you'd eaten that kebab.'

I won't dignify that with a response.

'And because no one owns the bit of air above this park, that person sitting over there is free to smoke away and pollute the atmosphere. I don't own the air, so I can't stop him. Imagine that the air was like your garden, or your front room – they belong to you, so nobody can pollute them without your say-so.

This is the basic idea proposed by Ronald Coase (1910–2013). He thought that externalities were a problem of poorly defined property rights. He argued that if property rights were made clear, meaning that everyone knew precisely who owned what, then people would be able to find a solution between themselves, with no need for state intervention. He imagines two neighbours: a noisy confectioner disturbing a quiet doctor. If the confectioner owned the right to make noise, then the doctor would simply have to offer him money to be quiet. If peace and quiet was worth more to the doctor than making a racket was to the confectioner, then they could come to a private deal.'

How would it work with the banana plantation?

'In the chlordecone example, imagine that the fishing communities had had the right to clean water. In this case, the plantation owners would have had to compensate the fishermen for the right to pollute. If this had been really expensive, the farmers would probably have found a cheaper way to deal with banana weevils. There's a joke in there somewhere about choosing the lesser of two weevils, but I leave that sort of thing to the Philosopher.'

But how would the fishing community have got together to negotiate this?

'Spot on, Monty. As Coase readily acknowledged, in most cases the sheer difficulty of negotiation would make this solution unrealistic. With one doctor and one confectioner you can just about imagine reaching a deal. But with large groups, as you had in the example of Martinique and Guadeloupe, it is hard to see how this would work in practice. The other issue is that outcomes may be different depending on who has the property right. Do the plantation owners have the right to pollute, or does the community have the right to clean water and land? The person who owns the property right is likely to get the better side of the deal. Nevertheless, this is an important idea, and might well be part of the solution.

There is another example that I really like, which involved a bit of "air rage". In 2014, a conflict over who had the right to the space in front of an aeroplane seat caused a United Airlines flight to be diverted.[3]

They were fighting over legroom?

'In essence. You've never experienced the joys of modern air transport, which involves, unless you're rich, being squeezed into tiny seats, with your knees rammed against the seat in front. It is enough to reduce the calmest person to a state of incoherent fury. What happened was that two passengers got involved in a very heated argument about whether one, a woman, had the right to recline her seat, or whether the other passenger, a man, had the right to the legroom. The man had bought a device called a Knee Defender, which stops the seat in front from reclining. The flight attendant asked him to remove this device and he refused. The woman reacted by throwing her drink over him. With chaos threatened, the flight crew made the decision to divert the plane. Now what would Coase have predicted if property rights were clearly established?'

I guess that if the woman had the right to recline, then the male passenger behind would have offered her some money not to. And if it had been worth it to her, she would have accepted. But if she valued reclining more, she would refuse.

'Exactly. But in practice I think both these examples, the Knee Defender and chlordecone, show that this solution is not, to say the least, without its challenges.'

OK, so clarifying property rights might help sometimes, but it's often, as in the poor fishermen, a red herring—

'Hang on, is that a rare Monty joke?'

What, oh, maybe… But that was the first way of dealing with externalities. You said there were three…

'Indeed. The next way to deal with negative externalities is by taxing them. These are also known as *Pigouvian taxes* after the British economist Arthur C. Pigou (1877–1959). If cigarettes or driving cause costs for others, then tax them. The congestion charge in London is a good example of this, as is the high tax on petrol. Champions of these types of taxes say they benefit society twice: as well as pricing in the negative effects, thereby deterring them, they also raise revenue for the government.

But these types of taxes also have problems.'

I'd have been disappointed if you hadn't said that.

'A common complaint is that they are regressive, in other words that they hit the poorest the hardest. This has been the accusation of those who oppose the idea of a sugar tax. The standard argument goes as follows. Sugar makes you fat and rots your teeth. This leads to increased healthcare costs, which fall on society as a whole. So the obvious solution is to tax sugar. This will increase the price so people will consume less of it. And those who do consume it will have to pay more tax, which takes account of the extra societal cost.'

Doesn't sound completely silly. But those problems… ?

'First that, as I said, it's regressive. If you're poor, you spend a bigger proportion of your income on food, so you'll be hit proportionately harder. And sugar provides a relatively cheap source of pleasure, which you're now going to hit with your cruel tax on fun. Others might argue that this is just an example of the nanny state, interfering with ordinary people's lives.'

So tax might help, but also has problems. The third solution?

'Perhaps the most obvious thing to do is to regulate. In some cases, with things that are unremittingly awful (like chlordecone), you might want to ban them. A less draconian response would be to limit the quantity of something. The EU cap-and-trade scheme for CO_2 emissions is an example of a hybrid system. In 2005 the EU created a market for greenhouse gases to try to combat climate change. They allocated annual carbon permits to firms, based on how much CO_2 these firms had been emitting in the past. The idea was to gradually reduce these permits over time to meet climate goals. Firms were also allowed to trade these permits. The system had the advantage that the cap on permits limited the total amount of CO_2 emissions (in Europe) and the trade bit meant there was an incentive for firms to try to reduce their emissions.'

Sounds good…

'Both regulation and taxation have a role in controlling negative externalities, but some free marketeers would say they interfere in the operation of the market in ways that must involve distortions and the dreaded inefficiencies. So, they'd argue, the cure is worse than the disease. But in most Western countries, we've decided that these are, in fact, a price worth paying.'

You've mentioned positive externalities a couple of times…

'Sure. So far we have been mainly talking about negative externalities, reasons markets go wrong because of bad consequences for third parties. Markets also "fail" because of positive externalities.'

Oh, and 'positive' makes it sound so… positive.

'The problem is that with some things there might be a great benefit to society as a whole, but no obvious or immediate benefit to any particular individual. The classic example is innovation. Conceptually, innovation is just the opposite of pollution in our earlier example. With pollution, someone is producing costs for third parties and not paying the price. With innovation, someone is potentially providing benefits for third parties and not being compensated. In a free market it can be pointless to invest a lot of time or money to invent something if it is easy for others just to copy your idea. The key problem is a lack of "appropriability". The person, or company, must be able to appropriate the value of the investments they make in inventing or creating something, or why would they bother? Indeed, you often find that people who invented things that became wildly popular got nothing for all their effort.'

Again, I think a few examples might help me get my head around this.

'Sure. A guy called John Walker invented the modern match in 1826 using a mixture of sulphur and other chemicals that ignited when scraped against something rough. Didn't make a penny, despite literally billions of matches being struck in the two hundred years since. Or Ron Klein, who invented the magnetic strip on the back of credit and debit cards, which massively oiled the wheels of commerce, making all of our lives easier. Not. A. Penny. Or Daisuke Inoue, who invented the concept of karaoke, thereby making the world a noisier and more embarrassing place.'

Let me guess – died in a pauper's grave?

'Well, I don't know about that, but his idea was commercialised by others who made a killing helping people to murder songs. Another example would be writing a book, like this.'

Like what? Aren't we just, er, you know, chewing the fat?

'Ah, yes, well, anyway, writing a book takes time and effort. If books could be copied and sold by pirates without paying the author, why would anyone bother writing them in the first place?'

So, you've set up the problem of positive externalities. How do you solve it?

'With the issue of innovations, you need to find a way of allowing the innovator to "appropriate" or acquire ownership of their idea. You can do this by giving people intellectual property rights. There are four main ways: copyright; patents; trademarks; and design rights. Copyright is for artistic works like books, music or drama. And it is an automatic right; the creator has the rights to his or her work by default. Patents are for inventions, but you have to register for a patent – and that's where our match man and the karaoke guy went wrong: they never filed a patent. A trademark protects logos and signs. If I showed you an apple with a bite taken out of it what would you think of?'

Those rectangle things Gabriel and Rosie are always looking at?

'Exactly. The Apple iPhone. The Nike swoosh would be another famous example. Finally, a design right protects the visual appearance or shape of an object. For example, the shape of the Coca-Cola bottle is a registered design.

All this deals with the appropriability problem. But there are other ways that the government encourages research and innovation. It will directly fund research, for example through universities, and it provides tax incentives for firms to spend money on research.'

OK. Got it. Innovation is an example of a positive externality. And to solve this, governments need to set up systems that protect intellectual property and provide direct support for basic research. But, just a thought, you've been going on about how great markets are, and all this stuff – protection, government investments, well it's not really very marketty, is it?

'Interesting point. And you could argue that there is too much protection for intellectual property. We need to balance the incentive to create against society's interest in free access to knowledge. The ultimate goal of such protection is not higher profits for the inventor, but social gain. The trend has been for intellectual property rights to get ever stronger. Intellectual property is very valuable to the owner, so people employ expensive lawyers and lobbyists. In the UK, copyright on a book now lasts for seventy years after the author's death. In the US, Amazon patented the "invention" of the one-click purchase. I think we have to ask, is this really innovation, is it really in society's interests?

A more controversial example than books or one-click purchasing is the strength of patent laws when it comes to pharmaceuticals. Drug companies have to invest heavily in new products, but then they can dominate the market and charge exorbitant fees. In the developed world, these might be affordable, but the developing world will be left without access.'

Hummm. So should we abolish intellectual property rights entirely?

'Some people have argued that.[4] But I think you want to be careful about situations where the costs of invention are enormous, and the costs of copying low. If you removed all property rights who would make a film, or develop a new drug? Nevertheless, there are convincing arguments that intellectual property rights are too broad, too long and too powerful.

Now, before we go home, I want to go on to talk about some other situations where markets might not work particularly well. There are certain characteristics of goods that impact how easy it is to sell them in a market. These are called "excludability" and "rivalry".'

You know I'm going to need some examples here...

'Think of an apple, or even better, think of your favourite treat, a rasher of bacon.'

Mmmmm.

'Bacon is an example of a good that is both *rival* and *excludable*. If you eat the rasher of bacon, then no one else can eat it. This is what we mean by rival. Also, if I am the seller of that bacon, it is pretty easy for me to stop you taking it if you have not paid for it. This is what we mean by excludable. Markets normally work pretty well for these types of goods, which we call *private goods*. But where goods are not rival or excludable you can expect problems.'

I am not sure I entirely get this non-rival, non-excludable thing. Can you give me some examples?

'Sure. Let's start with *public goods*. These are goods that are non-excludable and non-rivalrous. Things like national defence, irrigation projects, knowledge, weather forecasting. The defining characteristic of a public good like, say, clean air, is that if it is available to one person, then it can be available to everyone at no additional cost. Meaning that it isn't "used up" the way you use up that rasher of bacon. This is what we mean by *non-rival*. And it is hard, if not impossible, to exclude non-payers from getting the benefits of it. If the air is clean, we all get to breathe it in. This makes it *non-excludable*. The same argument would apply to national defence. It's neither rivalrous, in that the quality of being defended isn't used up by one person, or group of people, nor exclusive, in that you can't stop others from enjoying the great good of being defended.'

And why is this a problem?

'Well, it boils down to how these public goods are paid for. Everyone wants to be a freerider, enjoying the benefit without contributing to the cost. And if people manage to opt out, then the system might collapse. Think about trade unions. A trade union is an organisation that campaigns for and protects the rights of workers in a given industry. The union (assuming it's doing its job) will be able to secure a better deal for the workers than they'd be able to get for themselves if they were bargaining individually. This is why, historically, business hated unions. But union members have to pay a subscription – a few pounds each month to fund the union's activities. For any individual worker, if they opt out of the union, they will save the sub, but still enjoy the benefit of collective bargaining. For them it's a win-win. But if a majority of the workers opt out then the union dies, and all the workers lose.'

Hmmm… and the answer?

'When it comes to big things, like paying for defence, a fire service or a legal system, the simple answer is brute force. You force everyone to contribute through their taxes. When non-government institutions like unions (who can't use force) want you to pay for something that has these characteristics of non-rivalry and non-excludability, they often use a combination of tactics such as social pressure or offering small incentives.'

My head's beginning to hurt.

'Sorry, my little dog. But I've got one last thing to talk about. Some things are non-excludable, in that it's hard to stop people using them, but rivalrous, in that they can, in fact, be used up. This type of good is called a *common pool* resource. It is hard to exclude people from using this resource, but if one person consumes the resource there will be less available for others. The argument goes that free access, combined with unrestricted demand, will ultimately result in resource depletion. The problem is often referred to as the "tragedy of the commons" after an article written by Garrett Hardin in 1968.[5] A very sad example is overfishing.

For most of recent history there were, literally, plenty of fish in the sea. Anyone could go out and fish, and there were always enough fish left behind so that they could breed and reproduce. The coast of Newfoundland is just one terrible example of what can happen if unrestricted demand is placed on a common pool resource. This area was historically very rich in cod, but from the 1960s new technology allowed boats to massively increase their catch. Powerful new trawlers were not only catching ever-increasing loads of cod, but other non-commercial fish that were very important for the overall ecological system. In the early 1990s cod stocks suddenly collapsed: they had been so overfished that they were unable to replenish. In 1992 there was a ban on cod fishing in the area. Ten years later the cod had still not returned, and the jury is still out on how well the stock can bounce back.'

That is so sad. What can you do about this?

'One way to correct for this type of problem, which is like an extreme externality, is to use the solutions we talked about earlier. You could use taxation to limit demand. You could establish clear property rights. Or you could regulate. In Newfoundland the situation was so drastic they ended up by putting a moratorium on cod fishing. Before they reached this point, they tried to ban foreign trawlers, but domestic trawlers just took their place. They also tried setting quotas, but they set these quotas too high as they overestimated the supply of cod.'

Can you really not rely on people to be sensible about protecting the planet, and not poison us with lethal chemicals? Humans seem kinda dumb, sometimes, from the canine perspective.

'Generally, the approaches we've been discussing (tax, regulate, create markets) involve the heavy hand of government to force a solution. However, Elinor Ostrom (1933–2012) suggested that in certain cases it might be possible to overcome these problems without top-down regulation. Incidentally she was the first woman to be awarded the Nobel Memorial Prize in Economic Sciences. She argued that, left to themselves, local communities could manage common resources without leading to collapse. But as she herself was the first to admit, this solution is not a panacea. It is likely to work better where you have smaller, tight-knit communities, and they can observe people breaking the agreement.'

So, hang on, I'm doing some maths here, and something seems to be missing. We've looked at goods that are rivalrous and excludable, like my bacon. We've looked at goods that are neither rivalrous nor excludable, like defence, and we've looked at goods that are non-excludable, but rivalrous, like fish stocks. But what about—

'Excludable but non-rivalrous? You are a clever dog. Let's try to think of one. What this means is the type of good where it is possible for me to charge you to access it (in contrast to national defence) but it is non-rival, so that it does not cost me anything extra if you use it (your use of it won't diminish the ability of anyone else to use it). An example might be Netflix or, for that matter, almost any other internet entertainment service. This type of good often has a very high fixed cost of providing the good, but a very low (or zero) marginal cost. And in this case, you will tend to get monopolies, or at least the domination of the market by a very small number of large firms, as they have such an enormous advantage over small firms. This leads to all the problems of monopolies we discussed earlier.'

In the sad absence of that kebab, how about you give me a takeaway?

'You should be on the stage. The takeaway is that markets will work best for goods that are both rivalrous and excludable (*private goods*). The other combinations will cause problems that the market on its own won't be able to solve.

I've probably made it all seem much cleaner than the dirty, fuzzy reality, but the rivalrous–excludability pairing is a useful way of thinking about how and why markets flourish or fall on their faces.

What I really want to get across is that markets may work pretty well when it comes to *private goods*. But for the other categories, markets will be problematic, so we have to find ways to come together to provide these goods, or limit their overuse, or we will all be worse off. OK, Monty, I'm cold and dinner beckons for both of us.'

Now you're preaching to the choir. And I seem to recall there's some leftover casserole for your faithful hound.

Walk 9

The Market and Information: Why Red Bull No Longer Gives You Wings

What we talk about in this walk: Why markets need good information to function properly. How firms and governments solve the information problem (and why Red Bull got fined $13 million for its slogan: 'Red Bull gives you wings'). How information is a particular problem in insurance markets. How one online platform for drugs built a community of honest crooks. Why, even if we do have the right information, we sometimes still make the wrong choices.

It was a glorious autumn day, with sun shining through the yellowing leaves, so I thought we'd have a long walk on the Heath, ending up in the very dog-friendly café at Kenwood House. Monty's little old legs struggle with such a marathon, so I usually carry him on the first bit, as we wind up through the streets, though he insists I hide him under my coat if we bump into any of his canine pals, on the grounds that he'd 'never live it down' if word got round that he couldn't go the distance.

'OK, Monty,' I began, when we were on the dry woodland path leading from Whitestone Pond to the Arcadian glory of Kenwood, 'even the biggest supporters of free-market policies do sometimes put their hands up and admit that markets don't always work that well. On our last walk we talked about one type of market failure – the problem of externalities. Things like pollution and traffic congestion. Another situation when markets might work badly (or not at all) is when there are problems with information. The term used is *asymmetric information*: when one side of the deal knows something that the other side does not. One crucial assumption behind the model of a perfectly competitive market is that people know what they are getting when they make a trade. When this does not happen, markets malfunction.'

How big of a deal is this?

'It rather depends who you ask. But information problems are everywhere. A lender does not know how likely a borrower is to repay a loan. A dog-food manufacturer knows far more about what goes in the can than the buyers. That iPhone might look great on eBay, but until you get it in your hands, how do you know it's not a fake? If consumers are not confident that they are getting a good deal, then this will really affect the smooth running of any market. The key idea is that information problems will limit trade. In the extreme case markets may collapse entirely.'

A bit melodramatic, no?

'Perhaps, but it is not much of an overstatement. Markets really don't function without trust. Take the example of online marketplaces. One of the first was AuctionWeb, which later evolved into eBay. Its very first sale, back in 1995, was to Mark Fraser, who bought a laser pointer. But how did Fraser know that if he sent off his money the pointer would be sent to him? At the time he had to simply take it on trust. The laser pointer was dirt cheap (it was advertised as broken, and Fraser thought he would be able to fix it), and so he was prepared to take a gamble, but eBay needed some way of reassuring potential buyers that they wouldn't be conned. Without that, it would never have been more than a fun hobby for its founder, Pierre Omidyar, and he would never have become a billionaire.

So, in 1997 eBay started providing some crucial extra information: seller feedback. Suddenly here was an apparently objective way of assessing the trustworthiness of a seller.'

But how do people know if they can trust the online feedback?

'Excellent point. As soon as online customer ratings become valuable, then people will try to game the system, and fake reviews soon blighted online marketplaces.

In 2020 the *Financial Times* looked at the most prolific providers of feedback on Amazon in the UK and found suspicious activity from nine out of the top ten contributors.[1] And remember, the integrity of the market is founded on information. But here what we have is not information but … lies.'

So, is the information problem just an issue in online marketplaces?

'No, it goes back way before the internet. The classic theoretical example was put forward by the American economist George Akerlof.[2] He asked us to imagine that there were only two types of used car. There were the peaches, and there were the lemons. The peaches were perfect, the lemons were duds. The used car salesperson knows which is which, but the poor hapless buyer doesn't – it's quite easy to disguise a lemon as a peach. Therefore the buyer is reluctant to pay top dollar for a peach in case he gets home to find he's riding in a bona fide citrus fruit. So the buyers try to drive down the price. But if the seller knows he is actually selling a peach he will be reluctant to let it go for the lemon price. The upshot is that those with peaches will hold them back from the market, which will as a consequence be flooded with lemons.'

And so you make lemonade?

'Very funny. The point is that markets will not flourish if people don't have good information about the product for sale.'

You've made the case that this, er, asymmetric information thingy is a problem. I presume there's a solution?

'Businesses have come up with various fixes. For example, firms can offer you a warranty: a written guarantee that they will repair or replace whatever you have bought if it goes wrong within a certain period of time. This is designed to reassure you. In some cases, people will pay to get an expert opinion, for example when you pay a surveyor to give you a report on a house. Perhaps the most important way is through branding, and standardised products. Everywhere you look firms are trying to persuade you that their brand can be trusted. That new hipster café might have the best coffee, but Starbucks is hoping that you are not prepared to take the risk. Whether you go to one of their branches in London, Lahore or Los Angeles you know that you are going to understand the menu, that it will be clean, safe with decent Wi-Fi. You know what the vanilla latte will taste like, and that the toilet will be OK.

Branding is designed to reassure the customer, to let her know she is in safe hands. Coffee is just one example, but this rule applies to everything from your clothes to your toothpaste to the university you choose to study at. The John Lewis slogan "Never Knowingly Undersold" (now dropped) told middle-class Britain: you can trust us not to rip you off.[3] Nike's returns policy (sixty days) is a way to say: relax, we *know* our goods are of high quality. We are so confident that you will like them that we are prepared to give you sixty days to change your mind. Some companies now have a one-year returns policy. Levi Strauss telling us that they've been making jeans since 1853 lets us know that they would not still be here unless they kept their customers happy.'

If information is so important to keep markets functioning, why doesn't the government step in?

'It does. Self-regulation works pretty well in some cases, but often you do need more formal solutions. Those who extol the virtues of free markets and small governments often overlook just how much markets need rules and regulation and effective institutions to function. Governments often set rules for what information must be disclosed. For example, in the UK all packaged food has to have a label that tells you in detail what's in it. When you sell a house there is a long list of information that has to be disclosed if it might influence the buyer's decision, from obvious things like major building problems to whether you have been in any disputes with your neighbour.

Governments also set rules on fair advertising. In 2008 Danone got into trouble for the claims they made for the health benefits of their yogurts. They were fined $45 million and ordered to remove the terms "scientifically" and "clinically proven" from their packaging. In 2014 Red Bull were sued for their slogan "Red Bull gives you wings", on the grounds that, er, drinking Red Bull does not in fact cause you to grow wings.'[4]

Really? That's nuts!

'Yes. It was a bit daft. Nevertheless, it cost them $13 million. They had to pay $10 to every US consumer who had bought the drink since 2002. But this is just an extreme case of the underlying truth that markets need information to work well. The importance of this is hammered home by an example of a market that is plagued with information glitches: insurance.'

So what is the problem?

'Well, there are two main issues. Bad things happen in life. Cars crash, houses burn down, phones get stolen. Insurance is there to bail you out. The first problem is with what is called "adverse selection". Obviously, those who are the most likely to be affected by the bad event are the most likely to want the insurance. Those who know they are low risk might think that insurance is not a good deal.'

I am not sure I see why that is a problem.

'Insurance is all about the numbers. Take health insurance. Some people (young and healthy) will require virtually no healthcare. Others might have chronic diseases that will cost hundreds of thousands of pounds to treat. An insurance company makes its money by working out the average costs for all policyholders, and then adding a margin. But if people know their own personal risk, they might look at that average cost and decide it is not worth it. The healthiest people will be most likely to opt out, the sickest to get the best, most comprehensive insurance they can. And then the averages start changing. Premiums have to rise to cover the new, higher average (as the healthy people have started to opt out of the pool). Do you see where this is going? As the new price is higher, more people – the healthier ones – decide the price looks like a bad deal, so they opt out. The problem gets worse and worse so that health insurance ends up being extortionately expensive, and large sections of the population have no health cover.'

But this does not actually happen, does it?

'Sometimes. But there are ways of getting round it. In the UK we have tax-funded healthcare. This is a way of forcing everyone to contribute. This is actually a fantastically efficient way to fund healthcare. Where you do get private health insurance, health insurers like to insure large groups where individuals cannot select in or out. This is why health insurance is often done through employers. In America, Obamacare tried to get around the problem of adverse selection by making it compulsory to buy medical insurance. Again, they were trying to stop the young and healthy from opting out. In most countries (the US is a notable exception) people have decided that information problems in health insurance are so severe that a private market will not work.'

You said that there were two main problems. What is the second one?

'The second big problem for insurance is termed "moral hazard". Essentially, if you have insurance, you might be incentivised to be a little bit careless. Now this is probably not a huge problem with health insurance (when you go skydiving you are unlikely to stop checking your parachute just because your BUPA premiums are up to date). But it can be quite a big problem for other types of insurance. For example, if you have car insurance you might be a little less careful about where you park your car. Remember when Rosie threw her phone at Gabriel and smashed the screen? I suspect she'd have been a little less melodramatic if we didn't have phone insurance.

A more serious example of moral hazard was with the banking crisis in 2008. The financial crash largely happened because of risky loans made by the banks. When things were going well, these loans were being repaid, and the banks (and bankers) made money hand over fist. But when the loans turned bad, rather than paying the price of their folly, the lenders were bailed out by central banks. Ultimately the cost was borne by the taxpayer.'

That doesn't seem fair.

'It wasn't, but there was almost certainly no alternative. However undeserving the individual bankers may have been, the cost of not bailing out the banks (in terms of the economic chaos that would have resulted) would have been worse. But this was a very clear example of moral hazard: the bankers did not have to worry about the consequences of their actions when things went wrong, so they did not worry enough about the risk. Heads they win, tails we lose.'

So how do insurance companies deal with these issues – moral hazard and adverse selection?

'Well, to deal with moral hazard, companies often make you share the cost by using deductibles. For example, you might have to pay the first £100 of any claim. This can also be a sneaky way of teasing out more information. Those customers who are happy to have a high excess are likely to be the careful drivers. That eighteen-year-old who wants insurance with no deductible on a hire car? Perhaps that is a signal that they are not such a good risk.

In terms of the adverse selection problem, insurers will try to draw on a large pool of customers. Car insurance in the UK is compulsory. This reduces the problem of low-risk people selecting out.'

OK, I can see how good information is vital if insurance is going to work as it should. Any other examples?

'One case where you see all the problems caused by asymmetric information in stark clarity is the market for illegal drugs. Whatever you think about the ethics of recreational drugs, there are people who want to buy drugs and people who want to sell them, and markets have always emerged to put these two together. But increasingly, rather than having to buy drugs on dark and dangerous street corners, online platforms have emerged to trade drugs.

The most famous online drug market was the Silk Road, which tried to be the Amazon for illicit kicks. An online marketplace might be easier than hanging round dodgy parts of town at night, but information problems remain endemic. How do you know you are going to get what you ordered? The cocaine you expected could be baking powder mixed with a cattle dewormer. That ecstasy tab might just be aspirin. If you're lucky. It's not like John Lewis, there is no "Never Knowingly Undersold" promise, or sixty-day money back guarantee. You can't go to court or complain to the consumer ombudsman. One commentator on a dark web site (who had been repeatedly ripped off when trying to buy stolen credit cards) complained: "I want to do tons of business but I DO NOT want to be scammed. I wish there were people who were honest crooks."[5] Which sort of sums up the problem.'

How can these markets survive at all then, given what you've said about information?

'These marketplaces, like any marketplace, had to find a way to make sure that buyers and sellers trusted each other. The Silk Road did this in various ways that should be familiar. They set up a ratings system like eBay. And in case you worried about trusting the ratings, they also set up an escrow service: when you bought your drugs you paid the platform with bitcoin and when you confirmed online that you had received your drugs, the money was released to the seller. The platform also required new sellers to pay a bond to be allowed to sell in the marketplace at all. This bond was lost if too many buyers complained.'

And that worked?

'Yes and no. Silk Road operated from 2011 to 2013, and then was shut down by the FBI. Up until then its systems seemed to be functioning OK. But the people in charge of these marketplaces are not exactly model citizens. And if they were holding lots of bitcoin in escrow, plus all the bonds that sellers had to place to be allowed to trade, then there was an incentive for them just to run off with the money. This is exactly what happened with another online drugs platform, the Sheep Marketplace.[6] It announced that it had been hacked and all its bitcoin had been stolen. The suspicion was that they had just decided to take the money and run.'

We reached Kenwood House, gleaming white in the morning sunlight, and headed for the café, built in the former stables. I found a nice secluded table outside, tied Monty to the chair and went for coffee and a croissant for me, and a bowl of water and a sausage roll for him, as a reward for the long walk. He caught sight of the treat, tried to play it cool for a second or two, but then went into an annoying yap, which would normally be enough to get him his treat. But I was going to make him work for it.

'How about a little summing up of the first part of our walk, Monty?'

Really? We're going to do this when that thing is beckoning me with a delicious sausagey finger? Fine. So, what you are saying is that markets won't work unless there is good enough information for both sides to understand and trust the deal. There are private ways to get around this – things like money-back guarantees, online reviews and branding. Governments also ensure markets work by setting and enforcing rules – what information must be disclosed, and that advertising must not be misleading. And illegal markets find it even harder as they don't have a legal system to make sure that people play by the rules.

'Good. So far I've been taking it for granted that if people had the right knowledge, they would make better decisions. But what if people have the knowledge, but they are still not able to make rational choices? In other words, are people always the best judges of their own welfare? This is where the exciting field of behavioural economics comes in.'

Monty could only grunt as his face was full of sausage.

'Behavioural economics is a mixture of economics and psychology. Neoclassical economics assumes that we know what we want, we don't randomly change our mind, we make informed, rational decisions. If you make that assumption about rationality – that we know what's best for us, and how best to achieve it – then it's possible to make predictions, in the same way that a scientist could accurately predict the outcome of one billiard ball striking another.'

Sounds great. I think…

'But there is ample evidence that our choices are swayed by many factors that are *not* rational. Obviously, the fact that humans are sometimes illogical and make mistakes is not exactly news. And with that knowledge you might think that the scientific rug is pulled from under economics.'

D'oh!

'Except that it might be the case – and this is the line taken by behavioural economics – that people are *predictably* irrational.

The important idea is not that we make mistakes, but that many of these mistakes are, well, predictable.'

Ah, I see. You taketh with one hand, and giveth with another.

'Yeth, I mean yes. Behavioural economists have found various ways in which our irrationality takes predictable paths.'

Really? Predictable unpredictability sounds like a paradox...

'Suspiciously good word for a Maltese. Have you been hanging out with that collie at number fourteen? But, yes, there are certain irrational (in the sense of not necessarily leading to personal benefit) behaviours that can be predicted.'

Which are... ?

'Framing (how a choice is presented) dramatically affects our choices; procrastination and inertia are powerful, so the default matters; we are strongly influenced by what others do; we have a pronounced preference for fairness; certain arbitrary cues in our environment will change our choices—'

I assume you're going to go through these and explain...

'OK, let's start with framing. How a choice is presented – its framing – matters. If people are told that salami is "ninety percent fat-free" they are more likely to buy it than if told it is "ten percent fat".'[7]

Mmmmmm salami.

'Let's do an experiment (this is based on one conducted by Kahneman and Tversky, who helped found the discipline of behavioural economics).[8] I want you to imagine that a country is going to be attacked by an unusual disease that is expected to kill six hundred people. Two programmes are available to tackle the disease. If programme A is adopted, two hundred people will be saved. If programme B is adopted, there is a one-in-three probability that six hundred people will be saved, and a two-in-three probability that no people will be saved. Which programme would you choose?'

Well, I don't like the sound of B so I would go for A.

'And that is what the majority of people who were asked that question said. Now I want to ask you a different question. Imagine the same situation: again you have to choose between two programmes. If programme C is adopted four hundred people will die. If programme D is adopted there is a one-in-three probability that nobody will die, and a two-in-three probability that six hundred will die. Which would you choose?'

Oh well here I would go for programme D… Hang on a sec. Was that a trick?

'Yes, Monty, it was. Think about those questions again. The only difference between the two sets of questions was that in the first set I phrased it in terms of saving lives, while the second time it was phrased in terms of how many would die. Otherwise, the questions were effectively identical. They were just framed differently. Kahneman and Tversky's explanation for this is that people are generally risk *averse* (they don't like taking a gamble) when it comes to gains, and risk *seeking* when it comes to losses. And most people have the same intuitive reaction as you. The bottom line is that there is a long list of supposedly irrational factors that should not matter, but do.'

OK, I see that that is quite interesting – but does it really matter what a load of people think when answering hypothetical questions? I mean, this was not a real situation, was it. I'm not actually in charge of choosing medical programmes to respond to some horrible new disease.

'Good point, Monty. I would say two things here. First, that Kahneman and Tversky did ask real doctors that question and got a very similar response. Second, that there are many situations where the insights of behavioural economics have really improved outcomes for people. For example, the importance of what you make the default choice. Enrolment in workplace pension schemes dramatically increases when you must explicitly opt out rather than having to consciously decide to opt in. Another good example is organ donation. Some countries have a system where you have to opt in to donate your organs on your death. Others have adopted an opt-out system, where your consent is assumed. We all have a strong tendency to go with the default option – so when designing "choice architecture" be careful what you make the default. The key message: if you want people to do something, make it easy. Put fruit not chocolate by the cafeteria checkout.

The reverse is also true: if you don't want someone to do something, make it difficult.'

Is that why you keep the biscuits on the top shelf?

'We see firms using this strategy all the time. That month's free trial for a magazine? Very easy to take it out, quite hard to stop your subscription. In fact, cancelling all kinds of things, from insurance to gym membership, can be so bothersome you don't… bother.'

So behavioural economics seems pretty powerful.

'It has its critics. They claim that it makes no clear and testable predictions, which should be the sign of a good theory. Behavioural economics also tends to rely heavily on asking students what they would do in hypothetical situations, which is not always a good predictor of how people behave in the real world.'[9]

And what do you think?

'I think that behavioural economics is a useful addition to economics in helping us understand how the world works. Its central proposition is that there are many seemingly peripheral factors that turn out to strongly influence our behaviour. If you want to help people to save, be healthy, donate their organs, then it is probably wise to take this evidence seriously. Richard Thaler, the father of behavioural economics, has argued that he does not see behavioural economics as a revolution that will overthrow mainstream economics. Rather, it is a return to the kind of open-minded, intuitively motivated discipline that was first invented by Adam Smith, but with added number-crunching, and experiments.[10]

OK, I think we're done. Home?'

Home.

GDP: Not Everything That Counts Can Be Counted

What we talk about on this walk: A brief history of GDP – the number invented to answer the question: 'how is the economy doing?' Some Really Big Numbers. Problems with GDP, and some alternatives. How, despite its failings, GDP is a useful measure that correlates well with many other things we value (life expectancy and well-being).

Another fine if blustery day came along, with white clouds scudding across the blue sky. It was a day crying out for a walk up to a high place with a good view. We'd already done Primrose Hill, so that meant Parliament Hill. We took the train to Gospel Oak, and from there it was a ten-minute hike to the top of the hill, with a glorious view of the whole of London below us, from the shining towers of the City to the Gothic splendour of Westminster. It was once called Traitors Hill, perhaps because Guy Fawkes and some of his Gunpowder Plot buddies were supposed to have been planning to watch the original great firework display from here. It acquired its new name when Parliamentary troops congregated here during the Civil War. But now the only people congregating on the crest were tourists, holding on to their hats in the wind.

'OK, Monty, so far on our walks we have been talking mainly about relatively small-scale decisions made by individuals, firms or other groups and how these affect markets. That sort of thing is covered by the general term *microeconomics*. But now we are going to step back and look at the operation of the economy as a whole.'

I made an expansive gesture, taking in the vast panorama before us.

The big picture.

'Precisely. This branch is called—'

Let me guess, macroeconomics?

'Go to the top of the class.'

There's only one of me. Top and bottom are the same. Basic maths.

'Have it your way. But, yes, macroeconomics. Under this heading we'll look at things like unemployment, inflation, and what causes and limits economic growth. Although these issues are broad, and work on the wider level of the whole economy, they also have a real impact on our everyday lives.'

Got you. Big stuff, but not just theory. So, the microeconomics was like a little yappy dog, and the macro is a big bruiser, like that Newfoundland we sometimes see on the Heath. But they can both bite you on the bum.

'Er, yeah, I guess. We should start with GDP.'

Giant Dog Poo? Gaudily Dressed Pekinese? Gaunt Depressed Poodle…

'Finished?'

Sorry.

'Gross Domestic Product. Economists are notorious numerophiles, but the number they worship the most is GDP, and the very idea of an economy is inextricably linked to it.'

OK, sounds like the kind of thing I should know about. What is this thing called GDP?

'The basic idea is quite simple. GDP tries to put a figure on the value of all the goods and services being produced in a particular country. It might help if we go back a bit and look at the history. This giant and invisible thing we call the economy, and that we now try to measure using GDP, was really invented in the Great Depression.'

A bit of background…?

'The Great Depression started in 1929 and was the largest financial crisis seen in modern times. I don't want to go into detail about the causes of the Great Depression – it would take all day, and there's no real agreement among historians and economists – but it began as a massive crash in the stock market, which soon had dire consequences for the whole of society. Businesses collapsed, unemployment grew to levels not seen before or since, misery was everywhere. This desolation was plain to see, but remained curiously hard to grasp in cold mathematical terms. What was needed was a number, a single figure that could capture what was going on.

The US government turned to an economist and statistician called Simon Kuznets, who was tasked with finding a way to measure everything that got produced in the entire country in a given year. Every new car, every new dress, every bottle of beer, every house that got built, every visit to the doctor, had to be measured. In 1934 Kuznets published a report, *National Income,*

1929–1932, which became a surprise bestseller. For the first time, this book provided a way to answer the questions: What is going on in the economy? How bad are things? Are they getting better? Are they getting worse? Kuznets replaced vague notions with hard numbers, and very quickly politicians started talking about "the economy" using these figures. We went from a world without any solid idea of the reality of economic activity, to one in which these numbers were central.

Other countries soon adopted the concept. The beauty, from the point of view of politicians, was that once you can measure something, you can begin to think about controlling it. J.M. Keynes started to talk about the economy as something that the government could and should shape. After the Second World War, if a country wanted to receive aid from America it was compelled to produce an estimate of GDP. Knowing your GDP became as much a badge of nationhood as having a gaudy flag or a loss-making national airline. And once you have a single number, you can rank countries according to their GDP. In the Cold War battle of ideas between communism and capitalism, GDP was a way of showing who was winning. GDP is not just a number, but a weapon.'

OK, I think I've got the general idea. Leaving aside the ideological warfare point, GDP is just what goes on in the economy. But how do you actually measure GDP?

'This is the slightly more technical bit, but I will do my best. There is an old joke in economics that there are two things you don't want to watch being made – sausages and economics statistics. So this might get a bit messy, but at least it will give you an idea of some of the difficulties associated with GDP. A formal definition of GDP is the market value of all final goods and services produced within a country in a given period. The first thing to note is that GDP is a *flow* measure, not a *stock* measure.'

You have lost me there.

'What I mean is that GDP is not trying to measure the stock of a country's wealth, how much *stuff* there is. It's a measure of the *increase* in the amount of goods and services over a period of time. If a builder builds a house and sells it to you, that counts towards GDP. But in a few years when you sell that house on to someone else, that is not included in GDP as nothing new has been created.

And remember as well that GDP only measures production that takes place in a particular country (that is why it is called gross *domestic* product). It does not measure all the goods and services that we import.'

I think I'm getting there. But I'm still not sure how they measure this GDP thing.

'A little confusingly, there are three different ways of measuring GDP, but at least in theory they should all give the same answer. The first way is to simply add up the total value of goods and services produced. This is termed the *production approach*. The second way – the *income approach* – is to tot up the total value of everyone's income. Finally, the *expenditure approach* looks at the total value of what everyone has spent in the economy.'

So, how much is produced, how much is earned, how much is spent. And these three things should all give the same figure.

'That's it. To use a ridiculously simple example, if a farmer grew 100 apples and they had a market value of £1 each, then you could measure the contribution to GDP in terms of the value of this production (£1 x 100 = £100). Or you could measure it in terms of spending (consumers buy 100 apples for £1 each = £100). Or you could measure it in terms of income (the farmer gets £100 from selling his apples). In theory, whichever method you use, you should get the same number.

The expenditure approach is probably the easiest to get your little doggy head around, so let's go through that one. First think about the different groups there might be in an economy who are buying goods and services. There are households (that is us, Monty). There are firms. There is the government; they buy a lot of things. Then we have to take into account imports and exports. Remember that GDP is trying to put a value on all the goods and services created over a year in a particular country. Some of the goods and services we produce in the UK are bought by people living in other countries, so you have to add those in (that is our exports). And then a lot of what we buy is made in other countries, so you have to take that out (that is our imports).

Let me draw it out in the ground here with this stick. The GDP equation is—'

Wait, what? You promised no equations!

'I know I did… but this is an easy one. OK, here we go:

$$Y = C + I + G + (X - M)$$

"Y" stands for GDP (I don't know why, it's not my job to make up the symbols). "C" stands for household spending on newly produced final goods and services (apart from new homes, which get put in the investment category). "I" stands for investment; this is pretty much all spending done by firms. "G" stands for all government spending on goods and services. Then there are exports (X) and imports (M). The difference between exports and imports, net exports (X – M), is also called the trade balance. You add all that up, and you have an estimate for GDP. Got that?'

Not really. But I'm going to nod and encourage you to move on.

'OK, let me give you some real numbers, so you can see why all this matters. The first thing that might interest us is to look at which are the largest economies measured by GDP. According to World Bank data the five biggest economies in 2020 were: the US, China, Japan, Germany and the UK.'[1]

Fifth! Not bad for a small island.

'No, not bad, but sticking a dollar sign on it puts it into perspective. Measured in US dollars, US GDP was $20.9 trillion, China's was $14.7 trillion. The UK's GDP was $2.7 trillion.'

But there are lots more Americans and Chinese people…

'Which is why it can be more helpful to talk about GDP per capita (per person).[2] Because everything that is spent in an economy is also someone's income, GDP per capita is a pretty good indication of average income. China, for example, was second in our list, and their total GDP is huge (about three-quarters of the total of the US's). But they also have a huge population. China's per capita GDP in 2020 was only $10,500. In the US GDP per capita was $63,500. So it is really important to take population size into account.

At the other end of the scale, some countries have truly tiny GDPs. Take typical developing countries like Central African Republic or the Gambia. Their GDPs are $2,380 million and $1,868 million respectively.'

Not peanuts…

'That may still sound like a big number but per capita this means a GDP of $492 and $77 respectively.

One of the other things we might be interested in is how the GDP of various countries has changed over time. Looking at the period between 1952 to 2017, per capita GDP in China has increased from just over $1,000 in 1952 to over $13,000.[3] These figures have been adjusted to take account of inflation so they give you a sense of how real standards of living have changed. That is an extraordinary increase.'

What do you mean adjusted for inflation?

'The price of things tends to increase over the years. This is what is called inflation. When I was young you could buy a Freddo chocolate bar for 10p. Now one costs about 25p. If you are trying to measure how living standards have changed over time you need to take into account these changes in prices. If you are told that GDP has doubled, you want to know if that is because prices have increased, or a country is really producing more stuff. In the example above where I said that per capita GDP in China had increased from about $1,000 to $13,000, these figures were expressed in 2011 prices so that we could make meaningful comparisons. You won't be surprised to know that the way economists do this is rather complicated. The bottom line is that whenever you see comparisons of GDP across different years they will normally have been adjusted for inflation.'

OK I get it. GDP is really important. But, if I have understood you right, GDP only counts transactions where money changes hands. I know I am only a dog, but what about all the stuff you do that does not involve money?

'Spot on, Monty. GDP is an important number, but it is only one number. And there are a lot of things important to a good life that it does not measure. In fact there are many things that increase GDP, that actually make the country worse off. If you cut down a large forest, then GDP would go up when all the wood was sold, but the environmental cost would not be taken into account. War is another good example. Wars are expensive; governments have to buy weapons and steel and fuel, and so

GDP will go up. In a famous speech in 1968, Robert Kennedy took aim at this measure, which included spending on weapons and prisons, but failed to recognise some of the things that are most important to our well-being: our health, the quality of our education, the integrity of our public officials. Kennedy said that GDP measures "everything in short, except that which makes life worthwhile".[4] And while that might be a little harsh, there are many issues with GDP.

The first problem, as Kennedy pointed out, is that GDP does not include "negative externalities".[?]

Oh, I remember those – pollution, noise, crime.

'Exactly. When you empty a lake of all its fish, GDP will increase: it makes no allowances for the fact that you are depleting natural resources. GDP also does not capture any transactions in the informal economy.'

The one in shorts and a T-shirt?

'Keep working on that material. For economists, the informal economy is the known unknowns, the stuff that everyone knows goes on, but which is very hard for them to precisely measure. When a builder offers to knock a few quid off the bill if you pay in cash, or a taxi driver does not give you a receipt, that transaction is unlikely to be reported to the taxman, and so will not show up in GDP statistics. Even in developed countries, unreported activity can make up a large proportion of total economic activity. In 1987 Italy started to include its shadow economy in its official statistics and as a result GDP grew by eighteen percent overnight.[5]

This is even more of an issue in developing countries, where much economic activity takes place below the radar. In India, the vast majority of transactions are in cash, and many escape the taxman's notice. It is estimated that the black economy accounts for at least twenty percent of Indian GDP. In 2016, in an attempt to reduce this illicit activity, Prime Minister Narendra Modi announced that the largest Indian notes would no longer be legal tender. You had until the end of the year to go to a bank to exchange them for smaller notes or deposit the money in an account. After that, they were wastepaper. It caused huge disruption, with people queuing round the block for days waiting to exchange their old notes for new ones.'

So why bother?

'If you had a big stash of these notes (more than 250,000 rupees), then, before you could exchange them, you had to explain how you came by them. It served as a flashing light for the tax authorities, suggesting strongly that you'd been up to no good.'

Did it work?

'The tax take went up, which suggests that at least some activity may have moved from the black to the legitimate economy. But not many experts think it was worth the general chaos caused, and the other goals – to flush out counterfeit money and expose those who had been hiding their assets – didn't really happen. The latter, because the rich everywhere have got more cunning about hiding their wealth from tax authorities. But this was a good example to show you that GDP will account only for reported transactions, and, to avoid paying tax, many people use the shadow economy.

Another weakness of GDP is that, by definition, it does not capture transactions that you don't pay for. If I paid someone to take you for a walk then that would add to GDP. But if *I* do it then it doesn't. Is a country really better off if everyone pays someone else to walk their dog? If a mother decides to go to work, two jobs are created (her job, and whoever she pays to look after her child), and both increase GDP. Whenever people decide not to pay for something (to cook at home rather than eat out, to cut their own hair rather than go to a hairdresser, to grow their own vegetables rather than buy them) then this decreases GDP.

But who is to say that someone living in a country where people work fewer hours and lovingly cook their own food (and so, other things being equal, have lower GDP) does not have a better quality of life? Perhaps most obviously, GDP does not account at all for the value of leisure.'

You humans, spending all that time tapping at keyboards and peering at spreadsheets, and talking to screens. 'Zooming' makes it sound like you're on a rocket, but you're just sitting there trying to look like you know what you're doing. You need to be a bit more like dogs.

'You're not wrong. Another problem is that GDP tells us nothing about how income is distributed across a population. GDP growth might look good, but, as we discussed on our Inequality walk, if it is only going to the top one percent of the population then we might be less smug about it. On the BBC TV show *Question Time* (during the fractious debates about Brexit), a politics professor called Anand Menon suggested that Brexit would reduce Britain's GDP. A woman in the audience heckled, "That's your GDP, not ours." GDP deals in averages and aggregates, and so can hide a great deal of inequality and misery.

So far these problems are all to do with what GDP does and doesn't measure. But the changing nature of society has thrown up issues around the very concept of measurement itself. When GDP was invented, it was for a twentieth-century economy dominated by physical mass production: cars, vacuum cleaners, radios, whatever. For those goods, GDP works well as an index of economic activity. Though even here there are some problems. It is relatively easy to see that *more* of a certain good has been produced, but how do you account for improvements in quality? This year's TV might cost a little more than last year's, but it might also be much better. I bought a Mac laptop in 2002 for £1,499. I bought a much more powerful one this year for £999. If you don't account for the improvements in quality, then inflation will be overstated. Some things change so much it is hard to think of them as the same good. An iPhone is simply not the same thing as the phone that sat on the special phone table in my parents' house, or even the Motorola brick I had in 2000.

But GDP really starts to struggle when it tries to get to grips with services and digital goods, which increasingly dominate our economy. How do you compare the output of a surgeon today and twenty years ago? What about things provided by the government, like roads and education and health? For decades the value given to such output was simply the cost of provision. But does this give us an accurate way of valuing output?

Another measurement problem is how you value an economic activity that does not have a price. Think Wikipedia, Facebook, Zoom, YouTube. By global convention, zero priced goods are excluded from GDP. But whatever you think of these firms, they have added some value to our lives, which is not being well reflected in GDP.

Finally, the economist Diane Coyle argues that we tend to think about GDP as a natural object, like a mountain: a simple fact out there in the world that we can scientifically quantify, the way you'd measure the height of Mt Everest, rising sea levels or how many calories there are in a muffin. However, Coyle argues that GDP is not a material entity like these, it is a made-up idea, a human construct that we then adjust in numerous very complicated ways to take account of things like inflation and exchange rates.[6]

To sum all that up, GDP is a really important number, but you need to view it with a sceptical eye.'

If GDP has so many problems, why don't they just ditch it, and use some other way of working out how rich or poor we are?

'People have tried. The Himalayan nation of Bhutan, for instance, has produced a Gross National Happiness Index, which purports to capture a more holistic picture of well-being. It has four pillars: sustainable development, preservation of the environment, good governance and the preservation of Bhutanese culture.'

Well that sounds like a good idea.

'Perhaps. Some have argued that Bhutan's index is a bit of an empty slogan to deflect from the fact that Bhutan is very poor (its per capita GDP in 2020 was $3,000).[7] Or worse, that it is actually a cover for its somewhat repressive treatment of its Nepalese migrants (who gets to define what traditional "culture" is, and what gets included?). Nevertheless, few would disagree that happiness is a better index of well-being than money alone.

I think the human development index, as used by the United Nations, is a better measure. It takes into account life expectancy, literacy and education as well as standards of living. Incidentally it puts Bhutan at 129 (Niger is bottom at 189).'

Where does the United Kingdom sit?

'A rather respectable thirteenth place.'

Really? You'd never guess that from the way the Philosopher is always complaining and moaning.

'Norway (unsurprisingly) is top. The Better Life Index,[8] developed by the OECD*, is another interesting attempt to get round the shortcomings of GDP. It allows you to customise your own measure by deciding how much weight to put on various components, such as the quality of community, environment and life satisfaction. It has eleven categories that try to capture a more comprehensive picture of how good people's lives are.'

So why bother with GDP? You have given me a long list of all its problems, why not just use the other measures?

'GDP is undoubtedly flawed. Even Kuznets, who invented it, was unhappy with how his creation was being used, and was very clear that it should never be muddled up with well-being. But no single number can ever be expected to capture everything. And although it was never intended as a measure of it, GDP does correlate pretty well with other measures of human welfare. When you look at cross-country data you see that states with higher GDP tend to score higher on the things we all agree are important, such as life expectancy, and lower on things we think are bad, like infant mortality. The bottom line is that you can't expect GDP to do something it was never intended to do. And let's not forget that without GDP it would be almost impossible to talk about the economy at all, and so people like me would be out of a job.'

And I don't suppose I'd be getting all of these walks, which have undoubtedly improved my quality of life!

'True. But this one's gone on long enough. Let's head home.'

---

* The Organisation for Economic Co-operation and Development is a club of thirty-eight mostly rich industrialised countries including the US, UK, France and Germany.

Growth: How We Can Make the World a Better Place for the Gacoteras and the Chowdhurys

What we talk about on this walk: What is economic growth? How is it measured? How important is it? How is it distributed, both historically and geographically? Much of the world still lives in dire poverty – how can we make it a better place?

'On today's walk, Monty, I want to talk to you about growth.'

Ouch. I know I've put on a little weight lately, but you might have sugared the pill.

'Economic growth, Monty, as I'm sure you knew very well.'

Sure, but let's kill two birds with a brisk walk down to the park. And I know that one day I'll actually catch one of those infernal pigeons.

For a change I thought we'd go to Kilburn Grange Park. This is in the opposite direction to Hampstead, and in many ways it's a different world. The park itself is large and open, with tennis courts and well-appointed children's play areas, but it's surrounded by some of London's more deprived estates. Drinkers lurk in the shrubbery, and homeless people lie on benches. But for all that it's a place not of despair but of hope, with the children's ecstatic cries rising above the happy chatter of the mothers. And Monty gets to say hello to a few of the scruffy old dogs of Kilburn, widening his social circle beyond the pampered pooches of Hampstead. I unleashed him and he chased something that looked to be part Airedale, part wombat, then was chased in turn by a lumbering friendly giant like a baby hippo crossed with a hairbrush. Finally Monty had had enough, and came back to my bench, tongue lolling from a good old run-around.

'Ready for some brainwork?'

Neurones buzzing. Hit me.

'Right, growth. For most of history there was essentially no sustained improvement in humankind's standard of living. The average person in 1800 was no better off than someone from the Middle Ages. If you were barely clothed, fed and housed, you counted yourself lucky. Nor was there much variation from place to place around the world. The poor of Egypt or India or France lived much the same life, ruled by the demands of food production, and the whims of capricious and cruel masters.

The Industrial Revolution changed all that. Since then billions of people have been freed from lives of unremitting drudgery and poverty: lives of painful (and dangerous) manual labour for men, continuous household toil for women. For most, the twentieth century has changed life beyond recognition. The average person in the world is nearly six times richer since 1900.[1] But this change has been unevenly spread. Which raises key questions: why are people in the UK, US and Europe so much richer than 100 years ago? Why are people in sub-Saharan Africa still so poor? It is questions like these that are the heart of the study of economic growth.

But first, I want to introduce you to the Gacotera family.[2]

The Gacotera family live in the Philippines. Leo, forty, is a small-scale farmer. His wife Maria, thirty-six, is a housewife. They have three children. Leo works about forty-eight hours a week, and sometimes gets another twenty hours a week as a woodcutter. They live in a two-bedroom house that they built themselves with the help of family and friends. To call it a house is perhaps a bit misleading. It's been constructed and maintained with great ingenuity and care, but it remains a glorified shack, with a leaking roof, and precious little privacy. They have a toilet, a freezer, a mobile phone and some electricity, so, despite their hardships, they are better off than most of the world's people before 1870. They grow half of their food themselves, buying the rest. The family spend two hours a week fetching safe drinking water, and about seven hours a week collecting wood to use for cooking. They are planning to save so that they can replace that leaking roof. Their monthly income, measured in US dollars, is roughly equivalent to $194 for each adult (more on that calculation later).[3]

Is that so bad? Are they unhappy?

'Good question. The Gacotera family have a very basic standard of living compared to even the poorest family in a developed country, but they don't look too unhappy. They earn a little more than they spend, and there is scope in their lives for some relaxation. The children play with improvised toys. They aren't hungry, and there is hope for the future.

Now meet the Chowdhury family.[4] They live in India. Suresh is forty years old and collects fruit. His wife Basiniti is thirty years old and they have four children aged between ten and three. None of the children go to school. They live in a one-roomed – well, I am not sure what you would call it. In its wilder fantasies it might be a shack. Hovel might come closest. It has no electricity, water or toilet. It is a five-kilometre round trip to the nearest source of water, and this water is not safe to drink. Suresh spends over seventeen hours a week collecting the family's water, and four hours finding wood for cooking. They have an estimated monthly income per adult of about $30, all of which is spent on food. They hope to one day be able to buy a plot of land and have a home with a well. Now, it's impossible to see into the souls of others, but this level of poverty must cause unhappiness.'

That's pretty heartbreaking. I'm hoping this level of poverty is uncommon?

'It is not as unusual as you would hope. In 2017 about nine percent of the world's population lived below the extreme poverty line of $1.90 a day.[5]

Humanity has achieved great things over the past fifty years, using technology to revolutionise the lives of people in the developed world, so why are close to a tenth of the world's population living in such abject conditions?

The short answer is that they have been failed by their economies. The sustained period of economic growth that the UK, America and much of the developed world experienced has passed them by. When Adam Smith wrote *The Wealth of Nations* in 1776 the richest economies were about twice as wealthy as the poorest. Now the richest countries are more than forty times better off than the poorest.'

So why have developed nations, er, developed, and the others, er, not?

'That is the million-dollar question. The good news is that we do have a fair understanding of what makes rich countries rich. The bad news is that we do not seem to have come up with a recipe for making poor countries rich. But first I think we need to get a couple of technicalities out of the way.'

OK but keep it snappy.

'I'll do my best. First a definition. Growth is about measuring the increase in quantity and quality of economic goods and services that a society produces. Normally it is measured by how GDP changes from one period to the next. To make those comparisons over time meaningful, you have to adjust for inflation so you're measuring real growth, not just increases in prices.

The next problem is how to make meaningful comparisons *between* countries. To do this the figures are normally adjusted for differences in the cost of goods between different countries, using what is called purchasing power parity (PPP).'

Huh?

'It took me a while to get my head around it. If I told you that an Indian person earned 126,000 rupees and the average American person earned $50,000 who would you say was richer?'

No idea – I don't know what the difference is between rupees and dollars.

'Exactly. So to make a comparison you have to find some way of comparing what it means to live on $50,000 in the US with what it means to live on 126,000 rupees in India. You could do it by using market exchange rates. In 2017 126,000 rupees was the equivalent of about $2,000 dollars. But this is problematic. Because the cost of living is so much higher in the US than India, using this method overstates how much richer the average American is compared to the average Indian. So, economists use purchasing power parity (PPP) exchange rates, which take account of the fact that prices are very different in places like the US and India. Using a PPP conversion, the average Indian income in 2017 was more like $7,000.'

OK, so I have got the basic idea. You can show that over time the average person has got much richer, but the gap between rich and poor countries has also got much bigger. What's behind this?

'It's really to do with the way that relatively small differences in growth, say the difference between one and two percent, if continued for long enough can lead to vastly different outcomes.'

How vast?

'Imagine three different countries, Gondal, Exina and Alcona. In 1920, they all have a per capita GDP of £1,000. Let's say Gondal's economy grows at one percent. One hundred years later the Gondalians' GDP is £2,704. Exina grows at two percent, and its GDP is £7,244. But Alcona grows at four percent, and by 2020, its per capita GDP is £50,504. A small difference in the percentage makes a very big difference over time.'

Wow.

'Wow indeed. There's something called the "Rule of 70", which tells us to take seventy and divide it by the growth rate and this will give you the approximate time it takes to double. Take a growth rate of two percent. Seventy divided by two is thirty-five. So with growth of two percent a year, a country's income will roughly double every thirty-five years. As thirty-five years is about the length of a generation, this means that each generation will be twice as rich as their parents. If a country's rate of growth is seven percent (like China's), then income will double every ten years.

In short, the reason that some countries have been left behind is that they have failed to grow. The US became the richest country in the world because it had a long and unusually steady period of economic expansion, pretty much averaging two percent annual growth throughout the twentieth century. In 1865, when the American Civil War ended, GDP per capita was $4,637. By 2018 this had increased to $55,335. This is what a two percent increase year on year will do.'

And the rest of the world?

'Good data only becomes available from about 1960, so let's look at 1960–2009. Sub-Saharan Africa (SSA) started off poor, but not dramatically poorer than other countries. But it has had very low growth and has ended up as by far the most impoverished region. Asian countries started slightly above SSA in many cases but strong growth rates meant they generally ended up in the middle-income group of countries. Latin America in 1960 was doing relatively well, but its growth has been below average, and so it's stayed in the middle. OECD countries (a club of thirty-eight mostly rich industrialised countries including the US, UK, France and Germany) started off at the top and have ended up at the top, but have been joined there by others.'[6]

I get why growth is so important, but that still does not really answer my question of why some countries grow and others not. Where does this growth come from?

'Great question, Monty. And it is hard to think of a more important question than how to lift those remaining poor countries out of extreme poverty.

Economists think in terms of three basic drivers of productivity: *human capital, physical capital* and *technological efficiency.'*

You are going to have to do some more explaining.

'Let's start with *human capital.* It is an ugly phrase. It seems rather demeaning and dehumanising, as if a person were a piece of office machinery, like a photocopier, but it makes explicit the idea that well-educated, healthy people are more productive. And productivity is what determines our standard of living.

Next we have *physical capital.* This is all the equipment and machinery that you need to produce things. Think of a car plant: the buildings, the production line, the robot welders, the computers and printers needed to run the office.

Finally, we have what is called *technological efficiency* or *total factor productivity* (TFP). Basically, this is a catch-all term for everything else. It includes not just obvious technological advances, like the electric light bulb or the moving assembly line, but anything that improves efficiency, from incremental tinkering to how well countries are governed. We will talk more about this later. But some countries are, by any standards, very badly run. Think roads and transport, think legal systems, think taxation, think levels of corruption. Mess those up and it doesn't matter if you have clever workers and cutting-edge computers, your economy will still suck.'

And can you really measure these things: human capital, physical capital or technological efficiency?

'You can make estimates of human capital, and physical capital. You can't directly measure TFP, which is why it has famously been called "a measure of our ignorance".[7] But if you know a country's GDP, and you can estimate the first two, then you can go back and figure out what TFP might be. It can also be helpful to start thinking about productivity in this way. If you look at data across different countries, and see that for a particular country human capital is very low, then there is a clear policy implication: spend money on education.'

All sounds a bit vague to me. Also, if economists have all these theories and equations explaining growth, why hasn't the whole world developed?

'That is not an unfair criticism. There are some hypotheses. Some have argued that it is because of geography. Others emphasise the role of culture ("the Chinese like to save"). Finally, there is little doubt that effective institutions (good economic and political policies) can make a difference.'

Why would geography be a big deal?

'It is very striking that when you look at a world map most countries that are poor are located in the tropics, while those with high incomes have more temperate climates.

In *Guns, Germs and Steel*, Jared Diamond argues that geography is destiny.[8] Some countries simply have better natural resources than others. The epicentre of extreme poverty is Africa. If you look at the ten poorest countries in the world, the only one not in Africa is Afghanistan. The economist Jeffrey Sachs has argued that this must be more than just a coincidence and cannot be brushed aside with cultural explanations ("the people are lazy") or institutional justifications ("their leaders are corrupt"). Here the dominant condition is that of smallholder farmers who work tiny plots of land. Much of this land is so depleted it is impossible to farm productively. Malaria and other tropical diseases are endemic. They don't have safe water to drink. It is not corruption or idleness that is keeping them poor, Sachs argues, but the *Anopheles gambiae* mosquito.

Many of these poorest communities are also very isolated, living far from ports, which cuts them off from international trade. When Gap or Microsoft want to outsource their manufacturing, they are not going to venture 1,000 miles into the interior of the African continent.

The solution, for Sachs, is that the developed world needs to help the developing with these challenges. The invisible hand of the market is just not going to get people out of this poverty trap. Those of us who won the geographic lottery should pay to control malaria. Help farmers grow enough food. Give them fertiliser. Help with irrigation. Build roads.'

That seems pretty convincing.

'It is, but I don't think it explains absolutely everything. It assumes that agriculture is the only way out of the poverty trap, and in a modern, connected world, that needn't be the case.'

Which leads us on to…

'The cultural hypothesis argues that different values and cultural beliefs are what are fundamentally responsible for the differences in prosperity that we see around the world. In other words, our values are as important as our technical know-how. German sociologist Max Weber (1864–1920) argued that Protestant beliefs played a crucial part in the emergence of capitalism. His thesis was that Protestantism encouraged a set of values that led to the "spirit of capitalism" and so economic progress. The central cultural shift was away from one that focused on the afterlife, towards one that directed people to think of the present life as a way of honouring God. Wasting time was a sin, hard work a virtue. Consumption beyond one's basic needs was wasteful (and so sinful), which in turn encouraged the saving and investment that drove capitalism.'

Oh, and all that's true is it?

'Weber's approach has been widely criticised. Historians and economists have shown that the Industrial Revolution has roots that go back before Protestantism, and that deeper economic and technological factors were more important than the cultural shift he identified. But most do acknowledge that culture can play at least a peripheral role. For example, the frugality and temperance of many British Methodist and Quaker entrepreneurs in the eighteenth and nineteenth centuries is surely at least partly responsible for their success. But, no, the cultural explanation doesn't have too many close adherents these days.'

Which leaves…

'Our last explanation, a country's institutions. I think this is crucial in understanding differences in prosperity. To explain China's recent growth miracle by measuring how it increased its physical capital, or adopted foreign technology, would surely be to miss the point that it was fundamentally the result of a political decision by Deng Xiaoping to embrace markets.'

Can we just roll this back a step? You keep using that word 'institutions', what do you mean by it?

'When economists use the term institutions they are referring to all the formal and informal rules that shape our behaviour. And how society sets (and enforces) the rules really matters. Does that make sense?'

Yes. Sort of. Well, actually, no.

'Douglas North famously referred to institutions as the "rules of the game".[9] The formal rules are things like property law, company law, and the regulations guiding contracts and employment. Informal rules are all the social customs and conventions that shape how we cooperate.

People will only invest and work hard if they think they will reap some of the rewards. If the government (or the local warlord) just comes along and takes everything, then what's the point? A functioning justice system is crucial for the cooperation you need to go into business with someone. Commercial life becomes very difficult when contracts are unenforceable. Markets tend to function better when there is a healthy level of trust between citizens. You also need good regulations (protecting property rights and setting out quality standards requires plenty of government action). All of this is hard to measure.'

So, the more rules and regulations the better?

'More is not always better. Sometimes regulations get so onerous they are really just a way to extract bribes. The Peruvian economist Hernando de Soto carried out an experiment to illustrate this. He decided to find out how long it would take to set up a small shirt factory, while complying with all the laws and regulations in Peru. It took a painful 289 days. He had to get eleven different permits from seven different ministries. He was asked for bribes ten times. He tried to complete the process without stumping up for the bribes, but had to break his own rules twice or the experiment would have broken down entirely.

Partly inspired by his work, the World Bank established a measure called "Ease of Doing Business", which tries to capture levels of bureaucracy and corruption, and the good news is that Peru has now got a rather creditable score of 68.7 (the average for OECD high-income countries is 78.4).[10]

I could go on with the list of institutions that matter. But I think you've got the point. The good news is that, though geography might be intractable, institutions are something we can change, even if it is not always easy. And this should give us hope that economic failure is not set in stone.'

So, I've got that growth is a good thing, and that it can be helped along by investing in people, infrastructure and institutions. But can it go on forever?

'Logically, there must come a time when economic growth means that we've reached the point where there's simply nothing left, not a forest – indeed not a tree – not a fish in the ocean, just a barren lump of rock with perhaps just a few scuttling cockroaches and furtive rats and scabby pigeons, and us.'

Er, gone a bit post-apocalyptic there.

'Oh, sorry. But I was thinking about the fact that, historically, growth has come at the cost of terrible environmental degradation, and we can't let that continue for much longer. The question is just as contentious when you're looking at much shorter time frames, say what might happen in the next few decades. Again, economists don't agree about the extent to which the kind of growth rates we have seen in the past will carry forward into the future.'

Economists disagreeing? Quelle surprise.

'The world is complex. And I guess we will find out one way or the other soon enough. Some have argued that despite all the hype of new technology, we are looking at a future when growth will not rise as much as it did during the golden years of the twentieth century. As Paul Krugman has put it, "so much technoglitz; so little GDP".'[11]

Why do they think that growth is slowing down?

'Some argue it is just a temporary blip, that all radical new technology takes time to bed-in before the real gains are revealed. Robert J. Gordon has no time for such techno-utopians and argues that, in the US at least, growth rates peaked in the middle of the twentieth century.[12] He is doubtful that the standard of living for today's American youths will be double that of their parents. In *The Rise and Fall of American Growth* (2016), he contends that the twentieth century was a special century, and will not be repeated.'

What does he mean by special?

'Gordon believes that the transformation that occurred in living standards in the US in the first part of the twentieth century is fundamentally different from anything that has occurred before or after. (His focus is on the US, but many of his arguments apply to other countries too.) In 1870 hardly any American homes had running water, flushing toilets, light, or heating. Disease was everywhere. Seventy-five percent of the population was rural. There were no telephones, radios, no rural postal service, almost no paved roads. By 1940 the world was transformed.

Since 1970, most innovations have come in the fields of entertainment and communication. And while the iPhone is a magical thing, a flushing toilet beats it hands down when it comes to human well-being. Gordon says that some inventions are simply more important than others. He is sceptical that anything in our futures will quite match this level of change.'

Talking of home comforts, I think I felt a drop of rain...

'I think you're right. Back we go. But let's leave it with this thought. The most important question of economic history is why, after centuries of slumber, did the world's economy suddenly wake up? And what can we do to help the countries of the world where people like the Chowdhury family live, people who labour and toil and yet remain mired in hopeless poverty? How can we make sure that their children get a shot at a decent life?'

All Work and No Play Makes Jack a Dull Boy

What we talk about on this walk: The world of work, and how it has changed, for better and worse. We ask if people should be free to take 'bad' jobs (what about child labour?). Why we ought to be suspicious about unemployment statistics, and why capitalism needs unemployment. We ask if state benefits can be both generous and efficient. Finally, we talk about the future of work: Are robots coming for our jobs? (Probably, but this may well be a good thing.)

I found Monty stretched out in his favourite resting place: the warm impression left in Rosie's bed after she'd gone to school. He opened an eye, looked at me, and closed it again. If you were trying to explain the concepts of idleness, relaxation and ease you could do worse than to wave a lazy arm at Monty. Which was when I decided on today's topic.

'OK, Monty, like it or not we're going for a walk. And today we're going to talk about work and unemployment.'

Can't I just, you know, chillax a bit longer?

'Nah, up and at 'em. But I won't make it too taxing. We'll just pop down to the Poo Park.'

We found our usual bench, and got down to, well, work.

'Obviously it's not really a big part of your life, Monty, being a pampered pooch, but for most humans, work, after family, is the most important thing in our lives.'

Bummer.

'Sorta. Sorta not. Work is important. Not just because it pays the bills, but because for many of us, it is a powerful part of our identity. If you ask a person about themselves often the standard response will be framed around their job: a hairdresser, a doctor, an engineer, a teacher.'

Monty managed his first yawn of the day. *So, tell me about this interesting-sounding thing called work.*

'Let's start with the good news. For the average worker in the developed world, working hours have decreased dramatically over the last 150 years. Take Germany: between 1870 and 2017 average annual working hours decreased by more than fifty percent (from 3,284 hours to 1,354). Over the same time period UK working hours decreased by forty percent.[1] The data is less good for much of the developing world, but even there, working hours now (although often higher than in developed countries) fall far short of the punishing hours that were typical during the Industrial Revolution. And as well as shorter hours, working conditions – both in and out of the home – have improved immeasurably.

Take the US. Before the twentieth century most people worked in agriculture, or in heavy industry, or in domestic service. For men, work was hot, dirty and dangerous. For women it was relentless drudgery. But by the twenty-first century, in the developed world at least, when measured in terms of physical difficulty, exposure to the elements, risk of injury or death, work has gradually transitioned from being unpleasant to pleasant.'[2]

And on the other hand … ?

'There are still plenty of very bad jobs around. The International Labour Organization (ILO) estimated in 2017 that there are forty million people in modern slavery. Many of these are trapped in domestic work, construction or agriculture. Women and girls are disproportionately affected. Uzbekistan has come under pressure for its use of forced labour. Until very recently,[3] state employees including doctors, nurses, students and children as young as nine were forced to work in the cotton fields for around two months each year.[4] While the world of work has improved greatly for many of us, for some the reality is still pretty grim.'

Why doesn't the government just set laws to make sure that people are not badly treated at work?

'That is a good question, Monty. Typically, in the developed world, work is pretty tightly regulated. Things like the length of the working day, safety at work, job security, minimum wages are subject to legislation. But not all economists are in favour of these sorts of labour standards. Their argument is that if someone takes a job, however hard or badly paid, they must do so because they think it improves their situation.

Take child labour. It's something that appals us, and who wouldn't want to see it abolished? In 1993 the US government introduced a bill that would ban imports from countries employing children. Paul Krugman summarised the results: Bangladeshi factories stopped employing children. Great news, surely. But those children did not go back to school or return to happy homes. According to Oxfam most ended up in worse jobs, or on the street. A significant number were forced into prostitution.'[5]

Wait, so child labour is suddenly a good thing? I still feel really uncomfortable about this…

'Yes, I agree. The point is that those instant moral reactions we have must then be measured against the actual consequences of our decisions, and we might not always get the answers we want. Adam Smith's insight, that if an agreement between two parties is freely entered into, then it must benefit them both or it simply wouldn't happen, is hard to answer. But rather than asking if the choice was freely made, perhaps we need to ask whether that choice was made under conditions that ought to be – and can be – changed.[6] If the alternative to taking any job is starvation, can we really regard that as a free choice? So, it is worth remembering that although the experience of work has been transformed in the rich world, this is not the same for everyone.

That's work, Monty. Now I want to talk about its absence – unemployment. The first thing to say is that unemployment is unequivocally a bad thing.'

Why? Seems OK to me. I never did understand why you all rush around working so hard. Except Gabriel, obviously. Only ever seen him rush when he's late for a hot date.

'Take it from me, Monty, it is not much fun. When you lose your job you don't just lose your income, you lose your social status, social contacts, a daily structure.[7] It's not great for society either. It means that the economy is producing fewer goods and services than it would otherwise, and more money has to be spent on benefits. Economists often refer to three types of unemployment: *frictional, cyclical* and *structural.*

Frictional unemployment is caused when people move from job to job. Cyclical is when you lose your job due to a temporary downturn: think of the hits to the economy and employment caused by the 2008 financial crisis, or the Covid-19 pandemic.

These first two are not what keep economists, or politicians, awake at night. Structural unemployment is when there is a serious mismatch between what companies need and what workers can offer. And it is this type of unemployment that is really bad news. In Britain in the 1980s, the coal and steel industries collapsed. In the pages of an economic textbook those former coal miners and steel workers should have got on their bikes and found new jobs in expanding areas, such as the tech industry or service sector. In reality, such transitions are much harder. Communities that have been built around a single, dying industry took a hit from which some never fully recovered. Generations were blighted by unemployment and poverty and the social ills that go along with them. The Philosopher has a story about when the small mining town where he was brought up lost its pit. In the six months afterwards, four fishing-tackle shops opened up, funded by the redundancy payments. It was more or less one each for the fishermen in the town.'

OK, so some unemployment is inevitable, and not at all bad – I mean the frictional type you mentioned; some is bad, but temporary, rising and falling with short-term shocks and recoveries – the cyclical kind; and some is just plain bad, the structural.

'Got it.'

Now I'm wondering how you measure it. Measuring being a big deal for you economists…

'I was a little surprised to find out that, in the UK, it's actually done by a survey. The Office of National Statistics (ONS) picks a random group of 100,000 adults over the age of sixteen and asks them about their employment status. If they're out of work, and looking for a job, they count as unemployed.'

A surprisingly simple answer!

'It is simple, but this figure is a bit misleading.'

What's the issue? It sounds pretty clear to me.

'The unemployment rate counts those who are out of work and actively looking for a job. But it ignores those people who are out of work and *not* actively looking for a job. That seems fair enough, but it can miss some people you'd probably want to include in the unemployment figure.'

Like who?

'A student in the summer holidays, or a full-time parent, might respond to the ONS survey saying that they were neither working nor looking for a job, and they'd be quite rightly excluded from the figures. But what if you have been unemployed for a year, and because the economy is so terrible, and your prospects so dim, you've given up job hunting? As you are not actively looking for work, you wouldn't show up in the unemployment rate. Or what about someone who is highly trained, wants to work full-time, but can only find a part-time job in a call centre? You might think that people like this, the discouraged, or underemployed, should show up in the unemployment rate, but they don't. The key takeaway is that sometimes you should be suspicious of unemployment statistics. They don't always tell the whole story.'

I hear you. Lies, damn lies and statistics!

'I can't believe you've waited until our twelfth walk to say that... But the real problem for economists is explaining why unemployment exists at all.'

Huh?

'Economists think of the labour market, just as they do any other market, as the interaction of supply and demand. Businesses are on the demand side. They decide how many people to employ with the objective of maximising their profits. We workers are on the supply side. We are deciding how much we want to work. In a perfectly competitive market, the price of labour – just like the price of coffee or gold or cars – should simply settle at the point where supply is equal to demand. This logic strongly suggests that there should be no unemployment. Which is clearly not what we see in reality.'

So what's going on?

'The answer is that there are things happening here that the simple supply and demand story misses. There might be some areas of employment that function as a perfectly competitive market – Uber drivers would be one example. But most labour markets don't look like this.'

Why not?

'Economists have suggested two reasons: wage rigidity (or *sticky wages*) and the search theory of unemployment.'

Let's start with the sticky.

'Wage rigidity means that, for some reason or other, the market wage is set at a level higher than the market clearing rate.'

Huh?

'Think about that coffee. Coffee isn't ever "unemployed". If there's a glut, the price comes down until it meets demand. Wage rigidity stops that natural play of supply and demand, resulting in unemployment.'

But why does this happen?

'There are four basic explanations.'

Four!

'Sorry, that's economists for you. The first is that many countries have a legally enforced minimum wage. In the UK, as of April 2022, you have to pay everyone over twenty-three £9.50 an hour. Less if they are younger. Remember the law of demand? The rule that if the price of something goes up, demand for it will go down.

Some economists argue that if minimum wages are set too high, unemployment will be the inevitable result. Some win (those who get a better wage); others lose (their jobs). But although this might explain some unemployment (and this is debated),[8] it is hard to see it as a complete explanation. The UK only introduced a minimum wage in 1999 and you certainly had unemployment before that.

The second reason often given for wage rigidity is overly powerful trade unions. The unions' chief job is to bargain for better wages. Following the same logic as above, that may create winners (the unionised workers with better paid jobs), but it will also result in some losers – those who would have taken a job at a lower rate but now can't get a job at all.

Again, this can't really account for all unemployment. For example, in the US only about ten percent of the workforce is unionised, so it is hard to see that as a full explanation.[9]

The third reason to explain wage stickiness is that employers might choose, out of self-interest not altruism, to pay a higher wage than they actually need to.'

I don't get it. If all employers care about is making profits, why would they pay people more than they had to?

'Because employers care about productivity. And a motivated worker who does not want to lose their job is likely to work harder and so be more productive. Staff turnover, which is expensive and inconvenient for the employer, will go down.

The classic example of this is Henry Ford. In 1914 Ford announced it was doubling its wage rate to $5 a day. This generated headlines around the world, and crowds of applicants outside the Highland Park Plant. The context was Ford's development of the moving assembly line. This had hugely increased efficiency, reducing the time it took to build a Ford Model T from more than twelve hours to one hour and thirty-three minutes.'[10]

A good thing, surely… ?

'You'd think so, but the trouble was that previously skilled jobs had now become mind-numbingly repetitive and tedious. Many workers were not willing to put up with the relentlessly monotonous nature of life on the production line. Lateness and absenteeism soared, and many workers just walked out.

So that $5 a day was less about benevolence, and more about the need to make sure that workers thought very hard before quitting. If the alternative to your job is not another job paying the same rate, but a wage cut or the dole queue, then you'll behave. You'll moderate your demands for a pay rise. You'll resist going on strike. The logical consequence of this is that capitalism "needs" unemployment to make sure workers toe the line. Fail to perform at work and you'll be sacked, in the knowledge that there are plenty more saps ready and willing to take your place. Marx called these unemployed workers "the reserve army".'

Gulp. That all sounds pretty sinister.

'But I think an even more persuasive argument as to why wages are sticky is that offered by an economist called Truman Bewley. He wanted to solve the puzzle of why wages don't fall in a recession. If you think that the labour market follows the normal laws of supply and demand, you would expect wages to tumble when times are bad. If the demand for goods falls, demand for labour will fall too.

But this tends not to be what we see. Employers are curiously reluctant to cut wages – a pay freeze is far more normal. Bewley wanted to know why. He was an unusual economist in that rather than relying on number-crunching or theoretical models, he actually went out and asked people. What he discovered was that rather than militant unions being to blame, employers were worried about the damage to morale caused by pay cuts. They preferred to selectively lay people off rather than cause festering resentment among the whole workforce.'

OK, so if I've got this right, one cause of unemployment is that for various reasons, wages are set too high. What was the other story to explain unemployment?

'That was the *search theory of employment*. This perspective focuses on the idea that a certain amount of unemployment is inevitable. We all have to find jobs at one time or another. There are always vacancies and there are always people looking for a job. It is a bit like dating, although much less fun. But because of lack of information on each side, or a mismatch of skills, this process of matching vacancy to worker is not always seamless. But there are things that the government can do to make the process easier. Employers can be reluctant to take on young, untrained people – and for that reason unemployment is often much higher among the young. The danger is that unemployment can drift into unemployability. So there are many government schemes in the UK that provide subsidies to employers. The Kickstart Scheme is one. If an employer takes on a young person who was previously unemployed, the government will pay one hundred percent of their wages for the first six months.

A more contentious proposal is to make sure that unemployment benefits are not too cushy. When you are deciding to accept a job or not there will be a number of variables in the mix: how much you value your leisure (parents might place quite a high value on being at home). What you think you might get if you hold out and look for a bit longer (a highly trained accountant is likely to hold out till they find a job that matches their skills). And perhaps most importantly, simply how much cash you've got in your pocket. The unavoidable truth is that the more generous unemployment benefits are, the more picky people are when it comes to deciding whether or not to take a job. For this reason, the UK has particularly stingy unemployment benefits – currently for a single person they are about £75 a week, even less if you are under twenty-five.'

Wow. OK, I'm a dog, but even I know that's not much.

'There's a trade-off here. In a civilised society we want to help those in need. But we also want to encourage people to work. Unemployment benefits pay people to do nothing. This can be frustrating for those who feel they are working hard to support the feckless. But it can also be dangerous for those who are stuck at home watching daytime telly. There is considerable evidence that once people have been unemployed for more than six months, they become invisible to employers.[11] As a consequence, many countries have chipped away at unemployment benefits in order to keep incentives to work strong.'

That is a bit depressing. Is it beyond the wit of you people to find a way of helping the unemployed without putting them off finding work?

'The idea that lavish benefits discourage hard work is a bit of a mantra, particularly on the political right. It is not just economists and politicians who think this, but many voters. Generous unemployment benefits are generally not an election-winning strategy, though of course that's fed by the right-wing press, which loves to find and pillory some benefits cheat who's signed off on long-term sick pay while secretly climbing mountains, scuba diving and training as a bullfighter or ballet dancer.'

Has anyone managed to balance this?

'Actually, yes. Denmark has managed to design a system that is both generous *and* efficient. In Denmark unemployment benefits are worth more than eighty percent of your previous earnings. For parents it can be close to one hundred percent. You would think that this profligacy is hugely expensive, but Denmark spends far less than average on unemployment benefits. In the OECD, the average spent on unemployment benefits is 0.59% of GDP. The UK spends a paltry 0.15%. Yet Denmark spends only 0.07% of GDP.'[12]

What are they getting so right?

'The answer is that they have a very flexible labour market. Danish employers can pretty much fire people at will. Paradoxically, this helps keep employment strong. If firms don't have to worry that the person they employ is unsackable, they are more likely to take a chance in the first place. (As one of my old economics teachers put it – if you were trying to keep marriage rates high do you think banning divorce would be an effective policy?)

The flip side to Denmark's fire-at-will policy is a conspicuously generous safety net. Yet when Danish people lose a job, they find a new one faster than almost anyone else in the world.[13] This is because there is a team of people making very sure that you do not get used to sitting on that sofa. You have to submit a CV to a coach, and if you don't keep looking for work hard enough you can lose your benefits. Their system is best described as one of tough love. The state provides a generous safety net to cushion a very flexible labour market, but there is no hiding place for layabouts.'

Well why doesn't everyone just copy the Danes?

'I can't answer that, Monty, other than the extreme reluctance of politicians to be seen to increase rates of state benefits. But I should say that "getting to Denmark" has become a widely accepted metaphor for the question of how to get it right in the pursuit of a good society.

Look, Monty, we've had enough about unemployment, so before we go home, I'd like to talk a little about what the future of work might hold.'

Is this the bit where you tell me robots are coming... You know what I feel about robots.

'Oh, Monty, I know I shouldn't laugh about your irrational fear of our robot vacuum.'

It's not irrational. That thing is out to get me. I saw what it did to my second favourite toy rabbit. CHEWED IT UP. SPAT IT OUT. It's a monster.

'I promise you he, it, is not going to hurt you. But you are right, this is the bit where I tell you the robots are coming.

It's not just you with the Roomba: since the Industrial Revolution people have feared mechanisation. In 1589 Queen Elizabeth I refused William Lee a patent on his invention of a knitting machine, as she worried that it would put knitters out of work. The stocking frame operators of Nottingham (the original Luddites) destroyed the machines that threatened their jobs. Now we are frightened that artificial intelligence is coming for us. But should we be scared? The standard answer from economists is to say that these fears are overblown. They point out the hockey stick of history: automation in the past led to huge increases in productivity and living standards, so we should not fear for the future.'

Buuuut?

'Buuuuut, there are two issues for this narrative, both of which have implications for our future.

First, technological advance may have been just dandy for the West, but the consequences for much of the rest of the world were less benign. Huge increases in textile production in the UK were a disaster for places such as India and Egypt, once world leaders in the field. The collapse of the Indian cotton trade in the 1830s led to the then British Governor remarking that "the bones of the cotton-weavers are bleaching the plains of India".

Second, even in the West, rises in living standards driven by technology did not happen overnight, and the losses and gains were not spread equally. The Luddites are portrayed as backward and irrational, but the truth is that steam driven power-looms were destroying their livelihoods. By the 1820s, seventy-five percent of Blackburn's weavers were out of work, and back then that meant starvation or the horrors and degradation of the workhouse.'[14]

You are talking a lot about the past when we are meant to be discussing the future.

'As the saying goes: history might not repeat itself, but it sometimes rhymes.[15] Just as advances in technology in the past led to winners and losers, we should expect the same in the future. Robots and increasingly sophisticated AI is coming. Trying to hold this back is futile and possibly coun-terproductive. If self-driving cars can drive more safely, and more cheaply, should we really ban them to protect taxi driv-ers? History teaches us that in the place of these vanishing jobs, many of which are either boring or dangerous, new jobs will arise. But it is not much consolation to those who have been put out of work to say stop complaining, in the long run society will on average be better off. As Keynes liked to say, in the long run we're all dead.'

But why? If jobs are lost, how do you know there won't just be fewer jobs full stop? Which would be terrible, as you've already said that unemployment is an evil.

'So here I need to explain what is called "the lump of labour fallacy". This is the idea that there is only so much work to go around. History shows that this is not the case. Let's look at the US, again. In 1870, forty-six percent of people worked in agri-culture. By 2009 only one percent did.[16] Over the same period millions of women joined the labour force (female participa-tion rates went from about twenty-one percent to seventy-six percent). There was huge immigration. Yet unemployment rates did not explode. Why? By lowering costs of production, automation can create more demand. Whatever you were buying is now cheaper, so you have more money to spend on other goods and services. This increased demand leads to more jobs in other sectors. In the future, the economy may need fewer supermarket checkout staff but more yoga teachers or nurses.'

I am not sure what I am meant to take away from all this. Will increasing technology be good or bad?

'It will be both. If the past is any guide, progress comes at a cost. The pain will be felt immediately, the gains may take more time to really reveal themselves. We need to protect the losers.

Now, *you* may be able to snooze the rest of the day away but I have—'

Work to do.

Walk 13

Part I: Financial Markets in Theory: Why We Should Love Bankers

What we talk about on this walk: How the financial system should work (why we would have to invent banks if they did not exist). The three main elements of a financial system: The stock market, the bond market, banks (and why banking is based on a lie). When it goes wrong: Investment banking, financial innovation and the financial crisis of 2008. And for some light relief: How to get rich quick.

Today's walk had an actual purpose – over and above, that is, the usual one of getting Monty outside to take the air and perform his ablutions. I had to pay in a cheque, surely the most annoyingly old-fashioned and inefficient way of moving money around. It meant a walk up to Hampstead High Street and a visit to that once ubiquitous but now rarest and most exotic of creatures, a physical bank. It was all so old-fashioned I almost felt I should wear a bonnet and bloomers, and cycle there on a penny-farthing, though that would have been tricky with Monty.

We tend to assume that dogs crave greenery. We imagine they're happiest when peeing against some great oak or shimmering willow. But Monty seems just as content on an urban stroll, lampposts and traffic lights making excellent substitutes for trees. Monty also seems to like the purposefulness of going on an errand, as if he senses that he plays an important part in the occasion, deterring armed brigands and fending off attack by packs of ravening wolves.

So Monty was on the alert as we approached the bank, which made him growl at the three figures outside. It was a mini-demo, an offshoot of a bigger Extinction Rebellion protest happening in town. A white guy in dreadlocks, and what appeared to be a pensioner couple. It was a mild relief to see that the Philosopher wasn't among them, as this is his sort of thing. Each protester was holding a placard. WE CAN'T EAT MONEY, said one. PLANET NOT PROFIT, said another, and the third, in the hands of the dreadlocked guy, said, THE SYSTEM IS KILLING US. Monty growled, I smiled and apologised, and the crusty said, 'Have a nice day.'

Cheque paid in, we continued our walk around the charming back streets of Hampstead. It was once the playground of artists and writers, but now only bankers and oligarchs can afford even a flat here. I may have grumbled a little about this, on lines not dissimilar to those of the Extinction Rebellion gang.

Tell me then, why does everyone hate bankers?

'Well, moneylenders have always had an, how should I put it ... image problem. Jesus chased them out of the temple. Dante puts them in the seventh circle of hell, along with blasphemers, suicides and murderers.'

What's their punishment?

'Rained on by burning sand.'

Seems a little harsh…

'It does, but perhaps we can understand why financiers and their ilk might be unpopular. In Chambar, a town in south-eastern Pakistan, moneylenders charge poor farmers an average interest rate of eighty percent. The farmers have to pay it, because it's their only way of buying seed for the next year. No seed, no food, and they starve. If you think that's steep, let me introduce you to Wonga, who made a name for themselves in the UK providing short-term, high-cost credit to those who couldn't borrow money from anywhere else. Never mind eighty, in some cases Wonga were charging more than five *thousand* percent a year, driving some debtors, in an ironically sad echo of Dante, to suicide. And more august institutions are no more popular. Matt Taibbi (the *Rolling Stone* journalist) famously described the merchant bank Goldman Sachs as "a great vampire squid, wrapped around the face of humanity".[1]

I am waiting for one of your famous buts.

'You know my ways, Monty. Yes, there is a but. We might hate moneylenders, but we do need them. If banks did not exist, we would have to invent them.'

Er, why?

'Just as we need a market for other goods and services, we need a market for credit. Some people want to borrow. Some people want to save. An economy needs some way of connecting the two. Just to go back to those Pakistani farmers we feel are being ripped off. If the moneylenders didn't loan them the money to buy that seed, then their farms would fail.'

I am confused. All that sounds really sensible, so why do bankers have such a bad name?

'A country can be prosperous only if it has a well-functioning financial system. You need a system that allocates capital to those who can make best use of it. A system that allows people to safely store and smooth their income over their lifetime. One that can help protect you from risk. But you can have too much of a good thing,[2] as we saw in the financial crisis in 2008.

But this is a lot to take in without understanding the basics. I want to first explain how capital markets *should* work (and for the middle part of the twentieth century *did* work). Then we can unpick what went so wrong. Finally, we can talk about how to get rich quick.'

Oh, I like the sound of that last one.

'First things first. Financial markets have at their core three main components: the banking system, the stock market and the bond market. These three markets, however complicated they are made to sound, are ultimately answering three basic needs.

First, businesses need to raise capital to build factories and buy equipment. Entrepreneurs need to borrow to get their business up and running. Households need to borrow to buy a home or car, or to pay for further education. The modern economy could not survive without access to credit.'

Got it. First need, to borrow dosh to buy stuff you otherwise couldn't afford.

'Second, the financial system is there to help people manage their money across their lifetimes. Most people want to save for their retirement and need some way of transferring wealth to the future. You could just hide cash under your mattress, but apart from being uncomfortable that comes with some risk.'

Burglars? They wouldn't dare, not with your vicious guard dog on duty!

199

'Oh, they'd just bribe you with a sausage. But the real threat isn't from thieves, but from inflation. Inflation slowly erodes the value of your money. It is like an ice sculpture at a party – you can't see it melting away, but it is.[3] But if you can put your excess money to some productive use, not only will its value not shrink, but it might even grow. The world is full of prospective borrowers with good ideas, who are prepared to pay interest for the privilege of borrowing money.'

OK, need 2 is make the money you have do some work for you, and not just melt away. Need 3?

'Third, financial markets allow us to manage risk. The most obvious way is through insurance. But financial markets also make it easier to spread risk. Say you had £5,000 to invest. You could just buy shares in one company. But if that company gets into trouble, you would be completely wiped out. A much better idea is to put your £5,000 into a mutual fund: you buy a small share of a fund that owns a very large pool of different assets. This means your risk is spread: if one company tanks, you don't need to lose sleep, as hopefully it represents just a tiny proportion of your £5,000.

Bottom line – the three parts of the financial system (banks, stock markets, bond markets) are all, in their different ways, about addressing these three basic needs: raising capital, smoothing income, managing risk. That's it. Well, there is also a fourth element: speculation. But we will get on to that later when we talk about the financial crisis.'

I think that makes sense, but I am still going to need you to explain what banks do. And, frankly, stock and bond markets, no idea...

'We'll go through them in turn. Let's start with stock markets. Stock markets are a way for companies to raise money by selling shares – essentially small slices of a company – to investors they don't know. For instance, I own part of Facebook.'

Get you, fancy pants!

'Well, to be strictly accurate, I own one share in Facebook. One share in Facebook (now called Meta Platforms Inc.) is currently worth about $340.[4] And as there are currently roughly 2.8 billion shares outstanding, this means I own a tiny, tiny part of Meta/Facebook – 1/2,800,000,000th, to be precise. This is how it works. Typically, an individual might decide to set up a company investing some of their own cash, perhaps with help from friends or family. Jeff Bezos set up Amazon from the garage of his rented home, and his parents loaned him $250,000 to get it going.

If a company survives the tricky early period, it might decide to raise money to expand the business. It can do this by "going public"; that is, by selling shares in the company to the general public. These shares can then be traded on the stock market. And this is how small fry like me can end up buying shares in companies like Facebook.'

OK, got that.

'The next important part of the financial system is the bond market.'

Market I think I know, but what the heck is a bond?

'A bond is a way that governments or large companies borrow money. Think of a bond as being a bit like an IOU. You lend a company £100. In return they give you a bit of paper that says I owe the holder of this bit of paper £100 and I will pay it back in (say) ten years, and in the meantime I will pay ten percent interest a year. The important thing is that the bond (the IOU) is *transferable.'*

Why is that the important part?

'The transferable bit means that you can sell this bond to other people. What they will pay you for it will depend on the interest rate and the chance that the company will default on the debt, perhaps by going bust. So this bond now becomes something that itself can be traded. And that means a market.

Equity markets (which is another name for stock markets) are a way of companies raising money by selling shares in their business. Bond markets are a way of businesses raising money through debt. It's borrowing, but borrowing in a way that creates a tradeable product, the bond. Got it?'

Surprisingly, yes.

'Finally, we get to banks. The key thing about banking is that it is based on a lie.'

Huh?

'Well not so much a lie as a bit of a fudge. Let's take a step back. What do banks do? I said earlier that the financial system is there to connect savers to lenders, and banks and other financial institutions play a crucial role. Banks have three main functions: first, to identify profitable lending opportunities; second, to use short-run deposits to make long-run investments; third, to manage risk.'

Err, that's all just words.

'I know, I know. Let me fill this in a bit.

First, banks need to identify potentially profitable lending opportunities, and match them with people who want to save. It's a bit like dating, with the bank as a dating agency. In theory you don't need banks to do this. If I want to invest my money, I could try to find someone who I think has a good business idea and lend to them directly. But it's easy to see that that might not be very efficient. I don't have the time or knowledge or contacts to search out people with good ideas that are worth investing in.

It is much easier all round if you have an organisation that can specialise in this, and that can attract a large pool of people who either want to borrow or to lend and play matchmaker.

Second, banks can transform short-term liabilities into long-term investment. The technical term for this is maturity transformation.'

I think I understood about three of those words...

'Sorry, Monty. Translated, what I am trying to say is that you have to find a match between how long people want to lend for and how long people want to borrow for. Imagine if there were no banks, and I wanted to borrow money to buy a house. I would have to find someone who was prepared to lend me money for twenty-five or thirty years. That's a big ask. Again, banks can be the middleman. With a large enough pool of people wanting to either borrow or lend, they can bundle together lots of short-term loans into long-term investments.

And just to clarify, when you deposit your monthly pay cheque in a bank, whether you know it or not, you have become a lender.'

Well, let's hope your man Dante was wrong about that seventh circle of hell, and the burning sand...

'Quite! Banks will be using the money you deposit to lend out to other people. Typically, banks have lots of long-term lending (e.g. mortgages), matched with a pool of constantly renewed short-term borrowing (i.e. your deposits). This does, however, lead to one of the major instabilities with banks. Banking relies on confidence, and when that confidence goes there is a danger of a bank run. More on that shortly.

Third, banks help manage risk through diversification. We talked about this earlier. Going back to my example of a world without banks in which I wanted to borrow to buy a house. If you were the lender in that case, you would be taking on a serious risk. I might be a lazy good-for-nothing who ended up not paying you back. Banks lend to lots of different projects and so spread their risk. You as a depositor can then earn a return that is backed by lots of different investments.'[5]

OK, so I think I have got it. But what was that you said about banking running on confidence?

'There are two big problems that a bank can get into. A problem of solvency and a problem of liquidity.

A *solvency* crisis is when the bank's assets (things it owns that are worth money) are worth less than its liabilities (the money it owes other people).

A *liquidity* crisis is when a bank has assets that are worth more than its liabilities, but it cannot immediately sell those assets to satisfy a demand for immediate liabilities.

One thing that I always struggled to get my head around is the fact that when you deposit your money, say your monthly pay cheque, into your bank account, that counts as the bank's liability. The bank now owes you that money and has to pay it back to you on demand. But when a bank makes a loan to someone, that counts as an asset for the bank.'[6]

So why do banks have liquidity problems? Can't they make sure that they just have enough cash set aside to pay you back whenever you want?

'Banks make their money by lending out the money you deposit to other people. They count on us not wanting to withdraw our money all at once. And this is a socially good thing – we want banks to lend to people with bright ideas.

The problem is that the assets banks hold tend to be relatively long term and hard to turn back into cash. They are *illiquid*.[7] If a bank owns a bundle of mortgages, it can't suddenly call the loans in and demand that the person who borrowed the money pay back the full amount immediately.

On the other hand, the bank's liabilities – the money that customers, that you and I, deposit – are normally short term. We can walk in any time we want and take our cash out. In the jargon, banks borrow short and lend long. Normally this is not a problem. But if for some reason all the bank's depositors lose confidence, and try to take out their money, then you get a bank run. As long as we all trust that the bank will pay us back, we will leave our money there. As soon as we worry that they might run out of readies, we'll queue at the cashpoint until every folding note is extracted, and then we'll pound at the bank's plate-glass windows, and try to smash our way in, until the riot police come and drive us away with water cannon and tear gas.'

Steady on.

'Sorry, got carried away. This is why I said that banks run on trust. A lack of trust can become a dangerous self-fulfilling prophecy.'

You're saying it all goes wrong when trust fails, but I'm a bit puzzled as to why you'd trust banks in the first place. I wouldn't trust my bones with some other random dog...

'A very good question. This is a long-standing problem, so to shore up confidence, governments regulate banks to stop them from taking on too much risk. In theory. Governments also typically offer deposit insurance. In the UK, for example, customer deposits are protected up to £85,000. In practice, this government backing goes even further. The central bank can, and does, act as lender of last resort. In other words, if a bank is experiencing a liquidity problem the central bank can just lend the bank however much it needs to tide it over. (We will talk more about exactly what a central bank is later.)

This is what happened with Northern Rock. In 2007 the bank's customers, spooked by rumours that the bank had approached the government for emergency support, started to form queues around street corners to withdraw their deposits. It was the first bank run that the UK had seen in 150 years. But an even bigger issue is when the bank has a solvency problem.'

Remind me what that looks like again.

'This is when the value of the bank's assets is worth less than the value of its liabilities. Then the problem cannot be solved by just lending the bank some money to cover its short-term cash-flow problems – the central bank will have to let the bank go bankrupt, or it will have to bail it out.

I cannot emphasise this point too strongly: the banking sector only functions at all because of an explicit (and implicit) government guarantee. Banks are private companies, listed on the stock exchange. But ultimately the entire edifice of the financial system relies, when push comes to shove, on the backing of central governments.'

And is that not OK?

'It leads to one big problem: bankers have a strong incentive to take risks, knowing that if it goes wrong, someone else will pick up the bill. And that someone else is us. Heads they win, tails we lose. Which is precisely what happened in the financial crisis of 2008.'

I had a brief flashback to 2008. Gabriel and Rosie were both at junior school in Hampstead, and I'd usually walk them up on my way in to work. And I noticed something strange. Suddenly the streets were full of well-to-do middle-aged men, looking vaguely uncomfortable in weekend casual clothes. It took me a while to realise that these were financiers, laid off because of the crash. And that drove home what had happened to Hampstead.

The blue plaques on many of the houses showed that once this had been where artists and writers lived: D.H. Lawrence, Rabindranath Tagore, Edith Sitwell, Ben Nicholson – we'd strolled past them all. Now only the rich were here. I leave raving about inequality to the Philosopher. I think wealth creation is key for the good of any society; but it was impossible to think that any of these bankers, despite their millions, would be worth a blue plaque in the future. So even a free-markets person like me could feel a little thrill of *Schadenfreude* at their fall.

'Had enough of Hampstead?' I asked Monty.

I'm done.

So we set off home.

Part II: Financial Markets in Practice: When It Goes Wrong, and How to Get Rich Quick

'OK, Monty, we're going downhill on our way home, so we should talk about what happened when the whole financial system went downhill. And, as ever, it's often only when something goes wrong that you get a glimpse into its hidden workings.'

Like our toaster?

'Just like the toaster. So far, in describing what banks do, I was really talking about the banks that you see on the high street or advertised on TV. These are called commercial or retail banks. But there are also the banks that are a bit more elusive and obscure, called investment banks. These banks do not deal with the likes of you and me. They deal with very rich individuals and institutional investors…'

What's an institutional investor?

'Institutional investors are organisations like pension funds who invest the money that individuals have pooled together to save for retirement. Or sovereign wealth funds. For example, Norway has a state-owned fund that invests their oil revenue for the benefit of the Norwegian people. Investment banks got their name because they used to help companies raise money from these large institutional investors, by issuing shares and bonds. In addition to selling shares and bonds for their clients, investment banks also buy and sell shares and bonds with their own money, hoping to make a profit. This is called proprietary trading.

From the 1980s, we had the gradual rise of a new financial system in which these investment banks, and other financial institutions, increasingly moved away from "boring" banking, and got involved in the creation and trading of new financial products, such as securitised debt and derivatives.'

You're making my head hurt – securitised debt, derivatives. Do I really need to know?

'Sorry, Monty. It does get complicated. The bottom line is that weakened government regulation led to the development of increasingly complex financial products, and a subsequent speculative frenzy. This ultimately led to some banks going stony broke. But if you don't quite get it, don't feel too bad. At the height of the financial crisis in 2008 it became pretty clear that even Wall Street executives did not understand some of these novel products – and they were the ones buying and selling them.

Let me try to explain. In the old days, when someone borrowed money from a bank and bought something (a house, a car), that was that. You borrowed money from the Bradford and Bingley Building Society, and for the next twenty-five years you slowly paid the Bradford and Bingley Building Society back.

This meant that the Bradford and Bingley Building Society had a really strong incentive to make sure that you were a good credit risk. But then banks started reselling and securitising mortgages.'

Reselling sounds straightforward, but securitising?

'Bank A lends you money for a mortgage. You promise to give them a monthly payment for however long the mortgage lasts – say £1,000 a month for twenty-five years. For Bank A, this promise of a future stream of income is an asset. And they can sell this asset, say to Bank B. Bank B might buy lots and lots of mortgages from other banks and combine them with other similar mortgage loans. Now Bank B has this big pool of mortgages with (say) about £10 million coming in every month. This combined pool of mortgages can be *securitised*. What this means is that Bank B can divide this one giant pool of mortgages into lots of little slices (say 1,000 slices) and each of those slices can be bought and sold separately. If you own one slice, then you are entitled to 1/1000th of the money coming in each month. This is what is called a *mortgage-backed security*.'

OK. Got it.

'If you understand that then you, little doggy, understand more about the financial system than ninety-nine percent of people! Securitisation isn't necessarily a terrible idea. It's a way of allowing people to invest in mortgages with a reduced risk. If one of those mortgage borrowers defaults it really does not matter – the risk has been diversified.'

So, what is the problem? I presume there is one...

'The problem is that Bank A – and there were many Bank As – made lots and lots of loans to people who could not afford to repay them. These were the notorious "subprime" mortgages. The background to this was that the US government wanted to encourage home ownership, and so they relaxed regulation around home loans, making it easier for banks to lend to people with poor credit records. Banks increasingly pushed subprime lending, offering mortgages at attractively low initial interest rates, say five percent for the first three years.'

Yay!

'Which then went up to seventeen percent for the rest of the loan period.'

Boo!

'People thought five percent sounded OK, and, if the worst came to the worst and they couldn't afford the higher payments, they could just sell the house. And this all worked fine, as long as house prices were rising.'

I sense it's all about to go horribly wrong.

'Yep. I explained to you what a mortgage-backed security was. Well, this was only the beginning. Banks then turned these mortgage-backed securities into *collateralised debt obligations* (CDOs). Here the slices of debt that you buy and sell are not created equal. Some are riskier than others. This same principle was applied not just to mortgages, but also other consumer loans, such as credit-card debts. So now we have hugely complex bundles of debts being bought and sold on the market. This all started in the US but soon spread to other rich countries, as the old regulations that had restricted the ability of lending banks to sell on their loans to a third party were abolished.

And adding a further complication, there was something called a credit default swap (CDS), which was essentially insurance that paid out if a CDO defaulted.'

Isn't insurance usually a good idea? Doesn't that make things safer?

'Yes, in theory. The idea behind it all was to make things safer through diversification. (Well, to be more accurate, the idea behind all these things was to make the people who invented and sold them grotesquely rich.) CDSs acquired a particularly bad name because you could buy a CDS even if you didn't actually buy the asset that you were insuring. As a result, buying a CDS became the way that bankers gambled a company would go bankrupt. These CDSs were not regulated. This meant that financial institutions could issue and sell as many of these contracts (bets really) as they wanted.

In the end, although this was done under the cloak of diversifying risk, what it really enabled was wild speculation. When the crisis hit, it had all got so complicated that no one understood who owed what to whom.'[1]

You said this was all the doing of the investment banks. Did it have an impact on the boring banks – the ones I see on the high street?

'Yes, because many of the high street banks had bought these asset-backed securities (and their fancy relatives) and now owned a bunch of assets that were suddenly worth less than they thought. No financial institution was sure if who they were dealing with was financially sound. And as banks all lend and borrow from each other, you had both a *solvency* crisis and a *liquidity* crisis. It was a massive double whammy. The whole elaborate house of cards was about to collapse. Governments felt they couldn't let that happen, so they stepped in and propped up the banking system.

But those bankers who had created (and profited from) this insanely risky and complex system were able to walk away with their own personal fortunes intact. By one estimate the top five executives of Bear Stearns (one early casualty of the financial crisis) took out about $1.4 billion in cash and shares between 2000 and 2008.[2] As the saying goes: privatise the gains, socialise the losses.'

That is terrible. No wonder those guys were waving their placards back at the bank.

'You're not wrong. Capitalism, and quite possibly Western democracy, would not have advanced as it did without the development of the financial system. The growth of banks, investment banking, stock and bond markets, all that jazz, allowed firms to raise capital and pool risk. This was a good thing for society. We need banks. However, the deregulation of the financial system since the 1980s was, in retrospect, clearly a mistake. In the late 1990s mega banks were created that were too big to fail. If bankers took a risk and won, they got the prize, but when they gambled and lost the government picked up the bill.'

Now I get why people were angry.

'In many ways I think people were not angry enough. You know me, Monty. I like markets. I think people respond to financial incentives, and that hard work and responsibility should be encouraged. But the depth of ineptitude and venality among financiers was truly shocking. Bankers are very lucky that this is all so complex, and that no one really wants to make the effort to get their head around collateralised debt obligations and financial regulation. I think if people had really understood then these criminals would have been suitably punished.'

Well, my head hurts. Can we move on to something cheerier before we reach home? I vaguely recall you saying something about getting rich quick?

'Ah, yes, I did say that. That was a little bit of a fib. I needed some way to make you listen to all that stuff about collateralised debt obligations and credit default swaps. I am sorry to say that, just as there are no miracle weight-loss programmes, there are no miracle get-rich-quick schemes.'

Sometimes you are quite annoying.

'Sorry, but this is because of one of the most basic "laws" in economics. (I'm putting that in quote marks, Monty, because this is an economics law, not a physics law. So more of a tendency than an absolute ironclad certainty.) The reason it is very hard to get rich quick in investing is that there are very few bargains out there, for the very good reason that if there were, someone else would have snapped them up.'

But why?

'Suppose you were looking for a new house. That fancy Peke Penelope has agreed to shack up with you, and you are looking for a suitably swanky three-bedroom doghouse.'

I'm listening…

'You have a budget of £500,000. Some of the nicest ones in the area you want are £550,000. A few more that need some work doing are £450,000. But it is clear the market rate for the type of house you want is in this range. Suddenly your celebrity estate agent calls you up and says, "Monty, darling, I have a fabulous new house on my books. It is exactly what you wanted, the size you wanted, the area you wanted, and it is half the price it should be. Absolute bargain. You could sell it next week for twice the money." What would you think, Monty?'

I guess I might wonder why the seller was selling it for less than they could get. And if the estate agent thought that I could double my money overnight, why was she not buying it herself? Or if for some reason she couldn't, why would other buyers not also be after it – in which case I guess the price would just be bid up to the market rate.

'Did you really say all that?'

What?

'Never mind. But all spot on. There is no free lunch. The stock market works in just the same way. In a market where everyone is out to try to make money, the price of an asset reflects all available information. In economics, this idea is called the *efficient market hypothesis*. The implication is that there are no (or very few) obvious bargains out there. It is enormously hard to get rich quick.'

Well if you can't tell me how to get rich quick, can you tell me how to get rich slow?

'That I *can* have a go at. It is less exciting, but there is a basic set of sensible rules.

Rule one: *save, invest, repeat.* It's the old story as told by Mr Micawber: annual income 20 pounds, annual expenditure 19 pounds 19 shillings and 6 pence, result, happiness. Annual income 20 pounds, annual expenditure 20 pounds nought and 6, result, misery. You have to save. The first step is to stop borrowing. It is OK to borrow to buy a house, perhaps to pay for further education. But never, ever, ever take on credit card debt for anything other than a house loan or a profitable investment. Credit cards are the crack cocaine of personal finance. If that sounds too harsh, think of it like this. Every pound you pay to a credit card company in interest is stealing money from your future self.

Rule two: start early and invest for the long run. This is all about the miracle of compound interest. Remember the rule of seventy that we talked about earlier? That applies to personal finance too. Take the number seventy and divide it by the annual rate of interest that you are getting on your investments; this will give you roughly the number of years it will take your money to double. A quick quiz, Monty – if you are getting seven percent, how long will it take for your money to double?'

You promised me no maths. But, er, ten years I guess? Seventy divided by seven is ten, right?

'That's right, Monty, if you are getting returns of seven percent it will take about ten years for your money to double. This is the miracle of time and compound interest. Let me give you another example. Imagine that Great-Aunt Betty leaves you £20,000 in her will. You are twenty-five years old, and you could buy a car, or go on some fancy holidays. But being sensible you decide to put that £20,000 into an investment account. If that investment grew at ten percent a year, and even if you never added another penny to it for the rest of your life, it would be worth over £1 million by the time you were sixty-five. Now of course ten percent a year is a great return, and £1 million in twenty-five years' time won't be worth what it is today – inflation will have reduced the buying power of this money.[3] But still. Not bad.'[4]

I'm guessing it would buy me a bone or two. Rule three?

'Rule three: you need to take *some* risks.'

Hmmm... I thought you said that the point of the financial system – when it worked right, that is – was to reduce risks?

'Yes, it is. And well done, by the way, for listening. Let me explain. Riskier assets must offer a higher expected return or no one in their right mind would invest in them. If you had the choice between lending £100 to a bloke you met in the pub, or the UK government, and they were both offering you the same rate of interest, who would you choose to lend to?'

I'm guessing not the pub guy.

'Put another way: if you want safe assets you will have to accept lower returns. Lending to the government (which is what you do if you buy government bonds) is about as safe as it gets.'

Cool.

'But it doesn't pay out much.'

Uncool.

'Government bonds are likely to pay you less than you get (on average) if you invest in shares. Putting all your money in a cash savings account is even safer. But inflation is slowly eroding the value of your money. Remember, it's like that ice sculpture at a party – you can't see it melting away, but it is.

Another illustration. You've got £1,000 stashed under your bed. Inflation is running at five percent. In ten years' time, that £1,000 will only be worth, in terms of what you can buy with it, £570. So, your "safe" investment will have lost nearly half its value from the effects of inflation. And five percent inflation is not even that bad, historically. In the 1970s annual inflation in the UK was as high as twenty-four percent.'

Ouch!

'Oh, it could be worse. In November 1923, in Weimar Germany, inflation reached 29—'

Percent? Huge.

'No, 29,525 percent.'

Gulp.

'Not the worst, though. In post-Second World War Hungary inflation reached 41.9 quadrillion percent.'

I'll take your word for it that that's a big number.

'It is. A quadrillion has fifteen zeros. But we shouldn't get carried away. Inflation will erode savings, but it's unlikely to reach the levels of Weimar Germany or post-war Hungary. Buying shares is more risky than a bank account. Share prices go down as well as up. Sometimes by a lot. In 2020, when Covid-19 first hit, share prices fell by over thirty percent. But in the long run share prices have gone steadily up.'

OK, cash bad. Take some risk. Next rule…

'Rule four: diversify. Every time you are thinking of investing a large amount of money in a single share, repeat: Enron, Enron, Enron.'

Who?

'At one time Enron was America's seventh biggest company, and Wall Street's darling. It was rated as the most innovative large company in America by *Fortune* magazine for six consecutive years. At its peak, in 2000, its shares were worth about $90 each. In 2001 it suddenly declared bankruptcy. Financial "innovation" (read "fraud") had concealed huge debts. If you had placed all your money in Enron you would have lost everything.

So, you must make sure that any money you have is diversified. Never, no matter how much you believe in it, invest everything you own in one company or asset. There is one important caveat. You need to make sure that your assets are genuinely diversified. For example, if you have all your money in a variety of internet stocks, they may all be different companies, selling different products, with different management teams, but you are not really diversifying. It's still the internet.

If you want to invest in shares (and you should probably also invest in a spread of other assets) the most sensible advice is to invest in a fund (which is like a basket of different shares) and pick one with low fees.[5]

So Monty, simples. The catch is, just because something is simple doesn't mean it's easy. Let's recap. What are the four rules?'

Umm… Spend less than you earn. Think about the long term. Take some risk. Diversify. And that one about there being no bargains – the efficient something or other hypothesis.

'Excellent. So, the next time someone cold-calls you and tries to sell you an investment in a revolutionary new dog biscuit, promising suspiciously good returns, say ten percent, then one of three things must be true: 1. This kind and generous person must have stumbled on some secret undiscovered opportunity and, rather than make money from it themselves, they want to share this glorious thing with you. Or, 2. This is a high-risk investment, with a chance you'll lose your stake. Or 3. They are incompetent or dishonest. Normally, the answer is 3.'

Unless it's 1??

'It's never 1. OK, Monty, we are nearly home. Shall I sum this all up for you?'

Rather you than me.

'A credit system is essential for a modern economy. You need banks to act as the middlemen between those who want to save and those who want to borrow to invest. But banks need to go back to being boring. In the run-up to the financial crisis, large financial corporations were run primarily for the benefit of the people who manage them. For the most part, they still are. This is precisely why financial markets need to be tightly regulated. As many people have subsequently pointed out, it is hard not to think that the "masters of the universe" in charge of the financial system did not know (or want to know) what was going on.

Oh, and the best way to get rich quick is to rob a bank. As long as you're a banker.'

Walk 14

Money

What we talk about on this walk: Money, what it is, how it came to exist in its current form, the gold standard, inflation, quantitative easing and bitcoin.

Nothing excites Monty more than the abrupt snap and clatter, followed by the soft slapping sound, of letters being delivered. I'm not sure what ancient, atavistic instinct this triggers, whether it's the snapping jaws of some great predator, or the helpless struggles of something small enough for even our diminutive Monty to consider prey. But anyway, off he goes in a yapping scramble to the front door, where he barks at the retreating postman, snarls at the letters, scratches at them briefly with his nails (which we really must remember to get trimmed), then moves in for the kill. Alas, his dentition isn't up to much savaging these days, so he just gums the mail, leaving it sticky and smelling of dog breath.

This morning's Monty-mauled mail was the usual. A Boden catalogue, a leaflet from some or other political party, with a photo of a weakly smiling man with the look of a low-level sex offender relieved to have been given a non-custodial sentence, an interesting-looking letter intended for next door, and, finally, my bank statement. I thought about opening it, and then threw it down on the hallway table.

'Walkies?'

Monty had already grabbed his lead. I'm sometimes a little unkind about his very limited range of tricks. Does finding your lead count as a trick? Perhaps. Though sometimes halfway through the process he forgets, and seems to think the lead is a snake, and slips back into attack mode, shaking it until thoroughly subdued.

Where to?

'Let's go to the café. I can spend some money on an overpriced coffee and a dry croissant.'

KK.

'What?'

Oh, it's what Rosie says.

'And it means?'

No idea, I'm a dog, not a teenage girl. Let's get going.

'I thought it might be good to talk about something relatively straightforward today. We've been discussing things like GDP, inequality, productivity, markets, taxation, spending and the grotesque greed of bankers. All of these things involve, in one way or another, money. Many people might say that money isn't the most important thing in life – there's love, friendship, family—'

Dogs?

'I was coming to that. But very few people think that money is *unimportant*. And it's also something that we think we understand. Or, rather, it's so ubiquitous, so embedded in our lives that we don't think about it at all. I mean money as a concept, rather than it as a thing I can use to buy coffee. So that's today's mission: we're going to understand the meaning of money.'

Goody. So what is it then? Nice snappy answer, please.

'This is economics, so there's no such thing. One way to understand it is to think about what money does. If you read an economics textbook, it will tell you that money has three main jobs: it is a medium of exchange; it is a store of value; and it is a unit of account. The crucial thing to understand is that money is not real wealth. Real wealth is what a country can produce: land, food, shelter, clothes. Money is just the common unit that we have agreed to, that represents this economic value.

The traditional story of money goes something like this. In the beginning there was no money, there was only barter. You have a fish, I have a bunch of carrots, we swap. Kinda works. Indeed, for most of human history, this was the only game in town. But barter is not especially efficient as a means of trade. To use the technical term, you need a "double coincidence of wants". You have to want what I have, and I have to want what you have, or there's no deal. This can be very inconvenient. Then someone had a great idea: why don't we agree on one thing (and it can be pretty much anything) that we use as a common medium of exchange. Beaver pelts, salt, cows, cigarettes: all of these things have been used as a form of money, and all of these are referred to as *commodity money*.'

Huh?

'Commodity money – it means something that is a unit of exchange, but which also has a real value. People have a good use for beaver pelts and salt.'

And cigarettes?

'Cigarettes for a long time have been the standard unit of currency in prisons. Small, portable, hideable, with a recognised value. If there's something you want in prison, you pay in ciga-rettes.[1] Or you did. When smoking was banned in US prisons around 2004, cans of mackerel became the standard currency. A haircut cost two "macks". But just like cigarettes, macks count as commodity money because ultimately they can be con-sumed. That original use is still there. In principle you could use juicy bones as money...'

Now you're talking...

'The ultimate in commodity money is precious metal, most characteristically gold. It's still commodity money in that metals have a use – to forge into tools or weapons, or as decoration. And metals have other advantages. They are malleable, portable and (crucially) the supply of them is reasonably fixed. You can mine gold, but you can't just summon it up. It takes time and effort. If the supply of your money is fixed it makes it much easier to agree prices.

The next stage in the story of money is the development of paper bills that represent these gold coins.'

Why on earth would people want paper bills?

'Gold and other metals are heavy. If you are a trader travel-ling about you might find it a bit inconvenient to lug a huge load of heavy coins around. China was the first country to come up with the idea of paper money, in the eleventh century. There's a chapter in Marco Polo's account of his travels in thir-teenth-century China, with the helpfully descriptive title: *How the Great Khan Causes the Bark of Trees, Made into Something Like Paper, to Pass for Money All Over His Country*. China was surrounded by hostile states and its rulers did not want pre-cious gold and silver coins to be lost, so they told the people to use lower-value coins made of iron. This was pretty impractical as it took many more iron coins to buy something than if you were paying in gold. You'd need a wheelbarrow-full to buy a horse.'

Did you know that the Chinese invented the wheelbarrow?

'What? No. Is that even true? How do you ... oh, never mind. So, the merchants in Sichuan province came up with the idea of using IOUs. Rather than schlepp your wheelbarrow of iron coins to the horse trader, you would write a note promising to pay them a certain number of coins at a more convenient time.'

And they'd believe this? Very trusting, these Chinese horse sellers.

'Good point, Monty. There *is* a great amount of trust involved. It certainly helped if you knew where the issuer of the IOU lived, how wealthy he was, and how honest. The merchants started using these IOUs to trade with each other, not just the original issuer. The horse trader uses his IOU to "buy" a new cart. The cart seller uses it to buy a silk shawl. As long as everyone trusts that the person who has written the IOU is good for it, then these paper IOUs have become a private currency.

There's also something in it for the person who writes the IOU in the first place. If his IOUs are always being traded (and no one is actually coming to him to exchange the IOU for the coins) then, in effect, he has been given an interest-free loan.

The Chinese government saw all this and wanted a piece of the action. They outlawed the private currency and produced their own version, called the Jiaozi. Initially it was a huge success. And nicely illustrates the next part of the story: the invention of *fiat money*.'

What is fiat money?

'Fiat money is money that is not backed by any commodity (for example gold). When those Chinese merchants first created their IOUs, they could be exchanged for a specified amount of gold. When the Chinese government took over from the merchants, they also initially allowed people to exchange their Jiaozi for gold. But pretty soon they stopped doing that. From then on the paper money was backed by nothing more than the government saying that this is what it was worth. This is fiat money – "fiat" means "let it be done" in Latin. But there is a danger for rulers who can simply print money without having to worry if they have enough gold or silver in reserve to back it up. The temptation is to print just a bit more. And what happened then was what always happens when you print too much money: inflation. Eventually the Jiaozi was abandoned.

And this is essentially what we have now. There are no currencies today that are backed by gold. And it turns out that this has some advantages. And some disadvantages. But we will get on to that later when we talk about the gold standard.

So far I have been mainly referring to gold. And in Europe and the Middle East, gold coins were certainly used as a currency, but almost exclusively for high-value items or international trade. But most economies, from Roman times down to the eighteenth century, settled on silver as the standard unit of currency. The day-to-day world of buying food and clothes and candles and beer was conducted with silver coins, which contained a set weight of the metal. But silver began to lose its allure during the course of the seventeenth and eighteenth centuries, as silver currency was gradually debased.'

Debased? How?

'People would literally clip or shave the coins to extract a little of the valuable metal. So gold came to be seen as more trustworthy. There was also a shortage of silver, caused by the endless wars of the late eighteenth and early nineteenth centuries, as well as a draining of currency out of Europe to buy

Chinese goods; reciprocal trade wasn't an option there, as the West had almost nothing the Chinese wanted, whereas we craved their silks and porcelain. But it wasn't until 1821 that Britain officially adopted gold as the basis of our currency, backing up the paper banknotes. As Britain was then the leading industrial and commercial power in the world, other nations joined us on the gold standard.'

Well, from what you have just told me, moving to the gold standard seems not unsensible. Why would anyone trust a currency that is not backed by something real, like gold?

'That certainly became the orthodoxy. Without the confidence that the gold standard gave, it would have been very hard to get people to accept paper money. You knew you could take your banknote into the Bank of England and exchange it for an agreed amount of gold – which is where those words that are printed on notes that "promise to pay the bearer on demand" came from. (Now the Bank of England only agrees to exchange the notes for other notes and coins. You're out of luck if you ask for gold.) The main advantage of the gold standard is that when you are on it, money holds its value, as every bit of paper is backed by some amount of gold. Without that hard guarantee, the temptation for governments to print as much money as they like is almost irresistible, and that will lead to inflation, which, as we saw on our last walk, can have very damaging effects.'

So you've said. I have a question: if inflation is such an evil thing, why hasn't everyone just stuck to the gold standard?

'What really screwed the gold standard was the Great Depression. We've touched on it on other walks, as the Great Depression has become a battleground for many economic theories. But most economists think that sticking to the gold standard helped turn a stock market crash in 1929 into the biggest financial crisis in history.

In 1931 it looked like the world was falling apart; many people had borrowed money to invest in shares, and when the price of these shares collapsed, they had no way of paying back the loans. The panic then led to bank runs, as people were scared (correctly) that the banks did not have large enough reserves. And there is nothing that spreads faster than the panic of a bank run. Between the peak and the trough of the downturn, in the US GDP fell by thirty percent and unemployment soared.[2]

The chaos soon spread overseas. At the time the UK had the most important central bank in the world. And it was going to run out of gold. When you are on a gold standard the only way to stop people cashing in their money for gold is to raise interest rates.'

Why does that follow?

'If you take your savings out of the bank in exchange for a couple of bars of gold to store under your bed, you don't get any interest on that. So raising interest rates makes bank savings more attractive.'

Got it.

'So central banks, desperate to hold on to their gold reserves, raised interest rates.'

Which was… good?

'No! This is the exact opposite of what you should do in a crisis. When times are bad you want to lower interest rates to make it easier for businesses to borrow money to stay afloat and keep people employed.'

Ah.

'In the end the Great Depression forced countries off the gold standard. And you can see that the timing of when countries left the gold standard is closely linked to when they started to recover from the Great Depression. But this then, as predicted, leads to...'

Let me guess, inflation?

'Good dog. Without the forced discipline of the gold standard, many governments ended up putting their printing presses into overdrive. And when you have too much money chasing too few goods, inflation is the inevitable result. Over the past three decades the UK, along with many parts of the world, has experienced historically low inflation, with prices increasing one, two or three percent a year. But, as we are currently being reminded, this was not always normal. For the decades from the end of the Second World War to the 1970s, inflation was a huge part of everyday life. We're not talking inflation madness like Weimar or Hungary, but just that yearly grind with every pound in your pocket buying you progressively less. You can think of inflation as a silent thief, a pickpocket, a subtle swindler.'

Inflation sounds pretty terrible but, knowing you as I do, I suspect there's going to be another side to this...

'Hah, well, yes, you could say that with inflation, there are winners and losers.'

I knew it!

'In the jargon, it has *distributional effects*. Imagine that I want to borrow £1,000 from you, and I agree to pay it back next year with ten percent interest (so you would get £1,100 next year). Would you agree?'

Well, first, I'm a dog so unless you're talking about bones, I'm not interested. And second, I know there is going to be a catch...

'Just play along with me. If you agreed, and inflation was two percent, the real interest you would have got would be eight percent. So yes, that would be a good deal. But if some irresponsible government has allowed inflation to explode to one hundred percent a year, then that £1,100 I promised to pay back to you in one year's time will be worth much less than you had thought – about half as much. Crudely, unexpected bouts of inflation can be good for debtors and bad for lenders.'

Winners and losers!

'Yep, but the problem is that inflation redistributes wealth in a very arbitrary fashion. It might completely wipe out the small saver: think a widow who has scrimped and saved all her life to keep herself out of poverty in retirement. Less wealthy people often have more of their savings in cash, as they see this as less risky, and so they are particularly vulnerable to inflation. The rich investor is more likely to have most of their savings in assets such as property or shares, both of which hold their value much better. So, inflation might be a real windfall for them, especially if they have chosen just that moment to buy a big house with a large mortgage.

The other big problem is that once everyone begins to expect inflation you can enter a dangerous spiral. Getting out of it can be difficult. The way the US did it in the 1970s was to essentially trigger a recession, reducing demand to break the cycle. It worked, but it was very painful. Hovering behind these attempts to control prices is the terrifying spectre of hyperinflation.'

Tell me more about hyperinflation – I love a good horror story.

'In the last walk we touched on the most famous example: Germany in 1922–23. Germany had borrowed heavily to pay for the war, thinking that it would be easy to pay off the debts once it had won, by expropriating the wealth of the losers. But it lost, and the Allies imposed heavy reparations. To pay these debts, in a country devastated by war, the German government resorted to printing money. This sudden flood of paper money into the economy meant that prices ran out of control. A loaf of bread that cost 250 marks in January 1923 cost 200,000 million marks by November. The old were often hard-hit. One woman, who sold her house so she could live off the money, found that soon this money was not even enough to buy a loaf of bread. But some people made a fortune. Anyone who had been lucky enough to borrow money at just the right time to buy a fixed asset found they could pay back their entire loan with money that was now effectively worthless.'

Well, I hope all governments learned that lesson…

'Not really. A more recent example is Venezuela, where in 2018 you had to carry a bag of cash weighing about 14.6 kg to buy one chicken. One roll of toilet paper cost 2,600,000 bolivars, which would weigh 2.6 kg.'

It's not really my field, but why didn't they just, you know, use the banknotes… ?

'Perhaps they did. Interestingly, Freud pointed out the deep links – in our psyches but also in the wider culture – between money and excrement. Gold has been called the devil's shit. And, well, when we take you to the Poo Park, don't we call it doing your business?'

Er, moving on, why do governments keep making the same mistake?

'When a government wants to spend, often for very good reasons, such as pulling the country out of something like the Great Depression, they have to get the money from somewhere. In the absence of the fabled magic money tree, there are three choices: you can borrow money, you can tax people, or you can print money. Printing money can seem like the easy solution. This is why many countries have made central banks independent from the government, so that they can resist the pressure to print money. For example, in the UK the Bank of England (BoE) was made independent of the government in 1997, and one of its main responsibilities is to target two percent inflation. If the BoE misses this target by one percent either way, they have to write a letter to the Chancellor of the Exchequer to explain why, and what they are doing about it.'

Just a thought: if inflation is so bad, why don't they target zero percent inflation?

'That is a great question, Monty, and this always puzzled me too. Two percent inflation sounds like very little. And is so little that you would probably not notice much change in prices year to year. But it does still mean that prices will roughly double every thirty-five years. To make that concrete, if you retired at sixty with cash savings, by the time you got to ninety-five, your money would only be worth half as much.

But back to why governments target two percent inflation. One reason is that they want to avoid *deflation* (when prices on average fall) and another is because there are some benefits to low levels of inflation – even if some of these are a bit sneaky. Let's start with the problem of deflation.'

Problem… ? But deflation sounds great! Why would prices falling be a problem? I really don't understand this economics business…

'I thought exactly the same thing when I first heard about it. But let me explain. We talked already about inflation. But deflation has a different set of economic and psychological problems.'

Psychological? I thought we were talking about economics.

'It's really hard to take the psychology out of money, even if we don't go down the Freudian path. The most recent example of deflation is in Japan. The problems started with a banking crisis. People lost their jobs and they stopped buying things. Deflation creeps up gradually, slowly prices fall, but it went on year after year and people began to expect it (this is the psychological bit). If consumers think prices are just going to fall, then they put off buying things. Why buy a house if you expect the price to fall next year? And it was not just consumers that expected prices to collapse, but businesses. Why would a business borrow to invest if the money it has to repay will be worth more, in real terms, than the money it borrowed? A lack of investment and lower prices may lead to falling wages – even more bad news if you've just bought a house. Just as it is hard to break the cycle of inflation, it is also hard to break expectations that prices are always going to go down.

So what governments really want is stable prices, and increasing incomes. That keeps everyone happy and voting for your party.'

You said there was also a sneaky reason why governments target two not zero percent inflation.

'The slightly sneaky reason is that allowing a small amount of inflation is in essence a tax. And not just in the indirect sense that inflation reduces the value of your money. Inflation can be an easy way for governments to subtly increase their revenue. Many taxes are progressive. For example, with income tax, the more you earn, the higher the tax rate you pay. If the government keeps these tax thresholds at the same level, then each year, as wages rise to keep in line with inflation, more people will fall into the higher-rate tax brackets. But remember, if your wage has just increased in line with inflation, you are not in any real sense any better paid – you are just paying more tax. As Keynes put it: "By a continuing process of inflation, government can confiscate, secretly and unobserved, an important part of the wealth of their citizens." Or, in Milton Friedman's words, "Inflation is taxation without legislation."'

You are right, that is quite sneaky.

'Governments don't really like to point that out, so the rationale that central banks often cite is that there is some form of "rigidity" in the economy. So, a small amount of inflation can stimulate the economy.'

You have lost me again. What do you mean by rigidity?

'Another bit of slightly sneaky terminology creeping in. What they mean is that inflation makes it easier for firms to cut wages if they need to. If inflation is running at four percent, and your salary increases by two percent, you have effectively had a two percent wage cut. You might not be thrilled, but you might well shrug and accept it. If, however, there is no inflation, and your boss announces that they are going to cut your wages by two percent, well then you might think about downing tools and manning the barricades. This is what I meant about the importance of psychology to the economy. We'll talk more about unemployment in a later walk, but the point here is that giving firms a bit of wiggle room like this means you reduce unemployment, as the alternative for the firm might be to lay people off.

Finally, it also has to be said that just as inflation is good news for you if you owe money, the same goes for governments. The UK in the 1950s found itself saddled with public debts of around two hundred percent of GDP, due to the two world wars. Thomas Piketty argues that it was only the inflation of the 1950s (more than four percent a year) and the 1970s (around fifteen percent a year) that enabled UK public debt to fall to below forty percent of GDP in the 1980s. The UK national debt is rising again – as of today (August 2021) it stands at 106% of

GDP.[3] So it wouldn't surprise me in the least if the government let inflation drift up again, to eat into that pile of debt.'

We'd been sitting in our usual quiet corner of the café, but now my coffee was drunk, and my croissant reduced to crumbs, which I swept on to the floor for Monty to hoover.

'Since we are talking about money, before we go home we should probably talk about cryptocurrencies and, in particular, bitcoin.'

Isn't that the one the drug dealers like?

'That's the one. I'm going to focus on it here as it is the most established cryptocurrency, but there are many imitators. Bitcoin's development is shrouded in mystery. In 2008 "Satoshi Nakamoto" (a pseudonym for a person or group of people) created the first fifty coins. The idea was for a decentralised digital currency (so no actual notes or coins) free from the interference of central banks or governments. Since then, the value of bitcoin has fluctuated wildly. Before 2010 it was worth almost nothing. In November 2021 it was worth over £50,000.'

You are telling me that one bitcoin, one, was worth £50,000?

'Yup. The world is truly mad. As of today, one bitcoin is "only" worth £32,587. And that is roughly £32,587 more than I think they should be worth. In case it is not obvious, I am *definitely* in the camp of those who don't "get" it.'

You have my attention though. Explain this to me.

'Traditional currencies are issued by central banks who have a monopoly on the right to print money, and who also regulate and oversee the whole financial system. But with bitcoin there is no central authority. It is run through a peer-to-peer computer network of individual users, which is called blockchain. The actual bitcoins are generated by computers in this network. The computers solve very difficult problems, which takes time and energy. These problems are set to get harder and harder, which acts as a limit on the number of potential bitcoins. This means there is no way a profligate government can create more of them and "devalue" the currency. (But remember, just because something is scarce does not automatically mean it is valuable – the Philosopher claims he's the only person in the world who can whistle and burp at the same time, but the monetary value of that performance art is minimal.)

Sorry, back to where we were. The bitcoin network is also used to monitor the creation of these newly minted bitcoins and keep a record of all transactions. Bitcoin "miners" compete to validate transactions, and are rewarded with new coins. Everyone who is part of the system can see what is going on, and helps in its regulation. This means that you don't need pesky outside authorities (like governments or big banks) to enforce the rules.'

OK. I think I have a rough idea of what bitcoin is. But I'm still not sure why people should prefer it to dollars, or gold or shares.

'Bitcoin appeals to people for three main reasons. First, vaguely anarchic anti-government types like it because there is no evil central bank or monopolistic financial firm overseeing the process, and getting a cut of the spoils. Second, there's that built-in limit to the supply: bitcoin is fixed in quantity, so unlike normal currencies you don't have to worry about reckless governments printing money, and so inflating away its value. Finally (and perhaps this was the main factor initially), the allure of anonymity. Bitcoin appeals to crooks. Cash is obviously even more anonymous than bitcoin, but it is bulky and there are limits to how much money you can carry in a suitcase.

There's an entertaining story about Frank Sinatra, who in 1947 was widely rumoured to have transported a briefcase full of cash to Cuba, on behalf of his associates in the Mafia. It was alleged that there was either $2m or $3.5m in the briefcase, in $100 bills. Sinatra scoffed that it was impossible to fit that much cash into a briefcase, and offered the same amount of money to anyone who could do it. According to the *New York Times*, the novelist Norman Mailer did the maths and found that, with a bit of squeezing, you could fit $2m in the case. However, $3.5m was impossible. It's not thought that Sinatra honoured the bet.'

Er, and your point… ?

'Shifting $3.5m in bitcoin would have been – and probably is – a lot easier for the Mafia.

But even leaving the crime aspect aside, there are big problems with bitcoin. First let's think about why people buy assets. You could buy an asset because of its fundamental value, whether that's the income stream it will yield over the years or the pleasure you derive from owning it. Shares in a successful company should pay you dividends. You can live in a house (or rent it to someone else). You may get pleasure contemplating the beautiful art on your walls. There are also speculative reasons for holding an asset: you think the price will increase and that in the future you will be able to sell it to someone else for a profit. With many assets, you see a mix of both. But with bitcoin its only value is speculative: it only has value if you think you can sell it on for more than you paid for it. This means that it is particularly vulnerable to bubbles. It is a very good example of the "greater fool" theory.'

That sounds like my kind of theory.

'The greater fool theory is the idea that the price of an asset is determined by whether you can sell it for a higher price later on. The intrinsic value is not important; the only factor is demand – an asset will have value as long as there is a greater fool out there to buy it from you. I don't doubt that some people will make a lot of money out of bitcoin, and they will be the ones calling *me* a fool. But the value of bitcoin will only be sustained as long as there is an increasing market for greater fools.'

But what about things like gold and diamonds – they only have value because people think they do?

'That is a good comeback, although gold has that decorative value that we mentioned earlier, and diamonds, as well as making a very nice necklace, have important industrial uses. Cryptocurrencies have been described as digital gold, and it is reasonable to ask why the current value placed on bitcoin is any more ludicrous than that placed on gold or diamonds.

But there is a problem with this comparison to gold.[4] Gold has had financial status for more than six thousand years. It does not physically degrade (in contrast to bitcoin, which is an electronic entry on a ledger that requires active maintenance by interested and incentivised "miners"). And even so, gold has lost its status as a medium of exchange. Despite this, one can expect gold to be around physically for at least the next millennium. I am just not so confident that we can expect a system of decentralised computer ledgers to have that kind of longevity. In fact you might say that bitcoin relies on exactly the kind of conservative financial and societal structures that it seeks to undermine or circumvent.'

Neat.

'The other issue is that whatever you think about bitcoin as a long-term investment, it is certainly pretty useless as money.'

But it is called a currency?

'Remember earlier when we talked about the functions of money as a means of exchange and a unit of account? Bitcoins are simply far too volatile to work as money. For a company to set its prices in bitcoin would involve a huge gamble: what if the bitcoin price collapsed? So you thought you were selling your valuable bone collection for one bitcoin, when it was worth £50,000, but then the price collapses, and that one bitcoin now only equals £32,587.'

To be honest, I'd settle for that. I've already got most of the flavour out of them.

'OK, bad example, but you get my meaning. The argument about the stability that comes from governments not being able to simply print more bitcoins also has a flaw. It is true that there is a limit on how much bitcoin can be mined but this ignores the issue of the proliferation of competing virtual currencies such as ethereum and litecoin. One virtual currency may be fixed in supply, but if anyone can enter into the field then it is hard to see how the supply of virtual currencies in general can be limited.

And I don't know if this is an advantage or disadvantage, but bitcoin is not as anonymous as some in the early days hoped or thought. Your bitcoin "address" (where you want the bitcoins sent to or from) is anonymous. But if anyone is ever able to find out your bitcoin address – perhaps when you finally try to convert the bitcoins into something actually useful like, I don't know, real currency – then the blockchain will reveal the user's entire transaction history.

Another problem—'

Wow, you really don't like bitcoin, do you?

'It is fair to say that I am a sceptic. If none of that convinces you, how about the fact that the bitcoin system is hugely energy-intensive. Bitcoin miners compete to validate transactions and are rewarded with new coins. This requires a lot of hard computing, which all adds up to a lot of wasted energy.

According to research by Cambridge University, bitcoin uses more energy than Argentina.'

But £50,000 a coin. Surely that can't just be a bubble. I reckon you are just too much of a fogey to recognise the future when you see it.

'Perhaps. Ultimately, I think the biggest threat to bitcoin's long-term future is political. If you control the money supply, you control the economy. Maybe a decentralised virtual currency that is free of government control and regulation is a brilliant idea. But there is a reason why central banks are the only ones with the power to print money. I don't think governments are going to let the backers of crypto muscle in on their authority to control money. One thing is for sure, you should not hold in bitcoin anything that you cannot afford to a hundred percent lose. OK, time to pay the bill and go. Think they'll take bitcoin?'

I think we'd have more chance of paying with my old bone collection.

Part I: Depressions, Recessions and What Governments Can Do to Help: Fiscal Policy

What we talk about on this walk: Recessions and what causes them. What can the government do to make things better? Can we spend our way out of recessions (fiscal policy) or is monetary policy better (low interest rates and 'easy' money)? And what about quantitative easing (the modern version of printing money), or its even more radical cousin Modern Monetary Theory? Are these sensible last-ditch attempts to kick-start the economy, or are we going to end up like Zimbabwe, using bank notes as fuel?

The rain was falling out of a manic-depressive sky. Gabriel was in a sulk (girlfriend-related, as far as we could tell). Rosie was in a sulk (something to do with quadratic equations, or possibly sine curves). The Philosopher was in a sulk (a cracked filling). After the third or fourth door-slamming incident Monty looked at me, mournfully.

'OK, let's get out of here. How about a trip to the groomers, so you look pretty next time you bump into the Peke down the road?'

Anything's better than this. Everyone's so depressed.

I put raincoats on both of us, and took the big umbrella, with room enough for Monty, and out we went. Monty for once walked properly to heel, but only to stay under the brolly.

'It's not just people who slump into a depression, you know,' I said.

And I thought this trip was supposed to cheer me up... Haven't you talked enough about the Great Depression?

'Well, I thought we'd have more of a chat about when things go wrong with the economy, and what governments and central banks can do to help. We'll look at how governments use fiscal and monetary policies to guide economies out of recessions.'

Fiscal, monetary, more words.

'I know fiscal and monetary policies don't sound especially interesting, but I promise you they are important. And we're also at the point where economics and politics come together. This is where economists have to get down and dirty with the real world. Political protests, which we tend to see in terms of fights for freedom or democracy, are often grounded in economic dissatisfaction. The Tiananmen Square protests in China were triggered in part by spiralling prices. Inflation had hit eighteen percent and wages were not keeping up. A year earlier China had lifted price controls, causing panic buying and a rush to convert cash into gold.[1] Sharp rises in the price of bread were crucial in triggering the Arab Spring uprisings. When governments get this stuff wrong, it can end up in revolution.'

OK. OK. I'll pay attention. But before you start on all this fiscal and monetary stuff can you first explain to me what a recession is?

'Loosely speaking, a recession is when the economy goes into a decline. There's no universally accepted definition, but as a rule of thumb, a recession is defined as two consecutive quarters of falling GDP.'

And a depression is... a really bad recession?

'Kinda. One old joke goes that when your neighbour loses his job, it is an economic slowdown; when you lose your job, it is a recession. But when an economist loses their job, it becomes a depression! In some ways recessions are very hard to predict, but there's a strange regularity to them: since 1929, a recession has occurred about once every six years and lasted about one year. This series of expansions and contractions in GDP (which we call the business cycle) takes a human toll. Governments are expected to smooth them out, and economists to tell them how.'

OK, so what causes recessions?

'In general, they are caused by some shock to the economy. It might be a steep increase in fuel prices (the oil price shock in 1973), a stock market crash (1937, 2007), or a property bubble that bursts. In a developing country it might come from a sudden fall in the price of some commodity that they rely on – coffee or cocoa. Or, as we have all recently learned, a nasty little virus. Whatever the causes, the result is human suffering and hardship. And the most dangerous thing about them is that they can spread. A small recession can easily turn into a very big one.'

Er, why?

'Think of it like a chain reaction. Imagine that for whatever reason people got nervous about the economy. They start saving their money instead of spending it. Factories cut production, and shops cut staff. So unemployment rises. So people fear more for the future. It's a self-fulfilling prophecy: if we all believe that the economy is going to get worse, then it will get worse.

Covid-19 is the most recent example. UK GDP, as with many other countries, fell off a cliff in February 2020. Stock markets had huge falls. Unemployment shot up. Most countries went into recession. The International Monetary Fund described it as the worst decline since our old friend the Great Depression.[2] Governments were terrified that this would kick off a devastating downward spiral and quickly stepped in to try to halt the decline.'

What did they do? Did it work?

'Let me start with the first question, by examining what tools governments have in their economic toolbox. This brings us to fiscal policy and monetary policy.'

So, two tools. Who needs a toolbox for two tools?

'Yeah, OK, smart-arse. But these are actually two multitools, like a Leatherman and Swiss army knife. Multitool One is fiscal policy, which is all about how much the government taxes and spends. Multitool Two is monetary policy, which focuses on how much money is swilling around in the economy – think lower interest rates. The objectives of both are the same: to encourage customers and businesses to start spending and investing. Once you get that straight in your head, then suddenly all those scary-looking articles in the business sections of newspapers become that bit more comprehensible.

Let's kick off with fiscal policy. The key idea here is that, through tax and spending policies, governments can influence the amount of demand in an economy. If an economy is struggling, they might adopt what is called *loose fiscal policy*: increasing government spending, or decreasing taxes to try to encourage economic growth. A *tight fiscal policy* is, surprise surprise, the reverse: decreasing government spending, or increasing taxes. These act to hold back growth.'

Why would you want two completely opposite policies, when you only have one economy?

'It's all to do with economic cycles. We mentioned earlier how economies tend to have regular recessions, as well as regular booms. So, the theory is that you want a *counter-cyclical* fiscal policy, to keep the economy on an even keel. When times are bad, governments should increase public spending or reduce taxes, paid for, usually, by borrowing. If worried consumers are not spending or investing, then the government should do it for them. The hope is that this kicks off a positive spiral, or at least stops things from getting worse. And when times are good, government should do the reverse – reduce public spending or increase taxes.'

I get why governments would want to help get an economy out of recession, but why on earth would the government want to cool down an economy?

'The answer to that is that a responsible government needs to reduce the risk of unsustainable boom followed by a painful contraction. It's all a matter of balance. When the economy is cold, you stoke the boiler; when it's hot, you hold back the fuel.

The idea that governments can, and should, use fiscal policy to correct the economy is associated with Keynes, and emerged as a response to—'

Let me guess, the Great Depression?

'Clever clogs. Keynes argued that when an economy is struggling, government investment can jump-start it, in part due to the multiplier effect.'

What's a multiplier effect?

'It's really just the opposite of that death spiral the economy gets into when people lose faith. Imagine that there is a recession, people are nervous, they are saving their money instead of spending it. This means there is idle capacity: unemployed people who want to work, factories operating at below capacity. But if the government borrows money, builds roads and hospitals, then they can break out of this vicious circle. The people employed spend their wages on new shoes and restaurant meals and perhaps even on a car, and in turn that spending goes into other people's pockets, which feeds more into the economy, and suddenly we're back on the road again. Put more formally, the multiplier is the change in GDP resulting from a change in government expenditure. Keynesian economics in a nutshell.'

So how big is this multiplier effect?

'That is hotly debated. In a complex economy with a lot going on, it is next to impossible to prove exactly what the multiplier might be. However, there is some consensus that the multiplier is larger when the economy is below trend and closer to zero when the economy is already near its potential. There is also general agreement that economies should adopt counter-cyclical fiscal policy – they should spend cautiously in good times but be unafraid to turn on the taps when a crisis hits. If any economic policy is broadly uncontroversial, this is probably it.'

OK. So, when you're doing the 'loose' thing, what works better, cutting taxes or spending more?

'In theory either would do the job. Which you prefer is pretty much down to politics. Those on the right tend to favour tax cuts. Those on the left tend to want spending increases. But, objectively, if you want to stimulate an economy, it is easier to do it through spending rather than tax cuts. Tax cuts are more likely to go into savings as the rich, who are taxed more, can also save more, and the whole point of the stimulus is to encourage spending.

And this is the approach that most countries took during the Covid-19 crisis. They enormously expanded government spending. In the UK this means that our public debt has increased. A lot. For the year 2020/21 the UK's debt as a percentage of GDP was 106%. This is about double what it was in the 1970s. In a standard recession, even if politicians try to soften the blow, companies are allowed to go bust, and people to lose their jobs. But not this time. The UK government paid up to eighty percent of the wages of staff who were furloughed (i.e. temporarily laid off). It also provided businesses with grants and cheap loans in an attempt to keep them from going bust. The government also adopted expansionary monetary policy (cutting interest rates and other more radical measures, which we can talk about later).'

So, all this taxing and spending, the Keynesian malarkey, how much are we talking?

'If you want some actual numbers, for 2021/22 the estimate is that the government will bring in about £819 billion in tax. This is roughly £28,000 per household, though, obviously, rich households will pay more, poor households much less. And it will spend around £1,053 billion. So about £36,000 per household.'[3]

I know I'm not exactly a brainiac Border collie, but even I can tell that there's a bit of a gap there.

'You are right, Monty, currently the government is spending a lot more than it is bringing in in taxes. The furlough scheme alone was estimated to cost more than £100 billion.[4] But most economists think this was the right thing to do. In 2021/22 the government deficit (the shortfall between income and spending in one year) is estimated to be about £234 billion. This is the second highest it has been since the Second World War (only 2020/21 was higher). The expectation is that this deficit will begin to fall over the next five years, to reach about £73 billion. But remember, the deficit is different to the debt.'

Huh? Can you explain that to me?

'The UK's debt is the <u>total</u> amount that the country owes historically, while the deficit is what is added to that debt each year. Imagine that in our house we had total debt of £200,000 (adding up what we owed on our mortgage, credit card bills, and any other debt). And this year we were also spending £5,000 more than we brought in. Our *debt* would be £200,000, this year's *deficit* would be £5,000. So next year our debt would go up to £205,000. You are not alone if you get your debt and your deficits muddled up. Politicians do it all the time.'

Is there not some kind of catch? Surely the government can't just borrow more and more money – eventually it has to be paid back?

'We tend to think all borrowing is a bad thing. But borrowing by governments can be a good idea. If debt is used to invest in things that will increase the growth of an economy – for example investments in education, or infrastructure – then it can benefit the economy in the long run. Also, governments do not always need to aim for a balanced budget. It is more sensible to aim to balance the budget over an entire economic cycle – running a deficit in a recession, running a surplus in a boom.'

So, then governments should just spend their way out of recessions?

'There are some economists who think that a fiscal stimulus is *never* a good idea. They argue that all this talk of multipliers is exaggerated, and that government spending has a much smaller impact on the economy than its advocates suggest.[5] But in theory at least, most economists would agree that it is a good idea for governments to adopt a counter-cyclical fiscal policy (in other words, borrow money to spend in a recession).

However, this can be easier said than done. Let me outline three potential problems. The first is one you alluded to earlier when you said you could not understand why politicians would want to hold back an economy.'

My wisdom knows no depths.

'We vote for people who tell us what we want to hear. The idea behind counter-cyclical fiscal policy is that you would expand spending in a recession and cut it back when times are good. The trouble is that during boom times it is very hard for governments to hold back spending in the face of public pressure. Who, after all, ever campaigns for *less* money to be spent on the health service? What this means is that when recessions arrive, as they always do, there can be little room for expansion. More often, when things sour, governments find they actually have to cut back, when the economy needs the exact opposite. This is what happened with the disastrous and damaging austerity programme enacted by the UK coalition government after the 2007 crash. Public services were slashed by a government determined to reduce borrowing, just when the economy needed a cash injection.

The point is that counter-cyclical policy really needs to do what it says on the can. When the bad times come, it is essential that you haven't already burdened yourself with too much debt.'

OK. That makes sense.

'Another complication with fiscal stimulus is that you want to be sure that you really are in a slump. If there is no idle capacity – people looking for work, factories trying to expand – then government spending will inevitably stoke inflation.

And while we are on problems of timing, another difficulty with fiscal stimulus is that it takes time to organise. Politicians have to agree to it, and then find appropriate projects to spend the money on. By the time they have done that, the recession may already have passed. Covid-19 was unusual, as there was broad agreement that we were in a truly exceptional situation, so the fiscal stimulus was enacted in record time. Generally, tax cuts are much quicker, but, as we have said, the gains may be saved, not spent, which defeats the purpose.

OK Monty. That wraps up fiscal policy. And here we are at the groomers. He'll have you looking beautiful in no time.'

OK, but tell him, no bows. I draw the line at bows.

'You're the boss.'

Part II: Depressions, Recessions and What Governments Can Do to Help: Monetary Policy

I went and did a little shopping while Monty was having his hair and nails done. When I came to collect him, he looked like a drag queen, or perhaps a Kazakh oligarch's mistress, with huge, blow-dried hair and, of course, a bow. A pink bow. I expected to also see a furious expression on his little face, but he looked surprisingly placid. Either he'd had a cocktail with his pampering, or he hadn't looked in the mirror. I decided not to say anything.

'Who do you think is the most important person in the world?' I said, as we began our walk home.

You, of course.

'Too kind, Monty, but I think most would answer that it was people like prime ministers or presidents that have the most power. There is a reasonable argument to be made that it is really Jerome Powell, Andrew Bailey, Christine Lagarde.'

Never heard of 'em.

'These are the men and women who decide how easy it will be for you to get a job, how expensive your mortgage will be, how difficult it will be for you to borrow to buy a car. They are all heads of central banks and are in charge of monetary policy. Monetary policy is the other main lever the government has to influence the economy. The easiest bit of monetary policy to understand is the interest rate (we will work up to the other more complicated bits). If central bankers are worried that the economy is heading into a recession, they cut interest rates. If they want to dampen the economy, they raise interest rates. Remember interest rates are the price we pay to borrow money. The higher the interest rate the more it costs to borrow. As it becomes cheaper or more expensive to borrow, businesses and households will adjust their spending accordingly. Unlike fiscal policy, where you have to find appropriate projects to spend the money on, monetary policy can be enacted quicker than you could snaffle a cold sausage.'

Oh, sausage, you said… ?

'Sorry, another metaphorical sausage.'

Drat. Anyway, what exactly is a central bank?

'Most developed countries have come to the conclusion that monetary policy needs to be kept independent of political interference. That's the job of a central bank. The US has the Federal Reserve. Europe has the European Central Bank. We have the Bank of England. Central banks usually have two jobs. First, to maintain financial stability. This is a fancy way of saying that they are there to keep the financial plumbing working, so you can pay for things and transfer money. They monitor high street banks, and act as lender of last resort. But what I want to talk about here are the methods they use to control inflation.'

And how do they accomplish this miracle?

'The methods that central banks use vary depending on the country, but the basic principles are similar. They decide how much money is in circulation in the economy and how much it costs to borrow (the interest rate).'

I see. And that's what controls inflation?

'Yep. If an irresponsible government told its central bank to print huge amounts of cash, so too much money was chasing too few goods, then we've already seen what can happen: Germany in the 1920s or Venezuela more recently. Consequently, the goal of monetary policy at the Bank of England is to manage the supply of money while keeping inflation low and stable.'[1]

OK, money supply – I feel I ought to know what that means, but can't quite bring it into focus.

'The money supply means simply the total amount of money in circulation in an economy. This includes all the notes and coins, of course, but also all the deposits in banks that are readily accessible for spending. Ultimately, the amount of money created in an economy depends on the policy of the central banks.'

OK, that's the what, but what about the how?

'The Bank of England has two main ways to influence how much money is in circulation and how much it costs to borrow. One, they set the interest rate that they charge banks to borrow from them. Two, they can buy bonds to lower the interest rate on savings and loans through quantitative easing.[2] I will explain the first one, as that is a bit easier to get your head around.

The "Bank rate" is the interest rate that the Bank of England pays on central bank reserves held by commercial banks (think banks like Barclays, NatWest). This is the single most important interest rate in the UK. It is also called the BoE base rate, or even just "the interest rate". This rate influences the rate at which banks are willing to lend to each other in the money markets. Every day money flows in and out of all of our accounts. At the end of each day, the banks tally up their inflows and outflows against each other. Some might have a shortfall, some an excess. They will typically borrow or lend to each other overnight to balance it out. When banks are able to borrow from the central bank and each other at lower rates of interest, then they can in turn lend to their customers – people and businesses – at lower rates. At lower interest rates there will be more people willing and able to borrow. And the more banks lend, the more money there is in circulation.'[3]

Let me see if I have understood. What you are saying is that if the Bank of England sets low interest rates, this means that it is cheaper to borrow money, so commercial banks will lend more money, increasing the money supply, and that this is good because we will all spend more and so the economy will improve?

'In theory. The trouble was that after the financial crisis in 2007, central banks kept lowering the interest rate, until it got close to zero, and it still didn't spark a recovery in the economy. So, they started experimenting. This led to what is called quantitative easing (QE). Quantitative easing is when the central bank creates electronic money (they don't actually print it, they just enter some numbers in a spreadsheet) and uses that money to buy up assets (mainly government bonds) from commercial banks and other large financial institutions. The idea is that the central bank gets the asset, so it is not just giving banks money, and the bank now has more ready cash that it can go out and lend to businesses. Hopefully, this kick-starts growth in an economy.

Let's get some of the terminology out of the way. When people talk about quantitative easing, they will often refer to it as "asset purchases" or "expanding the balance sheet". Ben Bernanke (who was the chair of the Federal Reserve, the US central bank) has called it "credit easing".'

Why do they give it all these strange names? Are they deliberately trying to make it hard to understand?

'A cynic might say that that was *exactly* what they are trying to do. Money is about confidence. And printing money is usually regarded as the last refuge of failed states and banana republics. If the central bank announced that they were printing money, then people might start to lose trust in the currency. However, you can make a case for it...'

But wait, you keep telling me that printing money is a terrible idea.

'As so often, moderation is the watchword. The quantity theory of money implies that if you print more money, then in the long run prices will increase, as more money chases the same amount of stuff. But if the economy is getting more productive, so there is more stuff being produced with the same inputs, then some growth in the money supply is probably desirable. If monetary authorities want zero inflation, then they should aim to increase the supply of money in precise proportion to the growth of the economy. If they want inflation to run at a low level, then they should aim to have the money supply grow just a touch faster than the growth rate of output.[4] And in the short run, there is an argument that increasing the money supply can help stimulate the economy when there is a danger of a recession or depression. As long as they don't create too much of it.'

OK, that all sounds a bit, well, blurry. So, what was the actual impact of QE?

'People argue about it. There's some consensus that, after the financial crisis, when there was widespread fear that we were on the brink of some terrible economic meltdown, QE stopped the panic. It was better than doing nothing, and helped steer us away from a new Great Depression. The fears that QE would lead to inflation were unfounded. People did not rush out and buy more consumer goods. But those who could did buy assets like shares and houses. And those rising asset prices do not show up in the consumer price index, hence inflation staying low.'

So you are saying that QE (or printing money) did not impact prices for consumer goods, but did increase prices of assets – which are not part of inflation measures. Is that not a bit misleading?

'I think so, yes. The Bank of England's analysis of the impacts of QE concluded that, on the plus side, without QE many companies would have gone out of business.[5] It probably kept economic growth stronger, wages higher and unemployment lower than they would otherwise have been.'

And on the minus side?

'Well, as I said earlier, the price of assets like property and shares increased. This is great for those who already own them (the old, the rich), but less good for those who want to buy their first home or save up for their future (the young, the poor). And after Covid-19, we have had yet another huge wave of QE. Some people are worried that what started as an emergency measure has become institutionalised. It permits governments to continually borrow, and not face up to their debt problem.'

So what is the final verdict?

'Instinctively QE makes me nervous. The distinguished economist John Kay has argued that this policy of ultra-low interest rates has caused asset price inflation, pushing house purchases beyond the reach of many and rendering long-term saving more or less hopeless. In his words, the primary effect of monetary policy since 2008 has been to transfer wealth to those who already hold long-term assets – real and financial – from those who now never will.[6]

Perhaps the biggest problem is that almost no one understands QE, so for such an important area of policy you get very little public comment or criticism. And it's not just the public: most politicians don't get it, either. And the few people who *do* understand it don't all agree about its impact or value. However, for all its dangers, it was better than the alternative, which was *pain*. QE is morphine: great when you really need it, but too easy to get hooked on.'

Well, QE sounds a bit woo-woo to me...

'If you think QE is wacky, then wait till I tell you about Modern Monetary Theory (MMT). The best-known face of MMT is Stephanie Kelton.[7] The basic idea is that governments should first of all decide what it is they want to spend, and then print as much money as they need.'

Eh? But doesn't that go against everything you've been saying? What about inflation, and... and... people having to use wheelbarrows full of cash to pay for a loaf of bread?

'Kelton and the other MMT advocates don't say that inflation is unimportant. Their argument is that as long as there is unused economic capacity or unemployed labour then MMT will not be inflationary. If inflation does start to grow, then governments can easily control it by spending less or, ideally, by taxing the wealthy, thereby drawing off that excess spending capacity that drives inflation.'

Hmmm... not unpersuasive. And the case against? I assume there is one...

'As you've probably picked up, MMT is generally a policy advocated by the political left, and so of course the right hate it. For the right, MMT is a massive power grab by the state.[8] Its critics refuse to concede that inflation could really be kept under control under MMT, and then we are back to the argument that inflation is just a hidden taxation.

Critics of MMT also argue that, in the real world, government projects financed by printing money would not just draw on idle workers and idle factories but would inevitably siphon off some workers and raw materials from the private sector, once again creating the conditions for inflation.

There is also a good objection that if sovereign states embraced MMT too enthusiastically, then they might find that pretty quickly no one would lend to them in their own currency any more. There is a reason that Greece adopted the euro, and Venezuela borrows so much in US dollars.'

And what do you think?

'If QE makes me uncomfortable then MMT scares the pants off me. However, I am not entirely sure that there is such a big distinction between MMT and QE. The fact is that they bleed into each other. Kelton says that with MMT governments can and should print cash as long as it does not lead to inflation. And that rather seems to be the policy we have adopted with QE. The main distinction between the two is a matter of degree: how much the money supply expands and how you do it – indirectly through banks, or directly through government spending.'

You know, I've kinda lost track of where we are. This walk has been about how the government controls how much dosh is floating about in the economy. There's fiscal policy, which is about tax and spending, and monetary policy, which is about interest rates and also how much money you decide to print, or release into the wild by

*the quantitative easing thing. And governments and central banks
fiddle about with these two things to help nudge countries out of
recessions and prevent depressions. Have I got all that more or less
right?*

'That's pretty good, Monty. And, yep, we're nearly home, so
let's wrap it up. Up until the 1960s Keynesianism held sway.
This was the idea that fiscal policy was the best way to manage
recessions. If demand was weak then government spending
could pull economies out of recessions, or even stop them getting going in the first place. In the 1970s this idea fell out of
fashion. European and American economies, which had been
guided along broadly Keynesian principles, appeared to be fal-
tering. Growth was low, and both inflation and unemployment
were high.

Things were about to change. Led by the Thatcher and
Reagan administrations in the UK and the US, monetarism
became the new orthodoxy. The argument went that low interest rates would encourage people to do something more
productive with their money, spending or investing it.

By the 2000s interest rates had been pushed to historical
lows. After the financial crisis, central banks had little ammuni-
tion left. Interest rates had already been pushed to all intents
and purposes to zero, and consumers were still not willing to
spend, or investors to invest. To use Keynes's expression, it had
become like "pushing on a wet noodle". So, central banks began
experimenting with more radical monetary policies such as
quantitative easing. Then came Covid – and at this point even
the central bankers started to call for the use of fiscal policy
instead.

Is it possible that all fiscal and monetary actions that have
been taken in response to Covid-19 are storing up pain for the

future? Absolutely. Remember money is not real wealth. Modern fiat currencies have value only because people selling real things are prepared to accept them. A fiat currency has value only because it is scarce. And the central bank's job is to control that scarcity. But it is fair to say that if governments had not hugely expanded government spending (fiscal policy) and cut interest rates/engaged in QE (monetary policy) then the crisis would have been much worse, and many more people would have suffered as a result.

And, breathe. Home at last.'

Er, one thing. There was a dachshund back there. Looked at me funny. I could have sworn he… he… laughed at me. Being laughed at by a dachshund is like being called stupid by a boxer.

I glanced quickly at Monty's pink bow.

'Just your imagination, Monty.'

Walk 16

Going Global: Why International Trade Makes Us Richer (But Not All of Us)

What we talk about on this walk: Three periods of globalisation. Protectionism: does it keep (well-connected) companies fat and lazy or does it allow infant industries time to grow? Why free trade can be a win-win (it allows specialisation, economies of scale, competition – and you don't shoot your customer). The downsides of free trade (one good argument and two bad). Finally, what does this mean for the flow of money, and what does this mean for the flow of people?

Monty's frantic barking could mean only one thing: you've guessed it, the postman. Or, rather, this being 2021, the DHL delivery person. He handed me a squidgy package, and I knew what it contained.

'It's for you, Monty,' I said.

He had a quick, excited sniff, then lost interest. He knew.

I unwrapped it and presented Monty with his stylish new Pucci (as in Gucci, but for pooches, I suppose) overcoat.

Sure. For me. The way the mustard is for the hot dog.

'Well, whoever it's for, let's go and show it off to the world.'

I'm a bit tired today. Can't seem to get these old legs of mine working very well.

'Don't worry, we'll just have a short one, up and down the high street. And I know what we can discuss,' I said, looking at the label on the coat, which declared 'made in China'.

Five minutes later we were outside in the crisp sunshine, Monty looking very dapper, as well as snuggly warm, in his new coat.

So how is this all going to link up, then? I expect you have a master plan.

'Your coat has come a long way to keep you warm, Monty. So I thought for this, almost our last walk together, I'd talk about global trade.'

Last? Do you know something I don't… ?

'Oh, I don't mean last ever. I mean last walk where we talk economics.'

Phew. Global? Sounds interesting.

'It is. We've been a little bit insular up to now, mainly concentrating on Europe and North America. But as your stylish new coat demonstrates, buying almost anything these days, from a tin of beans to an electric car, suddenly embeds you in a network of trade that encompasses the whole world. Sometimes you only become conscious of this when things go wrong.'

Do tell.

'On 23 March 2021 the *Ever Given*, one of the largest container ships ever built, got wedged into the side of the Suez Canal, like a chicken bone stuck in a little dog's throat.'

Don't remind me – that was horrible. Put me off Kentucky Fried Chicken for life.

'We have begged you not to snaffle food you find in the street.'

Sometimes a dog's gotta do what a dog's gotta do.

'Anyway, for six days the *Ever Given* became a 200,000-tonne floating metaphor for all that can go wrong with globalisation. Something like twelve percent of global trade passes through the Suez Canal, and every day that the *Ever Given* was stuck held up a mind-boggling £7 billion in business.'

What a mess. Couldn't they just yank it out, the way you pulled that horrid bone out of my gullet?

'They tried, but it took six days.'

Whose fault was this fiasco?

'If you mean who owned the ship, then that's where it gets really complicated, but also highly revealing about the nature of global trade. The *Ever Given* was built in a Japanese shipyard, leased to a Taiwanese company and operated by a German shipping firm. But it is neither Japanese, Taiwanese nor German. It flies under the Panamanian flag, so operates under (the notoriously lax) Panamanian law. As for the crew, they are largely Indian nationals. And this, believe it or not, is a relatively simple story by the standards of international shipping. In 1999 the *Erika*, an oil tanker, sank off the coast of Brittany, heavily polluting the surrounding water. It took weeks to track down the ultimate owner from behind twelve layers of different shell companies.[1]

But the *Ever Given* is more than just a nice metaphor for globalisation; as we will get on to later, cheap transport, in particular shipping, has been one of the main driving forces behind globalisation.'

Globalisation? What exactly do you mean by that?

'Globalisation is the term used to describe our increasingly interdependent and interconnected world. In this chat, I'm mainly going to use the term to refer to the movement of goods and services around the world.'

So, international trade, then?

'Yes, but also the international flow of money and people. There's also a sense of globalisation, which is a little more amorphous and is about the flow of ideas and culture.'

OK, hit me, I know you have a plan – what's the agenda for today's walk?

'Let's start with some history. There is nothing new about trade – I've mentioned before that humans have traded and bartered, often across great distances, for millennia. Four thousand years ago, boats brought raw jade from Taiwan to the Philippines, where it was crafted into jewellery, and then traded on to other island communities. But what *is* new is just how much we trade and what we are trading in. World exports are now more than forty times larger than they were in 1913.[2]

More recently, you can think of globalisation as having three phases. The first was from around 1870 to the late 1920s, when it became cheaper and easier to move goods (and, almost as important, information) around the world. The second period was between 1929 and the Second World War, when globalisation stumbled and stalled. Many countries, suffering from the ravages of the First World War and the Great Depression, turned inwards and adopted highly protectionist policies.'

Protectionist?

'That just means countries either banned some imports or charged tariffs on their imports, making them more expensive, but helping home producers.

The third period was after the Second World War, when countries opened up again and trade exploded. This flourishing has been brought about by two technological advances. Modern container-shipping technology has made it so cheap to move goods around the world that transport costs have become almost irrelevant. This means that manufacturers are happy to set up factories wherever labour is cheapest, as the small extra cost of transport is more than balanced by the savings on the workforce. And then along came the internet, which abolished national boundaries for information.'

And protectionism gets in the way of all this? Why would anyone be in favour of it?

'For much of history international trade was seen as a zero-sum game. People thought about a country's wealth in terms of how much gold it had. Everything that a country did was to get more gold. To feed that gold lust, it was thought that a country should try to export as much as it could, and import as little as possible. Hence quotas and taxes on imports. It was Adam Smith, ever the revolutionary, who argued that wealth was not about how much gold a country had, but the standard of living of its people. He said get rid of tariffs and quotas and food will get cheaper, and people's standard of living will increase. Sure, some domestic producers might lose out, but they would move to other fields where the UK had an advantage.'

And did people listen to him?

'In Britain his arguments were influential. The Corn Laws and their repeal were a pivotal moment in this battle of ideas.'

The Corn Laws?

'In 1815 Britain had very high tariffs on grain. They could be as much as eighty percent. Powerful landowners wanted to keep cheap corn from being imported into Britain and undercutting them. But the (poor) consumer suffered. The situation came to a head with low harvests and the Irish Potato Famine of the late 1840s. Britain experienced scarcity and the Irish suffered starvation. The poor simply couldn't afford flour. Imports of cheaper corn became essential to prevent the famine that had devastated Ireland from hitting Britain as well. In 1846 the Corn Laws were repealed, ushering in a new era of free trade that would characterise British economic policy for the rest of the nineteenth century.[3] Today free trade is sometimes associated with big, nasty multinational corporations who exploit workers, but 175 years ago, it was a policy that helped the hungry, not the wealthy.'

And did other countries also follow and open up to trade?

'Not until much later. Britain was the industrial powerhouse of the world, and it could afford to be open. But other countries wanted to protect their infant industries. When the US gained independence, it adopted increasingly protectionist policies, as it wanted to allow its own manufacturing sector to develop. It was only after the Second World War that it began to embrace free trade. Germany did the same thing, protecting its developing manufacturing sector behind high tariff barriers.

And it is still a highly contentious subject. It's been a rough few years for those who believe in free trade. President Trump took the US into a trade war with China. "Our Country," he tweeted, "was built on Tariffs, and Tariffs are now leading us to great new Trade Deals – as opposed to the horrible and unfair Trade Deals that I inherited as your President. Other countries should not be allowed to come in and steal the wealth of our great USA. No longer!"[4] In the UK, the vote for Brexit could be seen as a protest against the effects of globalisation and free trade…'

So, if I have understood you right, protectionism is a bad thing, so why do people support it?

'There is a legitimate argument that import protection helps developing countries to build new industries. As we've seen, Germany and the US in the nineteenth century, and Japan and Korea in the twentieth, did exactly this. But you have to be careful. The costs of protectionism tend, as with the Corn Laws, to be borne by the poor, and the benefits go to the rich. Another form of protectionism is to give financial subsidies to home producers. Both the EU and the US have given huge sums to help domestic agricultural production, but these subsidies have largely gone to the wealthiest farmers. In the US, in 2019 the richest one percent of farmers received almost twenty-five percent of total subsidy payments. You have to ask who these tariffs are helping, and are they the people who really need help?'

OK, so far globalisation looks like a bit of a mixed blessing. From what you were saying, I'd thought there'd be more positives.

'Just getting to it.

The first argument for the benefits of globalisation goes back to Ricardo (remember him? He was the rich friend of Malthus that we talked about on one of our first walks). This is the theory of "comparative advantage". The basic idea is that countries should specialise in what they do best: French wine, Scottish whisky, Italian cloth, Saudi Arabian oil. Do what you do best, and trade. The idea is very easy to understand when we are talking about an "absolute advantage". If I am better at making dog collars and you are better at making dog leads, I have an absolute advantage at making collars and you have an absolute advantage in making leads. It is obvious in this case that I should spend all my time making collars, you should spend all your time making leads, and then we should trade. But what if I am better at making both? It is slightly counterintuitive but even then, it is better to specialise and trade.'

Huh – I don't quite see that.

'This is the idea of "comparative advantage". Emily Oster, Professor of Economics at Brown, gives a nice example. She tells of how she and her husband were deciding how to share out household tasks. And she was better at pretty much all of them – in particular cooking and doing the dishes. But she was *a lot* better at cooking (say ten times better) than her husband and only a little bit better (say twice as good) at doing the dishes. In this case you would say that she has the comparative advantage in cooking, and he has the comparative advantage in washing the dishes.[5] From an efficiency perspective, it makes no sense for them to share the cooking and washing of dishes equally. She should spend all her time on cooking, he should spend all his time on the dishes.

The same intuition applies to international trade. Even if one country is better at doing everything than another country, it is more efficient if they focus on making things where their advantage is highest. A country, like a person, should aim to do what they do best and then trade to get the other goods they need. Essentially, we are talking about the productivity gains from specialisation. Specialisation makes us productive, and trade allows us to specialise.

The second argument is that trade makes markets bigger, and bigger markets allow companies to spread fixed costs over more output. If I'm running a factory making engines for boats in Newcastle, I have certain fixed costs: designing the engine, for example. If my market is the north-east of England, then that fixed cost will be a large proportion of the total cost of production. If my market is the whole of the United Kingdom, the cost of designing the engine is spread over the much greater number of engines I can sell. And if the world is my market I can reach even more customers, without increasing those fixed costs. It's as if you had a sprinkler system attached to you, Monty, so one of your wees could be distributed to hundreds of trees at a time.'

A slightly strained example, but I get your drift.

'Third, globalisation increases competition. My boat engine company isn't just competing with other (perhaps badly run) domestic firms, but with firms all over the world. This is really all about creative destruction. It might in fact turn out that boat engines made in China are better and cheaper than my Newcastle-built ones. So I go bust. But that leads to an overall more efficient world, in which the consumers of boat engines win. Sometimes referred to as capitalism's sorting mechanism, creative destruction can be an enormous force for good, as new technologies and new companies displace the old.

Finally, there is the political argument. This is sometimes called the "Doux commerce" (meaning gentle, or soft, commerce) thesis.[6] It is the idea that trade promotes liberal values of tolerance, pluralism, reciprocity and cooperation. In short, businessmen do not shoot their customers. It was this argument that was behind the US's adoption of free trade policies after the Second World War, and was also the driving force behind the creation of the EU. In the words of the Schuman Declaration in 1950, European integration was intended "to make war [within Europe] not merely unthinkable but materially impossible".[7]

OK, that sounds quite convincing. Global free trade makes for a more efficient economy and, you say, a more peaceful world. But you've also said it has its critics…

'Free trade might increase the size of the pie, but this does not mean that everyone immediately gets more pie.'

We're back with the winners and losers again, aren't we?

'Yup. In theory the government can compensate the losers, which can still make everyone better off, but often in practice this does not happen.'

Who are the losers, the guys with no pies?

'The workers, particularly low-skilled workers, who lose their jobs in the industries that are exposed to foreign competition. The people building the boat engines in Newcastle. Look at what happened in Janesville, for example.'[8]

What happened in Janesville?

'General Motors (GM) opened their plant in Janesville, Wisconsin, in 1919. In 2007 Barack Obama gave a stirring speech about the auto industry at the Janesville plant ("This plant will be here for another 100 years"). In 2008 the plant was shut down. This was partly to do with oil prices, and the state of the US economy after the financial crisis, but also because of competition from European and Far Eastern car makers. Because the car factory closed, so did the plant that supplied the car seats, and so on. Some workers took local jobs that paid them less than half what they previously earned. Others commuted 270 miles to another GM plant, sharing an apartment during the week with other "GM gypsies". It can be hard – and humiliating – to reinvent oneself in midlife. When former GM workers went for retraining at the local college, a large number did not know how to turn a computer on, and many dropped out when they found that the instructors would not accept papers written by hand.

A decade on, unemployment in Janesville is less than four percent. On paper this might not look too bad. But the jobs that remain don't pay well, and the standard of living has declined.'

Winners and losers... But why should globalisation have made this worse?

'Before the boom in global trade, most trade was between countries with quite similar economies – for example between the US and Western Europe. But when China started to open up in the 1980s, this resulted in a tsunami of cheap Chinese imports. For consumers this was great, as the price of many goods in real terms has decreased. But for workers in certain industries, it was devastating.

Many economists underestimated this shock. And in some countries (e.g. the US), the social safety net is barely adequate, and so we saw a lot of political backlash. But it is important to note that this is only part of the story. The negative impact (for some) needs to be balanced by the positive impact trade has on price, quality and choice of product. The fact that consumers have more money to spend means that many new jobs would have been created. But it is little consolation to employees who have lost their jobs to know that in the long run workers will, on average, be better off.'

That does explain why lots of people are unhappy with globalisation. But is that it, or is there more bad news?

'Some argue that globalisation exploits the world's poor. Working conditions in developing countries are often appalling. And many people are deeply uncomfortable with the thought that an Indonesian worker sewed their trainers for sixty cents an hour. Surely we should insist that those workers receive decent wages, and work under humane conditions?'

Well, it is hard to argue with that, isn't it?

'The trouble with this argument is that while taking the job away from that Indonesian worker might make us feel better, it would almost certainly make life worse for the worker. This is something we touched on when we discussed inequality. Wages and working conditions in these factories may be, by our standards, terrible, but they are almost certainly an improvement over the alternative.'

But can't the sneaker makers just pay the workers more?

'The only reason that multinational companies operate outside their core is because of cheap labour. Everything else about running a factory in a developing country is far more difficult and expensive. Low wages are the only reason that developing countries have been able to compete. If you take that away from them, then you take away the potential to grow.'

That still makes me feel uncomfortable. But it is a hard point to argue with. Any more arguments against globalisation?

'It's sometimes argued, badly, I think, that globalisation is destroying the planet.'

But surely that's a great argument – you can't not want to save the planet?

'Of course I want to save the planet. It's just that I'm not sure that restricting trade is a good way to do it. Let's examine the facts. It's been said that with free trade you get a race to the bottom in terms of environmental standards. Companies will locate their factories wherever the environmental regulations are the laxest, and resist attempts to tighten rules protecting the environment. And this should be a concern. There is plenty of evidence from around the world of large corporations doing terrible things to the planet, from those pesticides in Martinique and Guadeloupe, to the Deepwater Horizon oil spill in the Gulf of Mexico.

However, the evidence does not seem to support the thrust that global development means a global environmental catastrophe. For example, China has seen its air quality stabilise or improve since the mid-1980s, at the same time as it has experienced both rapid growth and increased openness to trade.[9]

It's also been pointed out that international trade itself pollutes. This is a stronger argument. All this moving stuff about undoubtedly causes pollution. It's been calculated that shipping is responsible for three to four percent of greenhouse gas emissions. And so it's certainly the case that we should aim to move goods in as clean a way as possible. But the way to address this is to tax transport, not ban the trade.'

Well, I don't normally disagree with you, as it's you who puts my food out, gives me treats, buys me natty Chinese coats, but we might have to agree to disagree on that one. If we really care about the planet, surely we should try to buy things locally, to cut down on all those emissions?

'OK, that's fine, I like it when you fight. More trade will mean more emissions. But openness to trade can provide developing countries with access to cleaner, newer technology. However we finally defeat climate change, technology will play a role. And technology needs trade.

And unless you are really saying that you want to keep the world's poor poor, then this argument seems a bit hypocritical. By all means tax rich countries for polluting, but to deny poor countries trade, which may be the only way that they can claw their way out of poverty, is fundamentally unfair.

Again, I am not saying that any of these arguments should be ignored. There probably is a trade-off between economic output and the environment. But international trade may well make that trade-off easier (richer countries are able to afford better environmental standards). And I am just not sure that walling off poor countries, so that they stay poor, is the best way to think about it.'

Right, so, as we keep coming back to, there are ups and downs in this, but you think the ups are uppier than the downs are downy. What should countries do to make the downs less downy?

'The pretty widely accepted view is that countries should encourage free trade but protect the losers.'[10]

How?

'The standard list of recommendations includes things like making it easy for workers to relocate to where the new jobs are. Help workers retrain. An educated workforce with a flexible set of skills is going to find it easier to adapt to the new conditions. More radically, we might argue that those who have most benefited from globalisation should contribute more, meaning higher taxes on the rich, lower taxes for those at the bottom, to make sure that the gains from globalisation are shared with those who have lost out in the process.'

Given that this walk was supposed to be an antidote to the insularity of the others, we haven't talked much about what the poorer nations should do.

'Good point. Ha-Joon Chang,[11] a South Korean economist based at Cambridge University, has been highly critical of globalisation in its deregulatory, anti-protectionist formulation. He argues that the same rich countries that now tell poor ones to open up their economies developed their own by doing the reverse. The recent orthodoxy has been that protectionism keeps companies fat and lazy, but Chang argues that strategic protectionism is necessary to help poor countries develop. Unless infant domestic producers are able to develop the productive capabilities they need in the first place, they will never be able to grow big enough to compete in the long run.

Chang's own country Korea heavily protected its growing industries in the 1960s and 1970s, and the same strategy was

adopted by the Chinese government, driving their own astonishing rise. Their Made in China 2025 policy uses government
subsidies, tariffs and regulation to shape China's economy.[12]
Their government is happy to hobble foreign rivals. For example, Google and WhatsApp were not allowed entry to China's
market, which allowed them to develop their own rival, WeChat.

The second difficulty for poor countries is this idea of *compensation*. As I said, most economists in support of free trade
accept that it has winners and losers and argue that, so long as
we compensate the losers, it can still be a win-win. The trouble
is that, while in rich countries the welfare state may help the
poorest, in developing nations the welfare state is minimal or
non-existent. Discussion on the impact of free trade normally
looks at the winners in poor countries and losers in rich countries. But this is to miss the point that there will also be losers in
poor countries. You probably didn't want to be working for a
local drinks company when Coca-Cola entered your home
market.'

*What's the answer then? Is it good or bad that my new coat came
all the way from China in a container ship the size of a small town?*

'Calculating the net impact of free trade is complex.
International trade can bring many benefits. It allows producers
to specialise and make things more cheaply through economies
of scale. Competition can force companies to be more efficient.
It may spread innovation and help developing countries acquire
better technology. International trade has been an enormous
force for good. In the long run it may raise welfare. The bad
news is that people don't pay their bills *in the long run*. When a
factory closes, or an industry is entirely wiped out, it can result
in lasting devastation to individuals and communities.'

OK, thanks. I think. Home time?

'Almost. Just an *i* to dot and *t* to cross. So far, Monty, we have been talking about the trade in goods and services, which is what people normally think about when they talk about globalisation. But when you talk about globalisation you also need to think about two more things: the movement of money, and the movement of people across borders. Let's start with money. All this flow of goods and services between countries also means that *money* is flowing across borders. In 2020 the UK had a current account deficit of about 3.5% of GDP.'[13]

Sorry, that means absolutely nothing to me. If you are going to carry on like this, then I'm going to switch my attention to that delicious-looking Kentucky Fried Chicken carton.

'Don't you dare! OK, I'll keep it short and snappy. What this means is that in 2020 the UK spent more abroad than the rest of the world spent with us: 3.5% of our GDP more.'

When you say spending, what are you including?

'Good question. The current account balance mainly reflects the difference between how much we are exporting and how much we are importing (in terms of goods and services). If a country is running a deficit, this means it is importing more than it is exporting. If you want to be pedantic, the current account also includes the value of cross-border payments on investments such as dividends and interest payments; private transfers such as money sent home by expatriate workers; and official transfers such as international aid. But all of these are a much smaller part of the current account. If you add up all these different inflows and outflows then you get a country's current account balance.

If a country exported £50 billion worth of goods and services, and imported £100 billion, then the people it is trading with are going to want something in exchange for that other

£50 billion. This can come from savings, through borrowing, or through selling some of its assets. In short, if a country is consuming more than it is producing, it has to pay for the difference somehow. If the UK is running a current account deficit, then it means that foreign countries are accumulating UK assets.'

That sounds like we should be worried...

'It depends. A country might be importing lots of goods and services to build up their industrial base, running a large current account deficit, and borrowing to bridge the gap. If this means the country will be more productive in the long run, and so more than able to pay back the debt, then it can be a good thing. Other countries tend to want to lend to nations that have a high potential for growth. This pretty much described the situation in America when it was first developing. But if a country is importing more than it is producing *without* making investments that will increase its future productivity, then it may well be a problem. For countries, just like individuals, borrowing (or selling assets or drawing down on savings) to fund a productive investment can be a good idea, but borrowing just to spend money today without doing anything to raise your future income is storing up pain for later. Eventually the bill will come due. So, Monty, that is what international trade means for money. Now we get to people.'

I take it you are not talking about an actual trade in people, as in slavery?

'No, Monty. I'm talking about migration. Economists often wax lyrical about the benefits of free trade in goods and services. But what about people? When it comes to the free movement of labour, we have seen quite a bit of resistance. The EU has been unwavering in its commitment to the "four freedoms": the free movement of goods, services, capital and labour. But that is just within the EU. With very few exceptions, new workers are not allowed into the EU from outside. But even intra-European movement of labour caused serious problems, not least in the UK, where it was one of the drivers of Brexit.

The trouble is that in the short run there may well be a negative impact of immigration on wages and employment, in particular for the poorest. The new workers who come in will increase the pool of available labour and so firms will have more bargaining power, which inevitably means lower wages.

However, economists argue that this is not the end of the story. As firms are now getting cheaper workers, they will expand and invest. This will in turn increase the demand for workers and so wages should improve. In other words, while there might be a short-run negative impact on wages (and bear in mind that the "short run" can mean years or even decades), in the long run local workers should be no worse off. But because this is an area where you have seen most popular resistance, labour has for the most part not been globalised, and for political, cultural and language reasons remains largely national.

OK, Monty, I think we are done. Time to head home.'

So what is the verdict?

'In the long run international trade should lead to a growing economy. Consumers are made richer by cheap imports (remember a price cut is effectively a wage increase). This leads to increased demand and so rising demand for workers in other parts of the economy. But none of this is painless. When economists talk about frictions or transition costs, or displacement, this glosses over the very real suffering of those who are the losers in this game. When a person is made redundant because their job can be done more cheaply by someone in Vietnam, it is no consolation to say that on average the country will be richer. That individual will be poorer, and probably always will be. Markets, through competition, drive efficiency. Less efficient companies lose customers and ultimately go out of business. This is the idea of creative destruction. And international trade, by making markets bigger and more competitive, just intensifies that process. As Mark Twain might have put it (it's one of those unverifiable quotes), in words with which many of us will sympathise, "I'm in favour of progress, it's change I don't like."

Monty was looking a little shaky on his legs again, so I crouched down and, without any complaints, he stepped into my arms, and I carried him home, as he snored gently.

A Final Walk to the Churchyard

What we talk about on this walk: Economics is hard, necessarily so because it deals with complex issues. Sometimes it gets things wrong, but it's the best tool we have for understanding the nature of modern society, and even if the answers aren't always right, the questions are always crucial. Markets are a brilliantly efficient way of giving us many of the things we want. But they are far from perfect. And though they provide us with the means to live, they cannot help us with the things that make our lives worth living.

'Is that really snow?'

I was contemplating taking Monty out, perhaps just down to get some milk.

The Philosopher looked out at the street. 'It's not settling. It's more the snow version of drizzle. Snizzle, maybe.'

'Too cold to leave Monty tied up outside Waitrose. Anyway, there's talk of gangs kidnapping dogs.'

'Yeah, I heard. But I was thinking about that. He's an old dog. So far we've been quite lucky with vet bills. But that'll change...'

'What are you blathering on about?'

'Well, the dognapping epidemic. Maybe turn it to our advantage?'

'And you're suggesting...?'

'Exactly. Tie him up outside. Take your time in the shop. Come out. "Oh, Monty, where have you gone?" Think about it. We've had Monty's best years. His most productive years, in terms of how much pleasure he's able to output. So now's the time to release some equity. Or at least save some future unprofitable expenditure. Also, let's say he's stolen by the dognappers. They'll sell him on to some family, maybe with kids. A whole new generation will come to know and love Monty. Or a rich old lady. Maybe an oligarch's widow. Lonely. Needs company. She'd pamper him. Feed him sweetmeats prepared by his own chef. And if they can afford the dognappers' exorbitant fee, not to mention the doggy chef, they'll be able to afford the best vetinarial care for his declining years. It's a win-win-win.'

'"Vetinarial" isn't even a word. And he can hear you, you monster. I'm taking him out, but not to Waitrose. You can buy your own milk.'

At that moment Monty came padding into the kitchen. He gazed at both of us in turn, wondering what the atmosphere was all about.

'Walkies,' I said, brightly.

He didn't look desperately keen.

'Come on. We both need some fresh air.'

Outside it was very fresh indeed.

'Let's just go up to the churchyard.'

I meant the beautiful eighteenth-century church of St John in Hampstead. It's one of the best places in London to sit and think, and chat to your dog. We used to go there every day when we walked the children to their junior school, back when we were all a lot younger.

Oh, good. I like it there. But these old legs... Any chance of a carry?

'Of course.'

I scooped him up, tucked him under my coat, safe from the snizzle, and off we went. The church is only ten minutes away. As soon as you enter through the gates of the churchyard, you step out of time. London disappears, and you're lost, even in the bleak midwinter, in a place of green refuge. I put Monty down and he had a snuffle and a wee, but then looked back at me again, and I picked him up once more and let him sit on my knee as I sat on my favourite bench in the whole of London, which has a view of John Constable's tomb on one side, and then, over the wall, in the distance, the City of London, with its commerce and enterprising chaos.

'I think this is going to be our last economics talk, little friend.'

That's OK. Er, as long as you don't expect me to summarise everything we've gone through.

'Fine, let me sum up then, if I can. One of the things I was trying to get across was that economics is both hugely important and fiendishly complicated. If anything in economics appears obvious or simple, there's a good chance you've misunderstood it. There's a famous line from H.L. Mencken: "For every complex question, there is a simple and straightforward answer that is wrong."'

Hah.

'Economics deals with two levels of complexity: the human brain, which is the most intricate thing in the universe, and then the interaction of millions of those human brains in the market. So all the answers here are provisional, and hedged about with caveats and qualifications. But I hope that these walks have given you some way to start thinking about economic questions.'

Yeah, yeah. Got all that. Cut to the chase.

'OK, unlike the Philosopher, I'm a fan of markets, by which I mean the free exchange of goods and services. I'm not a free-market ultra: markets work best when the state can regulate and act as an honest broker, but the market system, when it works well, is a thing of elegant beauty. Specialisation and innovation have led to enormous increases in productivity. And both rely on markets. We can only specialise if there is some way to trade to get the other goods we need in exchange (what use are 4,800 pins to the pin maker?). Innovation only makes sense if you can sell your invention to others to buy the things you need. Who would put all that effort into designing a toaster just for their own use?

It is innovation, specialisation and markets that have been responsible for the greatest increase in human wealth and well-being that the world has ever seen. It meant we could escape the Malthusian trap, that death spiral of poverty, hunger and disease that would have otherwise resulted from the growth of human populations.

Almost everything that comforts and delights us in modern society is the result of the market: the toasters and other domestic appliances that save us from drudgery; the phones and TVs and games consoles that keep us from boredom. None of these are conceivable without that astonishing web of free human interactions facilitated by the market.

And there's a moral aspect to this, too – I mean above and beyond the morality of staving off destitution and starvation. Some people see free markets as a parable of personal freedom. The market enshrines individual choice. No central power can tell you what to want, to buy or to produce. Free marketeers like Friedman and Hayek have argued that there is an inseparable link between the freedom of consumers to choose and their broader political freedom.'

I feel you should be marching up and down, banging a drum.

'Sorry! That was a bit too cheerleadery. There are, of course, downsides. Markets leave people behind. As we've said time and time again, there are—'

Winners and losers.

'Winners and losers. And those losers have to be helped, not left to rot. And whatever Hayek and Friedman thought, there's no necessary link between free market economics and political freedom. That's something that Friedman should have known – he was an adviser to the brutal dictatorship of General Pinochet in Chile. So political rights don't just piggyback on the back of economic freedoms, but have to be fought for. But it's still true that they tend to hang out together.

But I guess there's something else, something I wanted to finish on. Even a markets person like me knows that the sort of things that markets are good at delivering – economic progress, financial security, technological advancement – although certainly important, are not everything. Not even close to being everything. Much of what we value escapes entirely the net of commerce. Friendship, love, beauty, faith, kindness, charity. There are things like the love of a person for a little dog—'

And of a little dog for a person!

'Thank you, Monty… where was I?'

How much you love me…

'Yes, I do, and how this love cannot be valued by the market.'

You realise, don't you, that that's what the Philosopher was getting at?

'Eh?'

All that guff in the kitchen about leaving me outside Waitrose for the dognappers. He was just saying the same thing in his own way. Letting you see how absurd it would be to use that kind of reasoning about little old me. Thinking of me as simply a cost or a commodity like the milk.

'Hmm, maybe you're right.'

You know I am.

I kissed the top of his white head.

'You think you're up to walking back down that hill?'

We can see how we go. If I get tired, you'll carry me?

Always.

Notes

Preamble

1   Heilbroner, R.L., 2011. *The Worldly Philosophers: The Lives, Times and Ideas of the Great Economic Thinkers*. Simon and Schuster.

Walk 1: The Toaster

1   Thwaites, T., 2011. *The Toaster Project: Or a Heroic Attempt to Build a Simple Electric Appliance from Scratch*. Chronicle Books.
2   Read, L.E., 1958. *I, pencil* (Vol. 8, No. 12, pp. 32–7). Freeman.

Walk 2: Part I: A Short History of Nearly Everything

1   Weber, M., 2002. *The Protestant Ethic and the "Spirit" of Capitalism and Other Writings*. Trans. and ed. Baehr, P.R. and Wells, G.C. Penguin Books.

Walk 3: Part II: Marx and the Revolution That Didn't Happen

1   Singer, P., 2018. *Marx: A Very Short Introduction*. Oxford University Press.

2   DiMaggio, P. ed., 2003. *The twenty-first-century firm: changing economic organization in international perspective.* Princeton University Press.

3   Marshall, A., 2009. *Principles of economics: unabridged eighth edition.* Cosimo, Inc.

4   In a letter to A.L. Bowley. Cited in https://www.core-econ.org/the-economy/book/text/08.html#great-economists-alfred-marshall

5   Taleb, N.N., 2005. *Fooled by randomness: The hidden role of chance in life and in the markets* (Vol. 1). Random House Trade Paperbacks.

Walk 4: Markets: Who Is in Charge of the Bread Supply for London?

1   Rogers, B., 2015. The social costs of Uber. *U. Chi. L. Rev. Dialogue, 82,* p.85.

2   Garber, P.M., 1990. Famous first bubbles. *Journal of Economic Perspectives, 4*(2), pp.35–54.

3   Friedman, M. and Friedman, R.D., 1990. *Free to choose.* Free to Choose Enterprise.

4   Stone, B., 2013. *The Everything Store: Jeff Bezos and the Age of Amazon.* Random House.

Walk 5: Household Behaviour: You Can't Always Get What You Want, But if You Try Real Hard...

1   Hyman, D.A., 2010. Convicts and convictions: some lessons from transportation for health reform. *U. Pa. L. Rev., 159,* p.1999.

2   Keynes, J.M., 2010. 'Economic possibilities for our grandchildren'. In *Essays in persuasion* (pp. 321–32). Palgrave Macmillan.

3   https://www.npr.org/sections/money/2015/07/
    24/426017148/episode-641-why-we-work-so-much

4   Juliet Schor: Why do we work so hard? https://www.you-
    tube.com/watch?v=FrIhloNEwT8

Walk 6: Firms: Monopolies, Oligopolies, Collusion and Competition

1   https://www.economist.com/books-and-arts/2004/08/05/
    what-an-art

2   Smith, A., 1937. *The wealth of nations [1776]* (Vol. 11937).
    na. – Book IV, Chapter VIII, p. 145, para. c27.

3   As of 2020: https://en.wikipedia.org/wiki/Starbucks

4   Epstein, E.J., 1982. Have you ever tried to sell a dia-
    mond? *Atlantic Monthly*, 23, p.363.

5   Note this is the marginal cost, the cost of making just one
    extra phone, and does not include the fixed costs such as
    development. The US dollar cost price was converted to
    pounds sterling using the average exchange rate for 2019.
    https://www.investopedia.com/financial-edge/0912/the-
    cost-of-making-an-iphone.aspx

6   https://guide.iacrc.org/case-example-of-collusive-
    bidding-by-contractors-2

7   Thiel, P.A. and Masters, B., 2014. *Zero to one: Notes on start-
    ups, or how to build the future*. Currency.

Walk 7: Winners and Losers: Capitalism, Markets and Inequality

1   With the bath metaphor, strictly speaking the plug repre-
    sents not just your spending but any depreciation in the
    value of your assets.

2 Okun, A.M. 1975. *Equality and Efficiency: The Big Tradeoff.* Washington DC, Brookings Institution.

3 All these figures have been adjusted from the originals used by Okun.

4 Milanović, B., 2012. Global income inequality by the numbers: in history and now. *World Bank Policy Research Working Paper* (6259).

5 Philippon, T. and Reshef, A., 2012. Wages and human capital in the US finance industry: 1909–2006. *The Quarterly Journal of Economics*, 127(4), pp.1551–1609.

6 Scheidel, W., 2018. *The great leveler.* Princeton University Press.

7 https://www.lse.ac.uk/Events/2020/06/202006151600/how-much-tax

Walk 8: When Markets Fail: Externalities, Public Goods and Common Pool Resources

1 https://www.bbc.co.uk/news/stories-54992051

2 https://www.bbc.co.uk/programmes/m000ph42

3 https://www.bbc.co.uk/news/28942485

4 Boldrin, M. and Levine, D.K., 2008. Against intellectual monopoly. Cambridge University Press.

5 Hardin, G., 1968. The tragedy of the commons: the population problem has no technical solution; it requires a fundamental extension in morality. *Science*, 162(3859), pp.1243–8. It should be noted that the concept was originated by William Forster Lloyd, who used the example of the problem of unregulated grazing on common land in Great Britain. Hardin developed this idea and applied it to the concept of human overpopulation. He argued that in nature, overpopulation is self-regulated. If parents only

relied on themselves, then the number of children they had was not a matter for wider society. If they could not feed their children they would die, and so the system would self-regulate. He argued that a welfare state would lead to a tragedy of the commons. If parents knew that the state would provide, they would overbreed and Malthusian tragedy would follow. Hmmn.

Walk 9: The Market and Information: Why Red Bull No Longer Gives You Wings

1   https://www.ft.com/content/bb03ba1c-add3-4440-9bf2-2a65566aef4a

2   Akerlof, G.A., 1978. The market for "lemons": Quality uncertainty and the market mechanism. In *Uncertainty in Economics* (pp. 235–51). Academic Press.

3   Dropped in 2020: https://www.bbc.co.uk/news/business-53881214

4   https://www.bbc.co.uk/news/newsbeat-29550003

5   https://aeon.co/essays/why-the-hidden-internet-can-t-be-a-libertarian-paradise

6   https://www.coindesk.com/markets/2013/12/03/users-track-100-million-in-stolen-bitcoin-after-sheep-marketplace-hack/

7   https://www.ft.com/content/380082b8-687c-11dd-a4e5-0000779fd18c

8   Tversky, A. and Kahneman, D., 1981. 'The framing of decisions and the psychology of choice'. *Science*, 211(4481), 453–8.

9   Gneezy, U. and List, J.A., 2006. 'Putting behavioral economics to work: Testing for gift exchange in labor markets using field experiments'. *Econometrica*, 74(5), 1365–84.

10 Thaler, R.H., 2016. Behavioral economics: Past, present, and future. *American Economic Review*, 106(7), 1577–1600.

Walk 10: GDP: Not Everything That Counts Can Be Counted

1   https://data.worldbank.org/indicator/NY.GDP.MKTP.CD
2   https://data.worldbank.org/indicator/NY.GDP.PCAP.CD
3   Note: to make comparison easier these figures are adjusted for price changes over time (inflation) and for price differences between countries – they are measured in international-$ in 2011 prices.
4   https://www.jfklibrary.org/learn/about-jfk/the-kennedy-family/robert-f-kennedy/robert-f-kennedy-speeches/remarks-at-the-university-of-kansas-march-18-1968
5   https://www.economist.com/finance-and-economics/2014/05/31/sex-drugs-and-gdp
6   Coyle, D., 2015. *GDP*. Princeton University Press.
7   Measured in current US$. See: https://data.worldbank.org/indicator/NY.GDP.PCAP.CD?name_desc=false
8   https://www.oecdbetterlifeindex.org

Walk 11: Growth: How We Can Make the World a Better Place for the Gacoteras and the Chowdhurys

1   https://ourworldindata.org/grapher/maddison-data-gdp-per-capita-in-2011us?tab=chart&year=1950&country=OWID_WRL. This is based on GDP per capita adjusted for price changes over time (inflation) and is measured in international -$ in 2011 prices.
2   https://www.gapminder.org/dollar-street/families/gacotera

3 This is a calculation that estimates that each adult can consume goods and services worth about $194 US each month. This includes things that they buy as well as an estimate for the things they produce themselves (e.g. food).

4 https://www.gapminder.org/dollar-street/families/chowdhury

5 https://www.worldbank.org/en/topic/measuringpoverty

6 Robert Barro Economic Growth & Prosperity: https://www.youtube.com/watch?v=z5yUUfZqp88

7 Jones, C.I., 2016. 'The facts of economic growth'. In *Handbook of macroeconomics* (Vol. 2, pp. 3–69). Elsevier. (They credit Abramovitz with this description p. 9.)

8 Diamond, J., 1997. *Guns, Germs and Steel: The Fates of Human Societies*. (p.186). Vintage.

9 North, D.C., 1991. Institutions, ideology, and economic performance. *Cato J.*, 11, p.477.

10 https://www.doingbusiness.org/en/data/doing-business-score

11 Krugman, P., 2021. Opinion. *The New York Times*. 25 May 2021.

12 Gordon, R.J., 2016. *The Rise and Fall of American Growth*. Princeton University Press.

Walk 12: All Work and No Play Makes Jack a Dull Boy

1 https://ourworldindata.org/working-more-than-ever

2 Gordon, R J., 2016. *The Rise and Fall of American Growth*. Princeton University Press.

3 https://www.ilo.org/washington/news/WCMS_767753/lang--en/index.htm

4 https://www.soas.ac.uk/cccac/events/cotton-sector-in-central-asia-2005/file49842.pdf

5   https://www.cato.org/economic-development-bulletin/ case-against-child-labor-prohibitions

6   This is the argument made by Chang, H.J., 2015. *Economics: the user's guide*. Bloomsbury Publishing USA.

7   De Neve, J.E. and Ward, G., 2017. 'Does work make you happy? evidence from the world happiness report'. *Harvard Business Review*, 4, pp. 1–7.

8   See Card & Krueger for the counterargument: Card, D. and Krueger, A.B., 1993. Minimum wages and employment: A case study of the fast food industry in New Jersey and Pennsylvania.

9   https://www.bls.gov/news.release/union2.nr0.htm

10   https://www.history.com/this-day-in-history/ fords-assembly-line-starts-rolling

11   Krueger, A.B., Cramer, J. and Cho, D., 2014. 'Are the long-term unemployed on the margins of the labor market?' *Brookings Papers on Economic Activity*, 2014(1), 229–99.

12   https://data.oecd.org/socialexp/public-unemploy-ment-spending.htm

13   https://www.economist.com/special-report/2021 /04/08/the-case-for-danish-welfare

14   Heilbroner, R.L. and Milberg, W., 2012. *The Making of Economic Society*. Pearson Education Company.

15   Often misattributed to Mark Twain.

16   Gordon, R.J., 2016. *The Rise and Fall of American Growth*. Princeton University Press.

Walk 13: Part I: Financial Markets in Theory: Why We Should Love Bankers

1   https://www.rollingstone.com/politics/politics-news/ the-great-american-bubble-machine-195229

2 Kay, J., 2016. *Other People's Money: Masters of the Universe or Servants of the People?* London: Profile Books Ltd.

3 With thanks to The Escape Artist for that metaphor: https://theescapeartist.me/2020/12/06/the-ice-sculpture-the-turkey-and-the-rollercoaster

4 As of 1 January 2022.

5 Diversification works most of the time. In the financial crisis of 2008, it turned out that the risks were not diversified but correlated.

6 Think about it from the bank's point of view. When they lend you money for a mortgage, you promise to give them a monthly stream of payments for however long the mortgage lasts – say £1,000 a month for 25 years. For the bank, this stream of money they expect from you is an asset.

7 Illiquid just means an asset that is not easily or quickly converted into cash.

Walk 13: Part II: Financial Markets in Practice: When It Goes Wrong, and How to Get Rich Quick

1 I really recommend this series of articles for anyone who wants to understand what went wrong: https://baseli-nescenario.com/financial-crisis-for-beginners

2 Bebchuk, L.A., Cohen, A. and Spamann, H., 2010. 'The wages of failure: Executive compensation at Bear Stearns and Lehman 2000–2008'. *Yale J. on Reg.*, 27, 257.

3 This also does not take into account any of the fees that you might pay on your investments, which can make a big difference.

4 https://theescapeartist.me/2016/01/21/the-3-numbers-that-can-make-you-a-millionaire

5   The fees you pay on your investments are very important. Imagine you had £100,000 invested. If this earned 6% a year for the next 25 years and had no costs or fees, you'd end up with about £430,000. If, however, you had paid 2% fees, after 25 years you would have about £260,000. Small differences in charges, because of the impact of compounding, can make a very big difference. https://investor.vanguard.com/investing/how-to-invest/impact-of-costs

Walk 14: Money

1   Radford, R.A., 1945. 'The economic organisation of a POW camp'. *Economica*, 12(48), 189–201.
2   https://www.britannica.com/event/Great-Depression
3   https://www.ons.gov.uk/economy/governmentpublicsectorandtaxes/publicspending/bulletins/ukgovernmentdebtanddeficitforeurostatmaast/march2021
4   Taleb, N.N., 2021. Bitcoin, Currencies and Fragility. https://www.researchgate.net/publication/353065461_Bitcoin_Currencies_and_Fragility

Walk 15: Part I: Depressions, Recessions and What Governments Can Do to Help: Fiscal Policy

1   https://www.marketplace.org/2019/06/05/economics-helped-spur-tiananmen-square-protests
2   https://www.bbc.co.uk/news/business-52273988
3   https://obr.uk/forecasts-in-depth/brief-guides-and-explainers/public-finances
4   https://www.bbc.co.uk/news/business-52663523
5   https://www.economist.com/finance-and-economics/2002/01/17/remember-fiscal-policy

Walk 15: Part II: Depressions, Recessions and What Governments Can Do to Help: Monetary Policy

1   https://www.bankofengland.co.uk/monetary-policy
2   https://www.bankofengland.co.uk/monetary-policy
3   If you really want the details read: McLeay, M., Radia, A. and Thomas, R., 2014. 'Money creation in the modern economy'. *Bank of England Quarterly Bulletin*, p. Q1.
4   https://saylordotorg.github.io/text_macroeconomics-theory-through-applications/s15-01-the-quantity-theory-of-money.html
5   https://www.bankofengland.co.uk/-/media/boe/files/news/2012/july/the-distributional-effects-of-asset-purchases-paper
6   https://www.johnkay.com/2016/09/10/essays-on-modern-monetary-policy-pt-3-the-folly-of-negative-rates
7   Kelton, S., 2020. *The Deficit Myth: Modern Monetary Theory and How to Build a Better Economy*. PublicAffairs.
8   Murphy, R., 2020. Book Review: 'The Deficit Myth: Modern Monetary Theory and the Birth of the People's Economy'. *Quarterly Journal of Austrian Economics*, 23(2), 232–51. https://doi.org/10.35297/qjae.010069

Walk 16: Going Global: Why International Trade Makes Us Richer (But Not All of Us)

1   Lanchester, J., 2021. 'Gargantuanisation'. *London Review of Books*. 22 April 2021.
2   These estimates are in constant prices (i.e. they have been adjusted for inflation) and are indexed at 1913 values. See: https://ourworldindata.org/trade-and-globalization

3   https://www.economist.com/by-invitation/2021/06/25/donald-boudreaux-and-douglas-irwin-on-free-trade-tips-from-1846

4   @realDonaldTrump tweet. 11:04 a.m., 15 Aug 2018. The full tweet: 'Our Country was built on Tariffs, and Tariffs are now leading us to great new Trade Deals – as opposed to the horrible and unfair Trade Deals that I inherited as your President. Other countries should not be allowed to come in and steal the wealth of our great USA. No longer!'

5   In the sense that this is the area in which he is relatively least bad. The *Economist* has a nice example with numbers in case this has not convinced you. https://www.economist.com/economics-a-to-z/c#node-21529435

6   Movsesian, M.L., 2017. 'Markets and morals: The limits of Doux Commerce'. *Wm. & Mary Bus. L. Rev.*, 9, 449.

7   https://www.economist.com/finance-and-economics/2016/12/08/economic-integration-and-the-four-freedoms

8   Goldstein, A., 2017. *Janesville: An American Story*. Simon and Schuster.

9   https://web.worldbank.org/archive/website01072/Globalization/WEB/PDF/ASSESS-4.PDF

10 https://www.economist.com/open-future/2018/05/04/a-healthy-re-examination-of-free-trades-benefits-and-shocks

11 Chang, H.J., 2015. *Economics: the user's guide*. Bloomsbury Publishing USA.

12 https://www.economist.com/finance-and-economics/2017/09/23/china-sets-its-sights-on-dominating-sunrise-industries

13 https://data.worldbank.org

Acknowledgements

Our thanks to our brilliant editor Sam Carter, as patient as he is diligent. And also to the whole superb Oneworld team, including Rida Vaquas, Holly Knox, Matilda Warner, Paul Nash, Laura McFarlane, Anne Bihan, Ben Summers, Mark Rusher, Lucy Cooper, Julian Ball and Francesca Dawes.

And to Charlie Campbell, who done the deal.

Thanks also from Rebecca to Professor Sandy Pepper of the LSE for his support, inspiration and encouragement over the years.

Index

Index

Index

Index

Index

Index

Index

Index

unemployment 183–92, 194, 228, 244, 246
  free trade and 270
  inflation and 234
  search theory of 186, 189
unemployment benefits 190–2
United States (US)
  economic growth 172, 178–9
  financial markets 211
  inflation 230
  monopolies 100–1
  protectionism 266–7
  work 83, 181–2, 194

variable costs 90
Veblen goods 77
veil of ignorance 111
virtual currencies, *see*
  cryptocurrencies

wage cuts 234
wage rigidity 186–8
wages
  capitalist system 35
  cheap labour 272
  income effect 83
  inflation 233
  migrants 278

  productivity 44
  surplus value 49
wants–needs distinction 84
warranties 140
Warren, Elizabeth 101
Watt, James 40
wealth
  accumulation of 105, 117
  banks 207
  income distinction 104
  money distinction 223, 260
  taxation of 118, 161, 257
wealth distribution 34, 48, 115–16, 230
Weber, Max 23, 175–6
welfare state 275
well-being indices 164–5
work/workers 35, 37, 44, 49, 50, 180–95
  bargaining power 30, 68, 106
  class conflict 48–9
  competition effects 92
  demand for 278
  free trade and 270, 274
  supply side market 186
  wealth distribution 34
working conditions 181, 271–2
working hours 80–1, 83, 84, 181

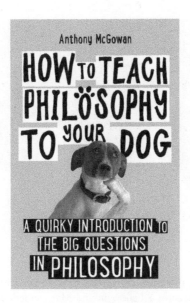

A *New Statesman* Best Book of the Year

Monty was just like any other dog. A scruffy and irascible Maltese terrier, he enjoyed barking at pugs and sniffing at trees. But after yet another dramatic confrontation with the local Rottweiler, Anthony McGowan realises it's high time he and Monty had a chat about what makes him a good or a bad dog.

And they don't stop at ethics. Taking his cue from Monty's canine antics, McGowan leads us on an enlightening jaunt through the world of philosophy.

Will Kant convince Monty to stop stealing cheesecake? How long will they put up with Socrates poking holes in every argument? Do they have free will to pursue answers to these questions? Join the dutiful duo as they set out to uncover who – if anyone – has the right end of the ethical stick and can tell us how best to live one's life.

But there is also a shadow over their conversations. Monty is not well… And so towards the end the biggest questions raise their heads: is there a God? Does life have a meaning? By the time of their last walk together, Monty – and the reader – will find that they have not just solved a few philosophical puzzles, but absorbed much of the history of Western philosophy.

© Nicky Milne

Dr Rebecca Campbell has a PhD from the London School of Economics where she is currently a Fellow in the Management Department, and Director of Studies of the prestigious Global Masters in Management. Before moving to LSE, she was the designer and CEO of successful fashion company Paddy Campbell. She lives in London.

Anthony McGowan has a BA, MPhil and PhD in philosophy, and has lectured widely on the subject. As an author for children and young adults he's won many awards, including the 2020 Carnegie Medal, while *How to Teach Philosophy to Your Dog*, also starring Monty, won widespread acclaim. He lives in London and shares custody of Monty.